Turn Left for the Gobi

PEKING TO PARIS THE HARD WAY

Phillip Haslam

Introduction

This is the story of our exploits in the 2007 Peking to Paris Rally. Whilst we always knew it was going to be a big event, we really didn't appreciate that it would effectively take over our lives in such a significant fashion.

We thought it would be a question of buying a suitable car, preparing it and driving the rally. Little did we know!

This is the story of how we chose a car, the quite unbelievable issues of preparation and, of course, the rally itself – driving halfway around the world through the most inhospitable terrain.

Did we make it! - of course we did - but what a journey!

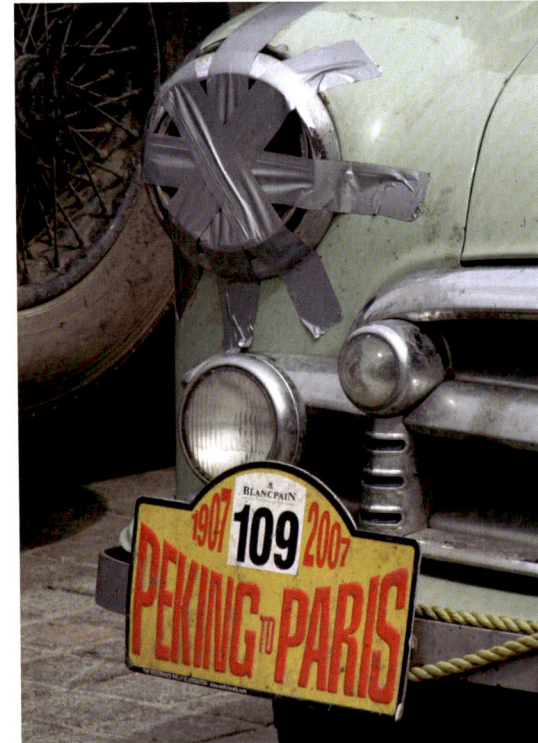

ISBN 978-0-9564326-0-5

Published December 2009 by
Phillip Haslam, Foolow, S32 5QR, England
Tel: 01433.630849 email haslam-foo@tiscali.co.uk

Printed in Great Britain by South Yorkshire Printers Ltd

Special thanks to Gerard Brown for the quite superb photographs on the front cover, the inside leaf and on pages 79, 80, 87, 92, 121, 124

Turn Left for the Gobi

PEKING TO PARIS THE HARD WAY

The story of Phillip and Yvonne Haslam's
participation in the 2007 Peking to Paris Endurance rally

by Phillip Haslam

THE BIG DECISION

It's the look on people's faces. When you mention you've done a rally from Peking to Paris. You see the listener firstly absorb the details of the extremities of the rally – Peking and Paris, then slowly you see the realisation dawn on their faces as to actually how far apart these two cities are, and the gigantic land mass that separates them.

Its only when you outline the journey through China, Mongolia, the Gobi Desert, Siberia, Central Russia, Moscow, St. Petersburg, Latvia, Lithuania, Estonia, Poland, Germany and France that the full scale of the adventure becomes clearer.

When describing the epic journey of crossing the Gobi Desert with endless days of open terrain, rock-strewn tracks and river crossings, the endless appalling pothole-strewn roads of Siberia, does the picture become clearer. Yes, it was the adventure of a lifetime.

We've tried to describe all of the elements of the epic adventure to so many people over so many months - The highlights, the low times, the fantastic scenery, the emotions yo-yo-ing up and down, the car preparation, the journey out to China, constantly keeping an eye on the clock, the amazing satellite navigation, the choice of a car, the gathering of spares, the consideration of medical matters, the ecstatic arrival into Paris, the coming down to earth upon arrival back home - that is when you start to realise how many elements there were to this journey. It is impossible to do justice to the whole story with just snapshots of our experiences, so we have decided to try and assemble as much of the story as possible.

Just before Christmas 2008 we were asked to do a talk in our local village hall about the Peking to Paris Rally. Everyone in the village followed our exploits, but I think people didn't really fully understand exactly what the journey was about, and the circumstances in which we travelled. The talk in Foolow village hall brought home to everybody the amazing project that we had undertaken, and people started to realise why the whole project had taken almost two years from conception to completion.

It was during the preparation for the village talk that we started to check through our notes, photographs, road books, spares list etc. that we realised how much information we had, but how much of the detail might slip away in the passage of time, unless we put some effort into recalling and recording as much detail as possible.

I have never written anything before, apart from, of course, the usual business correspondence, reports, etc. and I really don't feel that I have the consummate skills to simply sit down and write a book. We kept a huge amount of records on the car preparation before we left the UK, we constantly updated our blog on the internet as we travelled, and we also dictated notes onto a small hand-held Dictaphone as we travelled, outlining what we saw, what we did, and various anecdotes that we learned on a daily basis. I decided, therefore, to base these notes on a datal or diary system. It may be a little corny at times, but I feel that it's the easiest way to progress and, in any case, certainly during the rally, we were very much living on a 'day to day' basis so it is perhaps quite appropriate. Luckily, I kept some detailed diary notes at the very outset of the project, so again, I find it much more simple to relate to my daily diary rather than just dip into memories as they occur.

So here goes…………………

Chapter 1

HOW IT ALL BEGAN

Sitting in our house in Montauroux in January 2009, I had been trying to decide exactly where the initial ideal came from – without complete success. I am an avid reader of Octane and Classic & Sports Car magazines, and feel sure that I must have read something about the 1997 Peking-Paris somewhere in one of these journals. Certainly, something like that fired up my initial interest.

I began by reading as much about the Peking-Paris as I could possibly find. I started with Rosie Thomas' book 'Border Crossing', which I think on its own was possibly the major influence. Whilst I didn't find Rosie Thomas a very attractive character, nonetheless her narrative was both fascinating and compelling. She clearly had the ability to weave a wonderful story around her adventures, and her vivid descriptions of how she came to be involved in the rally, how she chose a partner (or indeed was herself chosen!), the preparation of the car and, of course, all of the trials and tribulations of the rally, were quite superb, and indeed I have re-read the book two or three times over the last couple of years.

I avidly read Sid Stelvio's (Philip Young) reports on the 1997 rally, and managed to obtain a DVD of the event, which gives a fine insight into endurance rallying across the world. In retrospect, the DVD with its jolly accompanying music and breathtaking photography, perhaps does not give an accurate reflection of the many difficulties that are to be encountered along the way, although I suppose this should hardly come as a surprise as, of course, it is the organiser's overview of the event, meant to encourage people to take part in the next one!

I managed to find a copy of 'Prince Borghese's Trail' written by Genevieve Obert, a writer for a US car magazine, who did the trip in a Hillman Hunter with Linda Dodwell as navigator. Once again, this proved to be a fascinating read, as it showed the rally from a somewhat different perspective. Rosie Thomas and her driver, Phil Bowen, were keenly competing in all of the time trials, wanting to achieve a high position on the leader board, whilst the two ladies were taking a more leisurely view of the whole trip!

The final pre-rally read was, perhaps the best of all. For Christmas 2006 Yvonne gave me a copy of Luigi Barzini's original descriptive narrative of the 1907 Peking to Paris. This book tells the story of how the original race came to be, with its central characters being Prince Borghese, the wealthy Italian prince, accompanied by his riding mechanic, Ettore Guizzardi, and Luigi Barzini, who was a prominent journalist of the time. Barzini telegraphed reports of the journey back to Italy throughout the whole journey (the blog of 1907!) and upon his return assembled these reports into a book, which became an absolute best seller in Italy.

I devoured the book and read it in two or three days flat – not being able to put it down. The descriptions were so graphic and even though they were on the road for sixty days, he managed to make each day seem like a separate, exciting adventure of its own.

Sitting here in 2009, I STILL find it difficult to conceive that, with the limited technology at his disposal, with the design of the car being in its infancy, and with the road infrastructure across the length of his journey being almost non-existent, they were able to complete the journey in such a relatively short time.

Incidentally, since I have returned I have also managed to obtain a copy of 'The Mad Motorists' which is another fine book written about the 1907 race. This book had taken a complete overview of the event and perhaps provides a more balanced view of the 1907 race and, of course, it covers all of the other competitors in the event.

So, how did the 1907 event come about?

In January 1907 the French newspaper "le Matin" put out a challenge.
"WILL ANYONE AGREE TO GO, THIS SUMMER,
FROM PEKING TO PARIS BY AUTOMOBILE"

This was really a ploy to increase sales of their newspaper, and it worked...... Forty cars entered but, eventually, only five teams took part. One of them was, of course the 35 year old Italian Prince Borghese, in a 40 horsepower 'Itala'. Apart from some strengthening to the bodywork and shock absorbers, and a modification to enable it to use low-grade petrol, there were no alterations to the engine or the chassis.

Once Prince Borghese had arrived in China, in preparation, he travelled the first 300 miles on horseback across Mongolia, to find a route. Using a wooden rod, the same width as his car, he measured the narrowest points between the rocky cliffs to ensure that he could get through.

There were no Regulations on this rally - only that the crews had to leave Peking in a motor car, and arrive in Paris. They started on 10th June 1907 at 8.00 am and took 60 days to reach Paris from Peking, beating the other teams by 3 weeks.

Prince Borghese was so far ahead of the field, that he had time to make a detour from Moscow to St. Petersburg to attend a dinner. St. Petersburg had not originally been on the route, which was through Mongolia, to Russia - Siberia, Moscow, then to Estonia, Latvia, Lithuania, Poland, Germany and, finally, Paris.

The Prince and the pauper

"Progress does not emerge from backing mediocrity or routine." – Le Matin

I believe it must have been somewhere in the region of 2004 that the first adverts appeared in the motoring press for the next running of the Peking-Paris, which was to be in 2007 to celebrate the centenary of the original race. Inspired by all the reading matter that I had devoured, I immediately sent off for an application form – originally simply to have an understanding of what the event was about. Once I had received the entry form and promotional literature, I suppose it was at that time that my imagination was finally fired up to contemplate taking on, for us, what would be an enormous undertaking.

I suppose I have always had an interest in cars since I was really young, when Dad took me off to Barnby Moor in Nottinghamshire in the early 1950s to watch the Monte Carlo rally cars checking in on their route from the start in Edinburgh to the completion in Monte Carlo. Indeed, I still have some grainy black and white photographs of that era – a particular favourite is a wonderful shot of Eric Carlsson thrashing his Saab through the Alps in deep snow – an inspirational photograph if ever there was one.

Through the 1990s Yvonne and I started to visit the Coys Festival at Silverstone in the summer and, via a series of strange coincidences, became interested in the cars driven by Sidney Allard. In 1998, we bought a black Allard 'M' type (the famous "black-grilled Allard" – don't ask – another story, another time!). In hindsight, the Allard was a great big, ugly brute, but as our first 'buy' it transported us into a world of weekend runs and fascinating drives across Europe. In our first year of ownership, we took the Allard on the Euroclassic Rally down through the centre of France to finish in Marseille, and in our second year, we took it right through Central Europe to finish in Salzburg. However, by that time we had 'got the bug'. The Allard had been terrific inasmuch as it had introduced us to a motoring pastime that took us through countries and towns we perhaps wouldn't have visited otherwise, and even more importantly introduced us to many, many friends in the motoring world. Driving the Allard and watching other classic cars constantly whipping by us made me start to think of the type of car that I would want to own eventually. I narrowed my criteria down to 1) must be pre-War, 2) must be open-top, 3) must have ample space to carry luggage on long distance rallies. We anguished long and hard for several months before eventually settling on a 1933 Aston Martin le Mans as our favoured car.

Famous Black Grilled Allard

It was on the Euroclassic route to Salzburg in 1999 that we finally completed a deal by phone to purchase our 'dream' car. After much haggling on a day-to-day basis throughout the whole rally, we arrived in Salzburg with the news that we had managed to buy Sir Malcolm Campbell's original

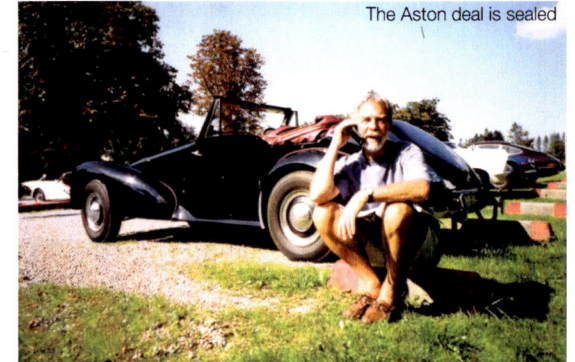

The Aston deal is sealed

Aston Martin 'le Mans' which came to us steeped in history and in magnificent condition, having been rebuilt, over a period of ten years, in St. Louis, Missouri. We bought the Aston in 2000 and it has given us many thousands of miles of amazing motoring. Later in 2000 we drove the car to Budapest and back and then in 2001 on the Euroclassic rally to Imola. The following year we drove to Valencia and back.

1933 Aston Martin Le Mans

We have done the Scottish Malts rally twice in the Aston, and perhaps our finest moment was being eligible to take part in the 2004 Mille Miglia in Italy. In 2006, we shipped the car to Buenos Aires and took part in the Argentinian Mille Millas, driving up and down the Andes and over into Chile. As I chat at the moment we have heard a whisper that we may again be eligible for the 2009 Mille Miglia – we shall see!

In 2002, I started to wonder about the possibility of running a 1950s sports car, which would allow us access into different types of events. We bought a somewhat battered Jaguar XK120 drophead from Twyford Moors in Clanfield, Sussex. Over the period of a year the car was completely stripped down and rebuilt, and in April 2003 we took delivery of the completed car. The XK has taken us around the whole of Ireland on the Irish Trial, completed four or five Scottish Malts rallies, done the 2004 and 2005 Rallye des Alpes, taken us to Istanbul and back (more of which later!) been literally thrashed around the Adelaide hills in the 'Classic Adelaide Rally', followed by a 4000 mile tour across Australia, and has just come back from a tour of Iceland, so as can be seen, our motoring interests had progressed significantly!

During the early part of the summer of 2005, Yvonne picked up the copy of the Rosie Thomas book and, whilst on the one hand, I am sure she enjoyed it,

XK 'as was'

XK in Classic Adelaide

on the other hand it posed more questions than it answered! Rosie Thomas dramatised the rally but also made it clear how potentially difficult such an exploit could be. In July 2005, we arrived in Montauroux in the XK prior to setting off a couple of weeks later for the Rallye des Alpes. It was sitting by the poolside in Montauroux that I really started to think seriously about entering the Peking-Paris, but Yvonne's initial response was perhaps not quite what I was expecting. She completely understood my desire to take part, but expressed a degree of concern over the privations and difficulties that could be encountered. Over a few days we talked through the pros and cons, but I was absolutely sure that I would only do the event if we could do it together. My view was that it was going to be an extraordinary trip half way round the world, but one that I would only consider doing with Yvonne, so that we could enjoy the experiences together. I must have put together a good argument as within a couple of days we had definitely agreed that we were both up for it and, over a glass of wine one evening, decided we would make an entry.

Dave and Jo Roberts joined us in Montauroux in their XK150 as we were doing the Rallye des Alpes together and, inevitably, the subject of the Peking-Paris came up. We suggested that they may also like to join us. Several glasses of the local rosé later we decided that we would 'go for it'. All the enthusiasm was there, we now just needed to turn it into fact.

Chapter 2

INITIAL PREPARATIONS

Having made the initial commitment to take part, eventually when the effects of the wine had worn off, it started to occur to us what lay ahead. Finding a car, preparing the car, procuring the spares, preparing ourselves mentally and physically and all the other thousands of minor details that we would inevitably have to consider.

As soon as we were back home in Foolow I contacted the Rally Office, who immediately made it clear that places were running short, and we would need to get our application in the post, together with a non-returnable cheque for £2000. This was 'The Big Commitment'.

Within a day or two we had confirmation of acceptance, and we were on the way. The prime requirement which occupied our minds for some weeks later, was exactly what car to contemplate taking.

With the acceptance of the entry fee came a substantial book, prepared by Philip Young, outlining all the requirements for preparing a car for an endurance rally such as this. I think it was reading through the document initially that gave us the first insight as to the complexities that were to confront us. To date, we had run our other two cars, which were generally well prepared, and had simply fired up the engine and turned up to the start of the various rallies we had entered. The only normal preparation was a good service and regular oil changes. It was quite clear from the rally preparation book that what was required of the car here was a somewhat different 'kettle of fish'. The organisers made it very clear that, whilst there was to be mechanical support on the event, it really only was to help out under extreme difficulties, and that it was each competitor's complete responsibility to ensure that he kept his car up to scratch all the way round, and it was his responsibility certainly to keep up with the rally on a day-by-day basis.

I read through the preparation book very enthusiastically and highlighted all of the points that I felt were relevant. It transpired that effectively the whole book was highlighted from end to end!

It was at this stage that I started to reflect on the one major concern I had – my complete lack of mechanical knowledge. I possess a great deal of enthusiasm and I am generally fairly willing but, sad to say, the intricacies of the mechanical side of the motor car had somewhat passed me by in my youth – and it did rather occur to me that it could be a little late to be learning now. Nonetheless, I determined to increase my learning curve somewhat and threw myself into ingesting as much knowledge as I possibly could.

I decided to set out my own initial criteria for the selection of a suitable car:-
Firstly it had to be open-topped. I could not contemplate driving half way around the world in a 'tin top'. All of our rallying to date had been in open topped cars, and we seem to have become quite hardly as the years have passed by. Several years ago now, Yvonne had recognised my passion for open-air motoring and had mostly (!!), willingly, acceded to it. So, open top it had to be.

We knew the terrain was going to be extremely tough going – the organisers made absolutely no bones about how difficult Mongolia was going to be. It was therefore essential that the car be extremely rugged and had good, simple, basic engineering principles. Clearly, nobody in central Mongolia was going to be able to fathom a complicated electronic glitch in a complex engine bay, but surely they would be able to sort out most engineering problems with a large hammer or welding gear! So, simple and strong it needed to be.

The organisers had made it abundantly clear that the quality of petrol we may expect in Mongolia was to be the poorest possibly available on the planet. Initially, they were talking about 70 to 75 octane petrol, and they put out the word that any car with a sophisticated high compression engine simply would not cope. So, low compression engine it had to be. Here we met our first stumbling block on my limited (none) engineering knowledge – what indeed was a low compression engine? It is amazing how quickly you pick up information once you start chatting to friends and colleagues, and I soon was a near expert on compression ratios!

There were one or two other issues, such as high ground clearance, ready availability of spares etc. etc. but really the first three items were possibly the most critical.

My first thoughts always centred around a pre-War car, but I soon came to the conclusion that anything that I really fancied taking on a trip such as this was well beyond my pocket. So a later classic then, something from the 40s or 50s. I was very much surprised to discover that my first criterion – a car being open top – was to preclude so many cars. Obviously the range of saloon cars available was absolutely enormous, but the list was drastically reduced as soon as the requirement for a convertible came into play.

It occurred to me that an American car was perhaps to be my starting place. American cars are reckoned to be extremely sturdy as, certainly in the 40s and 50s, a lot of American cars were travelling long distances on loose gravel roads, and in general the run-of-the mill American car was based on a sturdy truck engine. Chassis were usually extremely strong and most definitely spares would be available.

So, American it was to be, but where do we start looking.

A good friend of mine in Yorkshire, Richard, had a considerable collection of cars, amongst which were several American cars which, until now, I had given very little thought to. My interests to date had been for English thoroughbreds and I was really a little down on knowledge of American automobiles. Richard seemed to be a good starting place therefore.

In April 2005, I rang Richard and outlined my ideas and suggested we have lunch together so that he could give me some tips. Imagine my surprise, therefore, to find that Richard had also lodged his entry for the rally and, surprise, surprise, had entered an American car. At least I felt that my preliminary assessments had been in the right direction.

Lunch in Wetherby a week or so later was fascinating as I learnt more about American cars in a couple of hours than I had ever known in my whole life. Richard was an absolute font of knowledge and was hugely supportive.

At the end of lunch Richard told me of a strange circumstance that had lead to the surprising acquisition of a Chevrolet Bel Air into his collection, when really he didn't want one! Richard had bought a Plymouth convertible from someone via a newspaper advert and was delighted by the quality of his acquisition. Some months later the same chap called Richard to ask him if he would like to buy his 1950 Chevrolet Bel Air. Richard explained that he didn't require another car, as it was in so many ways similar to the Plymouth that he had already purchased. However, the vendor explained that he had recently been diagnosed with a potentially terminal illness and didn't want his wife to be saddled with the difficulties of selling the Chevrolet. He offered Richard the car at somewhere in the region of 50% of its 'real' value on the understanding that, should he survive the illness (which sadly he didn't), then he could have the car back at the same price. Richard, considerate and caring person that he is, had agreed the deal and the car was standing in his garage at home as we spoke.

He suggested that, with no obligation whatsoever, we might like to look over the car as he would be more than happy to pass it on to us should we be at all interested. Inevitably Richard's house was vaguely on our route back home, and it was with a degree of trepidation that we called to his home later than afternoon. Richard has an amazingly eclectic collection of cars all housed within a huge warehouse adjoining the rear of his house. The collection is quite astonishing firstly, in the breadth of its variety but, more importantly, in the superb quality of every vehicle. Richard had specialised in buying top quality cars, generally with extremely low mileages and, indeed, employed his own staff of three mechanics to oversee and look after his collection.

We had visited Richard's home on many occasions previously but I really wasn't prepared for the car I was confronted with.

First sight of Chevy

My first impression was that it was absolutely GIGANTIC, but my second thought was that it was in absolutely 'mint' condition. The car was such that, had someone explained that it had been wheeled off the production line that morning, it would have been easily believed. Every element of the car was just like new. Whoever had carried out the restoration had really started from the bottom upwards and, it appeared, everything was in absolutely prime condition.

Immaculate engine bay

Whoever had prepared the car had not only covered every detail, but had added on every conceivable extra that Chevrolet offered at the time. Every corner of the car was embellished with enormous chromium plated wings, brackets, cover strips, headlamp shades, stoneguards, over-riders, badge bars etc. etc. etc. Most eye-catchingly, it came with a pair of external spotlights affixed to each front door, which were capable of adjustment from inside the car via the most wonderfully engineered rotating chromium swivel handles, complete with onyx-like knurled knobs – the description is 'the dog's bollocks' in American automotive terms !!!!

Richard gave us an extensive tour of the car and, my, did it take a long time to walk right round the perimeter! On the one hand, I was absolutely over-whelmed by the sheer scale of the car and of the quality of the rebuild, on the other hand I was also taken aback by how soon this situation had occurred. I felt that finding a car was going to take a huge amount of thought, anguish, travelling etc. and here I was being presented with, 'perhaps', our Peking to Paris rally car within one and a half hours of having completed our exploratory talk over lunch!

Richard had outlined the details of the deal he had made with the owner, who in the meantime, sadly, had succumbed to his illness. Richard explained that he had no desire whatsoever to make any profit on the car and was quite happy to pass the car on to us for exactly the same price he had paid for it.

Imagine the dilemmas we were faced with on the drive home that evening. Was it the right car for us - my gosh wasn't it big - was it simply 'too good' to thrash half way round the world - was it all happening too soon - good Lord it was big……………

At this stage there really wasn't a huge rush, but nonetheless I couldn't help but think that this proposition was really too good to miss. I kept on thinking that the only down side was that I hadn't had the opportunity to look around too much, but I offset that by telling myself that no matter what, I couldn't have found a car in a better condition.

A week or so later we made the decision that we would buy the Chevy. I thought it would fulfil all the initial criteria I had set out and, anyway, Yvonne liked the colour!

So, the deal was done and we acquired a 1950 Chevrolet Bel Air convertible in 'blancmange' Green, complete with 216 cubic inch engine and three-speed manual column change gear box. It had the most amazing electrically operated power-hood, that was the equivalent of a small marquee. The interior was green leather with inset fabric panels of green and cream stripes, obviously never having been sat upon. The car even came with a magnificent set of white-wall tyres, the spare still had its rubber nobbles on the surface indicating that it had never been used.

Power Hood

Richard handed over all of the files, including detailed photographic records throughout its reconstruction.

We needed to house the Chevrolet at home, and one of my first requirements was to buy a flexible Carcoon-type container to house one of the other cars, thereby making space in the workshop for the arrival of the Chevy. Fortunately, Rodger, another great motoring friend from the village, offered space in his barn and we were able to erect the new flexible 'garage' to house the XK – thereby freeing up space in the garage at home.

Monday the 18th July dawned bright and sunny, and I set off on my bike to ride from Foolow to Monk Fryston. Sixty-five miles later, and to Richard's immense surprise I freewheeled up to the front door at lunchtime to pick up the Chevy. Rather surprisingly, given the enormous size of the car and its 'trunk', no matter how I tried my bike wouldn't fit into the car and I had to drive home with it sticking upright on the back seats! The car drove beautifully - to the end of Richard's drive – whereupon it seemed not easily to want to change from first into second gear. Surely this wasn't going to be a problem. (Little did I know!)

In the December previously, friend John and I were riding our bikes from Zeebrugge to Antwerp one sunny morning, when John told me to my total surprise that he had also decided to make an entry to the Peking to Paris. Astonishing really that a little village like Foolow would end up with two cars in the rally!

So here we were in July and I had my 'nearly-new' rally car and clearly all I was going to have to do was spend a relatively nominal sum of money on the car to complete the preparations ready for the start in Peking in 2007!

At this stage Dave and Jo were still hunting, and John and Joan also had not really decided what they would like to take. Mike and Josie from Hull were also taking part, and Mike had bought the remnants of a 1929 Chrysler 75 from Quebec. The bits were arriving in packing cases and Mike was shortly to start on an amazing rebuild.

So there we were, five couples in total, ourselves, Dave and Jo, Mike and Josie, John and Joan, Richard and Anne. We all knew there was plenty of work ahead of us, and Richard had a really bright idea that we should all get together at his house and arranged for Peter and Betty Banham to come and give us a general talk as to how we should prepare for our trip, not only the car preparation but all of the other incredibly important ancillary items. (Peter is perhaps one of the most widely respected Endurance Rally car preparers and stories of how he has coaxed cars that were seemingly lost causes to complete rallies are legion!). Whilst Peter took the men on one side to discuss car preparation, spring strengthening, low compression engines, sump guards and a million and one other aspects, Betty took the girls on one side to discuss navigation, border crossings, matters medical, clothes washing techniques, what foods to avoid, suitable clothing, advice on what foods to take, even suggesting a highly nutritious, calorie packed fruit cake!

My memory is that the journey home from Richard and Anne's was fairly quiet, as we all absorbed what we had let ourselves in for, and what considerable amount of work lay ahead for both driver and navigator.

2005
FIRST OUTINGS and STARTING THE RE-FURB

On August bank holiday Monday, we took the Chevrolet across to the Oulton Park Gold Cup Meeting and were, inevitably, drawn to the XK Club members. Keith Fell and Karen were there cooking up bacon sandwiches, with Keith taking time out to express extreme interest in our project. During the course of the afternoon we struck up an agreement that Keith would come to Foolow to work on the car, which would then give me the opportunity to work alongside him and get a basic understanding of exactly how it was put together. I was really relieved as it seemed to be a huge positive step in the right direction, and at last after months of thinking and talking we would get the opportunity to really get stuck in to working on the car.

Interior

The following day we took the car to Hope Show, or more accurately Yvonne drove the car to Hope Show, whilst I took the XK. During the afternoon the heavens opened and, as there was nowhere to shelter, six of us climbed into the Chevy for a bit of weather protection. A minor catastrophe when eventually it stopped raining, Joan who had been absently mindedly playing with a window winder in the rear seat, asked John to get out of the passenger door. Unfortunately, the rear wind-up quarter light had overlapped the passenger door window with the effect that when the door was opened it severely bent the quarter light, smashed the glass and broke the chromium frame. Poor Joan was absolutely beside herself and in tears and we all felt significantly more sorry for Joan than we had concerns for the car. Still, it was only a minor item, and as there wasn't too much work to do on the car.......

A month later Peter and Betty Banham came out to Foolow with Keith and Karen to do a detailed investigation on the car. Peter came up with all sorts of suggestions and everybody wrote frantic notes as to how we were to proceed. A little bit of bad news initially, inasmuch as Peter spotted a small rust stain on the block suggesting it might be cracked. I was a bit downhearted but was told that the engine could be cold stitched relatively easily. Nonetheless, cold stitching the engine seemed to me an 'engine out' job, which was certainly something I hadn't contemplated on my 'as new' car.

23rd October, and we were off to Gaydon to the first Peking-Paris rally seminar. The Chevy seemed to go well and we were running at 80 mph all the way. The seminar was a typical Philip Young production – hard hitting facts and cheap food! Having got our money and our commitment we were then made to realise exactly how tough the rally was going to be and what we might expect of the assistance crews (clearly very little, as there were three support crews to 135 cars!) Nonetheless, it was a great opportunity to meet other competitors and we formed the basis of what were to become some very good friendships. I checked the engine when we got home, and was a little disappointed to see water again showing through the side of the block.

John had announced that he had found a Rover 110 in Hull so, together with friend, Jim, we went off to Hull to take a look. The car was in excellent condition and John did the deal – though when the fond owner heard what John planned to do in the car, he visibly blanched. As always with these affairs, John's enthusiasm was somewhat blunted when, on the way home, one of the front tyres developed a huge blister – maybe the car had heard what was expected of it!

25 October. Heavens, the car won't start! Major problems with the battery. Our 6-volt battery won't take a charge (just found out that all American cars strangely are fitted with 6-volt systems – something we were warned against by the rally team at Gaydon a couple of days ago, looks like we shall have to do some thinking here). My battery charger is 12-volt and wouldn't charge the car, so I had to dash into Sheffield to buy a new 6-volt charger, unfortunately it failed, meaning I had to return to Sheffield and buy another one, it failed too. Eventually I borrowed a battery charger from Roger Thorpe in Castleton and, at least, we were able to get the car up and running.

28 October Keith and Karen came over for the day, and by now I had moved the car round to Andrew's garage in Foolow – it's a much bigger area and he has agreed to loan us his engine hoist. Once the bonnet was up, Keith noticed water leaking from the bottom hose. In no time at all Keith had the engine out, but very bad news was to come. Keith scraped the paint off the side of the block to discover that the engine had already been stitched from end to end previously. Lunchtime back at Spread Eagle House, we phoned around various engine stitching companies to discover that it would cost in the region of £2,600 to stitch the block. Keith's view was that we should simply scrap the engine and start again. Needless to say, I was a bit overwhelmed by this, but agreed eventually that it was the only course of action. Once the engine was out, we discovered that the clutch plate was worn and that the flywheel was cracked. What a day it had been. I was absolutely knackered from all the tugging and pulling with the engine and was not just a little dispirited with all the work that was needed.

Strangely, despite how I felt, I recall Yvonne and I went out to the Walnut Club Restaurant in Hathersage and had a particularly good evening. It's amazing what a bottle of wine and good company can do!

29th October Amazing. 9.00 am and Keith phoned to say that, on his way home yesterday evening, he pulled into a garage for some fuel and, whilst he was in the queue to pay, he picked up an American car magazine. Over breakfast early this morning, Keith read through the small ads and came across an identical Chevy engine block for the princely sum of £30. I dashed round to Andrew's, took some photographs of our engine so that we could check to ensure it matched exactly. Keith called later that day to pick up the photographs.

1st November Keith rang to say that indeed he had managed to buy the engine for £30 plus £100 carriage, and it was expected to be delivered on the 12th November. This seemed better news indeed and I was immediately cheered up.

5th November Keith rang with even better news. A friend of his who lived in Maidenhead, where the 'new' engine had been located turned out to be only five minutes away from where the engine was located; even better, he was coming up to Keith's the following day and would bring the engine with him. Suddenly the news was getting better, just five days had elapsed since the engine was discovered to be useless and here we were with a new engine, delivered in half the time we thought was possible, and saving the £100 carriage cost. Another high for me. I was to discover that the rally preparation process seemed to be based upon significant shifts in my morale, from extreme lows to extreme highs. Though I am bound to say that, as the months progressed, the proportion of lows managed to considerably outweigh the highs.

14th November So we had a new engine block but what now? I took a look at what £30 had bought me and was really disappointed. I don't know what I expected but it certainly wasn't the lump of grimy, oily iron that stood in front of me. This somehow had to be converted into a fully working engine that would be capable of dragging the Chevy, the two of us and two tons of luggage half way around the world.

A bit of phoning around soon established that there were very few people in the UK capable of working on Chevrolet engines. I eventually tracked down Adrian Bailey at Auto Services in Colne in Lancashire. As soon as I spoke to Adrian, I realised he had a huge knowledge of Chevrolets and he certainly talked a good story. I arranged to go and see him.

21st November I found my way across to Colne, possibly one of the most depressing places in the UK. It really didn't seem to have anything going for it. It had a complex one-way system that was almost impossible to navigate. The houses were of the type that had been bulldozed down fifty years ago in most other major cities. Seventy percent of the shops had closed down and, to boot, it was pouring with rain. Auto Services garage also didn't do anything to improve my initial views on Colne. It was housed in a cavernous, ancient unheated building filled from wall to wall with unrecognisable rusty wrecks and without a soul to be seen. Eventually, from between a pile of oily, filthy oil drums, an oily, filthy chap appeared and announced that it was Adrian himself. Despite initial appearances, clearly Adrian knew a thing or two about Chevrolets, and what spares he didn't have in stock, he had a contact for in the USA. Indeed, Adrian told me that what he didn't know about Chevrolets could be written on a very small piece of paper. Adrian told me that, despite the purchase of my new Chevy block, he would propose to swap this for a later model 1954 engine which had a pressurized oil system rather than the 'dip and splash' system that my engine had. (I later had the opportunity to see one of these dip and splash systems and was amazed to see that it was just as 'Heath Robinson' as the description suggests. As the crankshaft rotated, little swinging buckets dipped into the oil reservoir in the sump and splashed it all over the crankshaft – rather like those clocks that are driven by water splashing into a complex system of buckets which drive spindles etc.) So I was mightily relieved to think that our new engine would be a significantly improved model. Adrian agreed that, for the exchange of £5200, he would give me a new engine, completely rebuilt by the end of February 2006, complete with new carburettors, fuel pump and water pump etc. Furthermore, Adrian was able to gather together any spares that I should need, and we spent some considerable time listing spares for him to price up.

22nd November, I posted a cheque for £1500 to Adrian and crossed my fingers ready for the end of February.

24th November I fetched the Chevy back home from Andy's garage. It was an ideal day, freezing cold, and we were able to drag the car back round home with Andy's tractor, and pushed it into the workshop without damaging the grass. At least, now it was at home, I would be able to start some work on it myself.

26th November. I really felt that I was starting to get to grips with the car myself now. I stripped out the front and back seats and was most careful to collect all the nuts and bolts together and carefully label everything as to exactly where it came from. (This was in direct contrast to watching Keith perform. When he stripped the engine out, he simply dropped every possible combination of nut, bolt, washer,

spring, rods, arms, catches, cables, carburettors, manifolds etc. into one enormous box. I was horrified, as I could never see how everything could possibly go back together again and be a fully functioning engine. I clearly recall Keith giving me a very disdainful look!)

I also stripped off the chrome bumpers and over-riders etc. sprayed them with oil and wrapped everything in bubble wrap ready for reintroducing them back to the car who-knows-when.

28th November I phoned Michelin Tyres Research Department and they gave me some really sound advice on what tyres were available for our requirements. Our invaluable Rally Preparation Book made it clear that tyres should be upgraded from the normal 4-ply tread and 1-ply wall to 8-ply tread and 4-ply wall. The strong suggestion was that on endurance rallies such as this it was the walls that took almost as big a battering as the tyre treads themselves.

I spent the afternoon driving round scrap yards in Sheffield looking for new front seats for Yvonne and me. It really was one of the most depressing afternoons of my life. Firstly, it was snowing very heavily and, of course, scrap yards are not the most welcoming of places in any case, the cars were stacked two or three on top of each other, some crushed beyond recognition, others with their battered interiors and blood stains suggesting untold stories of heartache for someone, somewhere. I struggled round a couple of yards but was so utterly dispirited I returned home.

The seats I was looking for were individual front seats on their own runners, rather than the continuous bench seat that was originally fitted in the Chevy (ideal for a kiss and a cuddle at a drive-in movie, but less than ideal for a drive through the Gobi Desert). The seats needed to be fully adjustable and with good thigh and lumber supports. I also had a fancy for a velour finish rather than leather, as I felt that anything slippery would be less than ideal in hot, sticky conditions.

The thoughts of tramping round yet more scrap yards made me turn to eBay, and would you believe that within five minutes I found a pair of Rover 75 seats which were exactly what I was after. There was just an hour to run on the auction and there were no bids. 55 minutes and £25 later I was the proud owner of two fine seats that were to prove to be extraordinarily comfortable throughout the whole journey. Needless to say the best benefit was the knowledge that I didn't have to tramp the depressing scrap yards again.

1st December I had spotted on the drive down from Richard's initially that the speedo wasn't working so, when Keith came over, the first job we did was to strip it out ready for having it looked at. Sadly, the view under the dashboard horrified Keith who announced that the wiring was extremely poor with the outer casing cracked and fractured in many places. His view was that the whole of the car should be rewired. What? - on my 'new' car? Generally, however, we had a great day and stripped off the front and rear suspension.

6th December Got an email from the USA today to say that the cheapest solution for the speedo would be to buy a rebuilt one at a cost of $175. It was about twice as much as I had expected, but inevitably sent off an email of agreement.

7th December Buying the seats appeared to be simplicity itself. Organising the delivery, however, proved to be more complex than shipping the car to the other side of the world. I must say that two car seats are not the easiest thing to parcel and post, but nonetheless I didn't envisage quite such problems. The chap I was buying them from was a nurse and appeared to set off for work at 6.00 in the morning, not returning until 10.00 in the evening. He also appeared to work seven days a week, which gave little opportunity for the carriers to pick up the seats, and I recall that in the end, the chap had to take a day off work just to organise the collection!

8th December I took a trip across to Demon Tweeks for a bit of light relief. The idea was to buy quite a few parts for the car. It was only when I got there I realised how complex everything on a car is. I thought I had a reasonably simple shopping list –

seatbelts, bulbs, navigation light etc. I was faced with an enormous selection. Seatbelts came as lap only, lap and diagonal, 3-point, 4-point or 5-point fixings, together with a combination of every colour under the sun. Headlamp bulbs came with six different fixing types, not one of which was appropriate to the Chevy. Navigation lights had left-hand fixing with right-hand swivels, right-hand fixings with left-hand swivels, but inevitably not the precise combination that I required. I was also after some mesh headlamp guards – they came either the correct diameter with the wrong fixing lugs or correct fixing lugs with grills that were three times the diameter of the headlamps. Chastened, I returned home with precisely nothing, except more questions than answers.

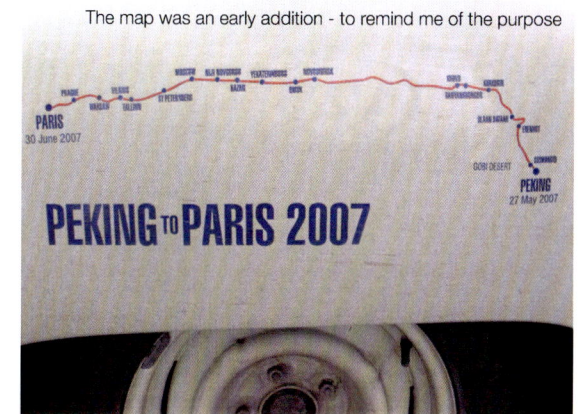
The map was an early addition - to remind me of the purpose

PEKING TO PARIS 2007

12th December I took the leaf and coil springs to GME Springs in Sheffield for re-tempering and, to my delight, they said they could do both types of springs which I thought saved me an extra journey. However, I then realised that it indeed created an additional journey, I had only taken one leaf and one coil, thinking they would be making new ones. I was told that it was cheaper to refurb the existing ones at about £100 per spring, so I returned home again and Yvonne took the other set of springs later in the afternoon. I spent a happy afternoon drawing details of the seat frame that I required to fix my smart new seats. The original bench seats were fixed through the floor with four bolts, and I was loath to start drilling new holes in the floor so devised a seating frame which would utilise the existing holes, carry my new seat guides and also provide a fixing for the console that I was thinking of fitting between the two front seats. It occurred to me that we would need to be carrying route books, maps, pens, pencils, watches, trip, GPS, water, sweets, dusters etc. etc. etc. and the idea of a central console seemed to be the perfect solution. The Chevy was so large inside that there was plenty of space to accommodate storage facilities.

19th December Jim Styles and Peter Bacon from Brosterfield Engineering in the village came round to take some precise measurements for my seating frame. Jim, as ever, was full of enthusiasm. Working as he did at the other end of the village, it really was a great bonus having someone like him with all of the facilities so close by.

20th December Jim rang this morning and, amazingly, he has finished the seating frame already. It's a brilliant job – very 'engineering' (i.e. absolutely huge and somewhat over designed!)

I set off down to Peter Banham's in the afternoon to pick up a set of seat belts he had obtained for me, and he also was going to source an alternator. On the way back I bought a whole load of timber to build the console in the car and also the storage bins in the rear.

22nd December Adrian rang in the morning with some good news and some bad news. The good news was that he had had the block crack tested and it is perfectly OK, but the head is cracked – he is going to have to source another.

Nipped over to Sheffield in the afternoon to pick up the springs from GME, which seemed excessively expensive at £352 – much more than I had expected – once again!

27th December I set off today to fit the seating frame into the car and fix the seats onto the frame. Not an entirely successful day. I found that the seating frame was not exactly the right size and when I used my new angle grinder to make the adaptations I burned a rather neat circular hole in the centre of my sweater. It took me all day to get the frame and seats into position, only to discover that the whole unit was too far back, and the seats wouldn't fully recline. (We had always had the idea that the seats should go back as far as possible for if there was ever the necessity for one of us to sleep whilst the other one drove.)

28th December The amazing Jim had returned the seat frame by lunchtime with new bits brazed on to move the whole unit further forward. I fitted the seats later in the day and everything worked perfectly. As it transpired, there was never the necessity for either of us to sleep in the car, so the whole exercise proved to be a trifle fruitless.

30th December I had a lot planned for today, and thought the overnight snowfall would ruin everything. Fortunately, the snow cleared as quickly as it arrived. I dashed off to Peter Banham's to pick up the alternator and pay for seat belts etc. and got back in time for Keith and Karen coming over. We managed to put the new rear springs on and one front coil, and spent some time measuring up for the seat belt fixings.

In the afternoon Adrian and his wife, Christine, called and it was really useful as we were able to discuss all sorts of things about the car. Adrian had a good look around and noted, for instance, that the car had its original 1950s front brakes but later 1950s rear brakes. This was quite helpful when arranging to order the appropriate spares. Keith stripped off the flywheel and asked Adrian to arrange for it to be balanced. Adrian seemed to think that this was a bit of a sophistication for a truck engine, but Keith, ever the perfectionist, felt that it would be worthwhile – it was only another £70 for heavens sake!

I decided it was time for me to start some fitting out work of my own, and it was really pleasant, at long last, to get involved with work which was within my own capabilities. Anything engineering, electrical or mechanical, I had little or no knowledge of at all, and was able only to follow the simplest of instructions. However, my general plan was to fit out the inside of the car with adequate storage. Having removed the existing back seat assembly completely, we were left with a huge void in which the general plan was to construct storage bins to carry all of our equipment. Chatting to various people over the months it had been suggested that prying hands may well relieve us of various pieces of our equipment during our journey and, therefore, I decided that it would be better to construct secure storage bins that were able to be locked. Also there was an enormous gap between the two front seats, and I had the idea to design and build a console unit that filled this substantial gap. The plan was to fill a unit that was large enough to carry our maps, road books and route cards whilst having separate compartments for pens, pencils and navigator's miscellaneous detritus, compartments for water bottle, thermos flask, and panels upon which we could mount stop watches, trip meter and GPS equipment. I also was keen to incorporate a radio so that we could drive our iPod and listen to the hundreds of tunes we had recorded specially for our journey (as it transpired, there was so much to see and do on the whole trip that we never once turned the equipment on!).

2006

1st January Another year dawns, but I'm afraid that festivities cannot take precedence over the need to push on with the work. I took the broken rear quarter light window out today and it proved to be an extremely ticklish job. I couldn't even work out how to take off the winding handle initially – it was an embarrassingly poor start. It's a bit like buying a new car and not being able to find out how to open the door. Two or three phone calls later I discovered that Mr. Chevrolet had devised the most cunning spring-loaded chromium cover plate, which secreted the completely hidden fixing pin, which required a £250 specialised tool to remove it. Nonetheless, a hammer and a large assortment of nails, and four hours later, produced success. I spent the rest of the day cutting up timber for the rear storage bins and designed the metal support brackets, all of which were taken round to Jim's for fabrication.

20th January Back from France today, having had a two-week Chevy-free break, except, of course, that I have been making copious notes and produced dozens of free-hand sketches.

I picked up all the brackets from Jim, which he had completed; inevitably, again they need a little bit of fine tuning – they are so complex in shape.

I was somewhat disappointed when I got the speedo back today from the States.

I was expecting to get back the whole unit, but only the tiny centre portion arrived. You don't get much for 175 dollars (plus, as it transpired, a further 35 dollars for import duty!)

I spoke to Adrian, who told me that the engine is on its way and, indeed, all the parts are going to Clay Cross tomorrow for specialised machining. I finished off the day by ordering a new wiring loom from 'Chevys of the 40s'.

22nd January I stripped out the oil gauge, amps and fuel gauges today, which was a much easier job than I expected. I think that's the first time so far I've found myself in the position of making a statement like this!

23rd January I posted off the rest of the speedo to Dick Reynolds in the States, and I can already feel UK Customs rubbing their hands in the background.

I picked up the last bits of brackets from Jim and Hammerite-painted them all.

26th January My handwritten notes say "Great day – at last". Adrian rang early with his suggestion for a spares list – cost at £2,000 plus. He suggested a deal whereby he would take back any unused parts with a 50% handling charge. Not much of a bargain there, I thought, but he didn't seem to be open to negotiation and where else am I going to get the parts from. He told me that the engine was still on course for the end of February.

I spent the rest of the day fabricating the console, making steel brackets and starting to build the rear bins. I really felt as though I had a long but successful day.

2nd February I took a trip to the throbbing metropolis of Colne today to talk about spares. As I arrived and was hovering about in the seedy area that was rather lightheartedly called ' his office' I happened to overhear Adrian on the 'phone talking to his supplier in the States, and was horrified to discover that the pistons and the rings that had been delivered were the wrong size. Nonetheless, I was told 'we shall overcome'. Adrian produced an enormous box of spares and I could see that I was going to have some difficulty in deciding what to take and what not to take. I could barely lift the box off the floor!

Back home in the afternoon to take a further look at the storage bins in the rear of the car and, given the huge quantity of spares I had been presented with in the morning, started to worry about space in the car. I therefore decided to increase the size of the rear bins by building a second tier in which we thought we could house all our plastic boxes containing medical supplies and food etc. This would be an ideal location as it would be within relatively easy reach.

3rd February A full day, but, again, with not much to show for it. A bit more timber work done and the back panel to the bins was fixed. With the car being such an irregular shape, joinery work was ten times more difficult than, say, fixing a cupboard in the kitchen. The shapes, curves and profiles meant that everything had to be put in, adjusted, put back, re-adjusted, and on and on. There were many days like this when I seemed to work for 7 or 8 hours, but when I stood back at the end of the day, could barely see what I'd done. I was starting to find some difficulty in explaining myself away, as whenever Yvonne came up to the workshop to deliver coffee and cakes, the car looked to her exactly the same as it had done three days previously. I'm sure she thought I had another woman stashed away in the workshop.

5th February I did a bit more work on the interior today, and the rear compartment was almost finished. However, I had a sobering moment when trying my first fixing of the seat belts which I had bought at great expense. The seat belts worked really well, as they clamped us back into the seat as they were designed to do. However, the handbrake on the Chevy was an 'umbrella' type which protruded out from under the dashboard, and in my seatbelt bondage I couldn't reach to within a foot of the handbrake. Clearly, some rethinking would have to be done!

Around this time we lunched with Dave and Jo and started to think what we could do to give the cars their big 'shakedown'. Philip Young had constantly warned against turning up in Peking without having properly tested out the car over significant distances. Indeed, this message certainly came home to me as friends, David and Adele Cohen, who did the 1997 Peking-Paris in a Stutz Bearcat, told how they had just managed to finish the car an hour before it was rolled into its packing case for shipping to China. The car was a complete nightmare from the word 'go' and in fact only made two days of the rally before it succumbed to an irreparable electrical problem – a one dollar component had failed and the Chinese authorities wouldn't allow electrical equipment to be shipped into the country! The sum total for David and Adele was an extraordinarily expensive three days rallying. We decided that we would very much take Philip Young's advice on board and started to plan a long, circuitous drive around Europe. We eventually plumped on Istanbul as our 'target' destination and were thinking in terms of a September start date. At least we had a date to focus on and by this time Dave and Jo had bought a lovely 1954 two-seater Sunbeam Alpine. It was a great looking car but in slightly suspect condition in one or two areas. Dave and Jo were just about to embark on a similar project to ours.

6th February I called to Bielowski's – our local friendly upholstery – to see about some vinyl fabric for covering our rear bins and central console. I couldn't believe it, they had only one spare roll of vinyl and it was exactly, not just near, but exactly the right coloured vinyl. I know in the grand plan of things this wasn't a major component for the project, but you need some good 'breaks' for heaven's sake!

New interior - seats Terratrip central console etc

14th February Keith had suggested I bought a

new, heavy-duty battery, and thought Halfords would be a good bet. Easy job there, I thought, just nip to Halfords and pick up a battery. Wrong again. No surprise therefore to discover that there was a myriad of choice. I was so overwhelmed that initially I was in need of medical attention, but I made the whole thing easier on myself by simply choosing one that fitted in the rectangular tray that already existed.

19th February We had been told that we needed to buy a Terratrip trip meter, which was essential for accurate measuring of the road distances, therefore allowing us to precisely follow the details in the route book. Clearly, this was an absolutely essential piece of equipment and must not only be precisely accurate, but also totally reliable. It needed to be built into a position where both of us could see it clearly and Yvonne could operate the re-set button easily. I devised a hugely complex bracket affair made up out of aluminium plate which would both provide a fixing for the Terratrip and also house our new fusebox behind it. It was quite a challenge but one I enjoyed and rose to with enthusiasm. Remember the Terratrip – it WILL reappear.

20th February Adrian rang in the morning to advise me that he had a problem with the oil pump as the wrong type had been sent. However, he was hoping for a delivery from the States in about a week, and suggested the engine would be ready for 2nd March, so almost on time.

Keith and Pete, (the auto-electrical wiring guru) came over to start the wiring in the car and all seemed to go really well. We ordered all sorts of connectors, brackets, crimping tools and cabling through Vehicle Wiring, who promised to deliver the following day. Pete fitted the airhorns which sounded great, but there was a stumbling block when it came to sorting out the bulbs in the front spotlamps. It will be recalled that we had decided to uprate the electrical system from 6-volt to 12-volt and it meant, of course, everything, just everything, had to be changed. The headlamps were easy, as it was a fairly simple matter to track down sealed beams, but the spotlights were a different kettle of fish, and we simply could not find the correct bulbs. Pete solved this by spending literally hours with the original reflectors, some new bulbs, a yard of copper strip and a bucketful of solder. He eventually managed to make up completely new fittings which were so successful that they

survive to this day.

21st February Keith and Pete finished the first phase of the rewiring by lunchtime and spent the rest of the afternoon changing the wheel bearings and fitting the front suspension.

26th February I finally completed all of the internal woodwork to both the console and the rear bins – a momentous day. The following day I took the console to Bielowski's for him to cover in our magnificent green vinyl.

1st March Spoke to Adrian and, glory be, the engine is finished, exactly on time!

3rd March We were shortly off on a relaxing non-car holiday to India, Nepal, Bhutan and Sri Lanka, so it was important to get everything set up for the engine installation to happen whilst we were away. Keith arranged to pick up the engine on 7th March and I sent Adrian a large cheque for the engine and spares. Hopefully, there should be no hitches.

Jim from Brosterfield Engineering popped round in the afternoon and measured up for the lids for my rear bins. He was planning on making them from rigid aluminium panels and had offered to fit complete piano hinges and locks etc. I felt that the lids needed to be reasonably rigid in case we had to stand on them at some stage or another.

Over the last few months John had been working hard on the preparation of his Rover. However, he received a phone call from Peter Banham telling him that he knew of a fully rally-prepared Rover P4 which was for sale. This car had done several long endurance rallies and had, in fact, completed the "Around the World in 80 Days Rally" with its former owner. What a dilemma for John – what to do. On the one hand John's plans were well on the way but, on the other hand, this was an opportunity almost too good to miss. Rapidly the decision was made, and John, perhaps very wisely, decided to switch cars. A deal was quickly done and a very relieved looking Rover 110 was put back on the market, looking for a buyer who would, perhaps, give it an easier life.

2nd April We managed to put Chevy related issues behind us for three weeks and came back fully refreshed. The engine was, indeed, fitted into the car – but not running yet. I was a little disappointed as I expected it to be fully operational. Apparently, there had been problems with the distributor cap etc. etc. etc. which had slowed things down.

5th April I decided that we should have cigarette lighter power points mounted both under the bonnet and in the boot. I had bought a rather smart fluorescent strip light as my portable work light, and decided that it would be useful to be able to plug it in independently either front and rear of the car. I also fashioned a smart protective container for the light out of a short length of 50 mm waste pipe, covered both ends by caps from Yvonne's furniture polish tins which happened to fit perfectly. To this day she can't work out where the caps went.

9th April We received a missive in the post from Philip Young today, which was extremely hard-hitting, lots of instructions as to what we should be doing with our cars. Most concerning, however, were the new 'mandatory' regulations suggesting that it would be necessary to fit a roll-bar and full harnesses. I was absolutely apoplectic. The rally organisers had been telling us for months that we should be working on our cars and preparing them for the rally and it was only now at this very late date that they suddenly decided to introduce new measures. However, they were extremely radical issues, and for us to fit a roll bar at this stage would have meant stripping out the whole of the rear bins that I had spent weeks making. I was so frustrated, I hardly slept a wink that night.

10th April Needless to say, first call of the day was to Philip Young suggesting that it was totally out of order to be introducing such radical issues at such a late stage. Mercifully, he agreed to change the wording, and whilst he was still insisting on a full harness, he simply made the inclusion of a roll-bar a 'recommendation'. At least I

shall get a full night's sleep tonight.

Big day today. Keith and Pete came over and, for the first time, the engine was started up. What a relief – an enormous step forward for mankind.

In the afternoon, I nipped over to Jim Stiles' again for him to weld up the throttle connection which had broken. He had already made up the cupboard doors for the rear bins etc. which were a great job – it made the whole of my construction look most professional. I asked him to make up brackets for the alternator and also to fabricate some new bumpers. Jim is great to work with as he is so full of enthusiasm and so accommodating.

13th April Peter Bacon from Brosterfield Engineering came round to precisely measure for bumpers etc. and brought some slim pieces of aluminium to use as formers. The bumper fixing positions are quite complicated and he thinks he can mock up our 'new', simple bumpers with his aluminium strips.

Over the last week or two I have been wrestling with a problem as to what to do about tyres for the car. I simply could not find the correct combination. What people considered to be the right tyres simply wouldn't fit our wheels and anything that was available to fit the wheels didn't seem to measure up in quality to cope with the demanding terrain that we knew we would be confronted with. Clearly, correct tyre choice was to be of paramount importance and I decided to approach the problem from a different angle and look for wheels that would accommodate the correct tyres, but of course would have the correct hole combination to fit the Chevy wheels. Adrian produced a solution as he has found four six-inch wide, fifteen-inch wheels in his workshop and ordered an additional one from the USA to make up a full set – just a 4 to 5 week wait for the fifth wheel.

Part of the rally recommendations were that we needed an expansion tank and we spent some time in working out the very complex shape that was needed to fit in the restricted space available. Northampton Radiators seemed to be the company that specialised in these, so we ordered one at the cost of slightly in excess of £200. It occurred to me it would have been less expensive to have hollowed one out of a gold ingot!

With raising the suspension on the car we managed to create yet another problem – that of having non-standard shock absorber lengths. Furthermore, the shock absorbers were unusual in that they had a pin fixing on each end and it was simply not possible to find a standard unit that would suit. Keith put me in touch with Bilstein in Nottingham who would purpose make some new ones for us. I took our elder grandson, Calum, with me and we called back through Chesterfield to drop off the broken rear quarterlight to Auto Windscreens for them to remake it.

5th May An administrative day today. We ordered the Garmin GPS (upon the Rally organisers instruction, all competitors had to have the identical GPS as the plan was to download waypoints which could be followed as the rally progressed). Northampton Radiators told me they had posted off the expansion tank; Bilstein confirmed the shock absorbers would be ready within a day or two, and Auto Windscreens rang to say the rear quarterlight was ready. I spent some time at Markovitz, our local builders' merchants, buying wire cables and clamps for fastening down the engine mountings. Philip Young had put the fear of God up all of us by telling us that the terrain would be so tough in places that it would be necessary for us to wire the engine down to the mounting blocks – for fear it should jump off! I must say, at this stage, it was almost impossible to envisage what sort of terrain would encourage our hugely heavy engine to separate itself away from the chassis.

17th May Big delivery today, the shock absorbers arrived, the Garmin arrived, a new radiator cap appeared and a very smart new set of red seat belts. Following the issue of not being able to reach the handbrake, Peter Banham had recommended that we bought some Schroth electrically tensioned seatbelts. Inevitably, these were a special order from central Germany and, judging by the price, were handmade from the fine soft underbelly of a Yak owned by the Royal family of some far distant land; they were the haute couture of seat belts.

I really must stop wingeing on about how expensive things are, it's just that at every twist and turn I seem to be needing something highly specialised which gave the appropriate supplier the opportunity to reach into thin air for a price, then double it!

19th May Keith, Karen and Pete came over for the day. Another big day – Pete completed the electrics, I made up the central console, Keith fitted the front shockers – which turned out to be the very devil of a job. Keith also drilled into a useful surface of steel ducting to fix the expansion tank. I stripped down the rear quarter window and fixed it into position. Mercifully, it was much easier to put back together than it was to take out. All the hinged lids to the storage bins were fixed into place, and the pièce de resistance was Keith's inventive siting for the Terratrip sensor. Peter Banham had been adamant that the Terratrip should not be driven off the speedo cable as, if the speedo cable failed, you not only of course lost the speedo but also the trip meter. The Terratrip has a small sensor which needs to 'look at' a series of whirling bolts in order to pick up a reading. Keith's cunning plan was that he would insert the sensor within the brake drum and manufactured a bracket so that the sensor could be mounted whilst reading the fixing bolts inside the drum. It was a cracking idea, as apparently, one of the major complaints for Terratrips is the difficulties of achieving and maintaining the 1 mm clearance gap under the car – particularly where sand and rocks are bashing about.

20th May Keith and Karen stayed over last night so a good, early start this morning. I had bought a couple of sheets of steel and we started with the initial fixings for both the sump guard and petrol tank guard. Keith also finished off the expansion tank, fitted the alternator, mounted two coils on the inner wing, fitted the rear shock absorbers, then concentrated on the horrendous job of fitting the oil pressure line behind the speedo. There was hardly any room to work in and the language that emanated from the depths of the dashboard made the stuff I hear at my local football match pale into insignificance!

26th May 2006 The rally organisers had come up with an idea for a weekend event, the purpose of which was so that competitors could meet and get to know each other - there were to be lectures on car preparation, safety, hygiene, food preparation, and finally a practice run to familiarize ourselves with the Garmin GPS system. The choice of venue at Haythrop Hall in the Cotswolds sounded magnificent, however, the joy of the venue was somewhat short-lived when we discovered that the accommodation was akin to 'Cell block H'. It didn't take us too

Light relief on 'The Malts'

long to work out that this was Philip Young's clever introduction to endurance rallying by attempting to replicate the standard of the forthcoming Russian hotel accommodation! There were, inevitably, a lot of 'mutterings' amongst the crews about a rip-off for this £600 weekend. Nonetheless, we had a terrific time meeting fellow competitors and, indeed, starting relationships that would clearly last for many years to come. It was at dinner one evening that three crews of us decided to form

a team to enter for the team prize. The common factor between ourselves, Richard and Nicola and Jose and Maria, was that we all owned Aston Martins – but weren't taking them on the rally! It was a little contrived but over a bottle of wine seemed a particularly good idea. We were to be called 'The Dry Martinis'. Even at this early stage, we decided to book a team dinner and Richard, who knew a wonderful restaurant in Tallin (Estonia) agreed to book for a year hence. At least it should inspire us to make Tallin come hell or high water.

17th June Again, Yvonne and I had a break from Chevy work by doing the Scottish Malts rally in our XK together with Dave and Jo. Whilst on the rally Dave had some particularly bad news when he learned that both the A and B frames in his Sunbeam were beyond redemption, and he was obliged to have the car transported to Peterborough to have the work carried out, as he present mechanics didn't have the expertise for this particularly complex job. We both took consolation over some particularly fine malt whiskies whilst discussing the comparable issues of endurance rally car preparation.

Upon our return, I started work on the vinyl covering of the rear bins and, when they were completed, they were looking good. Although I say so myself, the bins look quite professional. What a great colour match the vinyl is!

19th June Keith and Peter came over and we got the engine running again. Keith connected up the alternator and Pete wired up for the seat belts. We got the seats bolted in permanently and the sump guard is almost completed.

20th June Keith and Pete here all day, and the bonnet was fixed into position. This sounds an easy job but, my goodness me, how difficult it was. Firstly, the bonnet is absolutely enormous and, being of American manufacture, is incredibly heavy. It's a remarkable piece of design in that the whole bonnet is cleverly hinged on a latticework of moving parts and completely counter-balanced by a pair of gigantic springs that are fixed at the bottom by a bolt that is both impossible to see and impossible to reach. Nonetheless, persistence and bad language will always succeed, and eventually the bonnet was in place. I really do hope we never have a problem with this!

The next problem was that the starter motor packed in. Pete took it off and managed to totally repair it and we eventually had our first run – four and a half miles. However, the engine sounded 'dog rough', absolutely 'dog rough'. I 'phoned Adrian who told me that it's just 'easing in'.

Peter finally wired up the spotlights, secured the seat belts, provided us with a foot switch for the air horns inside the passenger compartment (this was a Betty Banham suggestion to clear the crowds out of the way, and I imagined Yvonne taking to this with alacrity!!!) and eventually replaced all the inner panels.

Catastrophe! Keith has spotted water pouring from the bottom of the engine compartment. Remember that flat easy piece of ducting that the expansion tank was bolted to? Well, unknown to anyone, the heater radiator was directly beneath the ducting and we drilled into the core in two places. The expansion tank had to be taken off and the whole of the heater duct disassembled. We are going to need to sort this one!

Peter from Brosterfield came round today (twice). He has reworked the sump guards a couple of times and was a complete star. It's quite an added difficulty having to cart the equipment to the other end of the village each time there is an adaptation to be made, but Peter uncomplainingly took it in his stride.

Later in the day, Adrian rang to say that he had re-thought the situation regarding the rough sounding engine, and wanted to come over and take a look inside the engine compartment.

Rallying in the Alps

Sadly, the final frustration of the day was that the starter motor failed again, and clearly was going to require "a dose of looking at".

21st June I took the starter motor into Dowding & Mills in Sheffield and was delighted to hear that they think they can repair the motor by Friday. Also Serck took a look at the radiator core and decided that they could replace that by Friday. Fingers crossed.

22nd June Big day for me. I sorted out the cubbyhole latch! Don't ask.

26th June The heater radiator has been re-cored at a cost of £200, and the starter motor repaired at a cost of £150. Where do they get these round figures from?

Adrian and his foreman, Alan, came over to Foolow and stripped the whole of the front of the car down. Bumpers off, radiator out etc. Eventually to discover that the front two gears were not meshing correctly and he confirmed he would have to take it back to Colne to sort it out. Adrian also told me with great delight that, in his view, the front sump guard was 'duff' – far too weak. "I'd have never made it like that myself". It seems to be the old issue of somebody wanting to assert his own authority by picking away at someone else's work. It is quite clear at this stage that Adrian and Keith have utter disregard for each other, and are both looking for opportunities to 'points score'.

27th June 6.45 in the morning and there is a rattle at the door. Alan has turned up with a trailer to collect the car. Adrian rang to say that the problem was that the front gears needed replacement.

30th June Adrian rang and the job has been done. A new set of cogs has been manufactured and fitted. However, he tells me that the starter motor has 'had it'. It started up the engine, but he couldn't stop the starter motor from running. I asked him to sort it out himself if he could but it was hardly a case of a well-spent £150 with Dowding & Mills.

We are off to France shortly, so Adrian has agreed to deliver the car back complete with new starter motor and new wheels before 22nd July.

9th August Back from competing in the Rallye des Alpes in the XK. A hugely successful trip, sunny weather, great rallying, no Chevrolet problems. The car is back from Adrian, and Keith and Pete arrived to fit the heater radiator etc. plus lots of other bits and bobs.

10th August Bad, bad day. The bonnet didn't appear to fit properly and was chipping the paint where it met the front corners of the wing. I stripped off the whole front apron of the car to see if I could find out why it was happening – needlessly, as it transpired. We then realised what the pile of spare washers were doing on the bench – no-one could remember where they had come from. It turned out that the wings had to be forced apart and these spacer washers dropped in between the radiator to hold the wings the correct distance apart. A couple of hours sorted out this little job. A piece of 3" x 2" timber was cut slightly oversized, wedged in between the wings then gently, oh so gently, hammered into place, forcing the wings apart. The washers were dropped into place and, hey presto, the bonnet closed perfectly.

Keith fitted a spare electric petrol pump and filter. This gives me an easy chance to switch over from one pump to another if there should ever be a problem.

I was rolling about under the car trying to look reasonably knowledgeable, when I spotted a loose spring on the handbrake, and also, remarkably, found a loose bolt holding the gearbox down. It was a good job I had spotted these two items, but they were quickly both sorted.

The final issue of the day produced yet another horrific problem. In order to operate the electric hood, it was necessary to fire up the engine and pull on a large handle in the car. This, in turn, activated a hydraulic pump which drove the hydraulic rams to raise or lower the hood. I was in the process of trying out the system when there was a screech from Keith to say that there was fluid pouring everywhere down the inside of the bulkhead but, worse than this, it appeared to be a corrosive fluid that was having a dreadful effect on the paintwork. Hastily, the pump was turned off and the corrosive fluid mopped up – mercifully the paintwork damage was minimal and was mainly restricted to the inside of the bulkhead.

There were two issues here, why was the thing leaking so badly, and what on earth was the product in the hydraulics? Where would I find a solution to this one? I emailed 'Chevys of the 40s' in the USA and waited with bated breath.

13th August Keith had decided that the hydraulic fluid was, indeed, brake fluid and it was that which had such a corrosive effect on the paintwork. We decided to replace this with proper hydraulic fluid.

Bad news from 'Chevys of the 40s', the hood valve that had broken was simply not replaceable; no-one had an idea of where to go from here.

I took my new six inch wheels round to Brosterfield Engineering for them to double weld all the seams. Keith had made the point that there was not much sense in having super strong suspension and the best all-terrain tyres in the world, for the wheels to crack up at their weakest point.

14th August The wheels are delivered back fully welded and Jim and Peter brought the bumpers back at the same time. I spent most of the day fitting them, as they still needed a bit of bending and tweeking. Eventually I took them all off again to give them a coat of paint.

15th August Good Lord! I took the car to Roger Thorpe at Castleton and it has passed its MOT! I then went off to a small company in Chapel-en-le-Frith who have agreed to powder coat the wheels an exact colour match at £25 per wheel. Disappointingly, the car seems to be 'missing' quite badly, which is really frustrating.

A bit of good news at the end of the day, Jim Stiles tells me that he feels he can fix the hydraulic switch for the hood. Jim is a man of many talents and has spent years working on hydraulic equipment for lifting and drilling. According to him it's "no bother".

17th August A 6.30 am start for me, in awful weather, driving across to Keith's home in Staffordshire. It was a horrible drive. The car was 'missing' badly and it was wallowing awfully on corners. How on earth am I going to drag this thing half-way round the world?

Keith stripped down the carburettor but it didn't seem to solve the problem. We rang Adrian and he has offered to change over the carburettor for a spare he has when we go there next Tuesday.

Keith came up with a bright idea to drill holes in the front brake drums for easy access to the adjustment on the brakes. Currently, the only way to adjust the brakes is to remove the wheels and the drums, and it's a real fiddle. Keith's idea is going to avoid a lot of hassle and I can't imagine why 'Mr. Chevrolet' didn't think about it in the first place.

On the way back home I called in at Jim's to talk about fixing the hydraulics for the hood, and he has shown me an enormous valve, which appears to be a part off a JCB. Over-engineered, or what?

19th August Our trip to Istanbul is now just around the corner, and we are putting together all the spares and trying to think through what we will need to take.

21st August Nipped round to see Jim and was hugely disappointed to discover that he now cannot use the JCB hydraulic switch. However, he has overcome this by having the original Bakerlite part completely remade in aluminium, telling me that he has organised this through a mate of his at Goldcrest Engineering. Rather surprisingly, this turned out to be John Turner, a very good friend of mine from long ago, and it was great that he was able to help us out with this rather unusual request.

22nd August The new wheels were colour-coated and the car taken back to Roger Thorpe's at Castleton to have my new Goodyear 'All Terrain' tyres fitted. They really looked 'the business' and, indeed, proved to be a great success on the rally. The only problem was that the tyres, being so huge and knobbly, were incredibly difficult to get into the rear wheel arches and the eventual solution was to let the tyres down, fit the wheels in place, and then inflate them. This did not bode well for if we have a puncture en route. It's a problem that I never thought of, nor indeed had anyone else.

The enormous plus was that the new wheels and tyres had absolutely transformed the handling of the car. It meant that I could now push it hard into corners and, with the new stiffened suspension, it had made an enormous difference with the 'blancmange' effect being almost totally eliminated!

The car was still extremely 'asthmatic' so I took it over to Adrian's. We had only done about 190 miles in the car and it really was not going very well at all. Adrian told me that it merely wants running-in and the whole thing will settle down. Whilst we were there, he took the opportunity to severely criticise the suspension which he said was hopeless and far too strong with no give. We left feeling extremely low.

23rd August Yvonne and I set off for a running-in trip around Kirkby Lonsdale in the Lake District, taking the mileage up to about 480. The car was going very, very poorly indeed; there was no pull whatsoever, so we turned back to Adrian's for him to adjust the timing and the carburration. I complained that there was an awful noise coming from the engine, so Alan, the foreman, went with me in the car for a short run. He, of course, was aware of my total lack of mechanical knowledge and, playing on this, told me that it really wasn't a problem because the noise "is just coming from behind the dashboard". I really didn't believe that he was correct, but agreed to keep running the car for a little longer to see if it settles down.

As a fascinating aside, whilst I was chatting to Adrian, Yvonne was chatting to Alan the foreman, and boastfully he told her that he used Marijuana, grew it in fact, and had just introduced his father-in-law to it, to relieve aches and pains. He also said that, when he was younger he'd done the odd job on behalf of anyone who'd had a grudge or been owed money, and said that turning up on somebody's doorstep with a bin lid in his hand, always had the right effect!

During my conversation with Adrian, he happened to drop out a gem. Referring to a recently upgraded car he was finishing, he remarked that he "made his money out of the idiots who came through his garage door". I drew his attention to the inappropriateness of this remark, given our current circumstances, and I must say that momentarily he looked most embarrassed and, of course, protested that this didn't refer to us!!!

The fuel guage has stopped working now – when will these problems stop? The outcome was that we ran out of petrol on the way home. Luckily, a chap pulled up to try and help us and was good enough to run me to the nearest fuel station, about 3 or 4 miles away. I filled up a can, dashed round to pay and we leapt in his car to go back to the Chevy and Yvonne, only to discover that I had managed to leave the petrol can standing on the forecourt of the garage. What an idiot I felt, how on earth were we going to manoeuvre our way half way around the world!

A final ignominy was that it poured with rain on the way home, and the car leaked really badly around the perimeter of the hood. Everything inside the car was completely awash.

We were both thoroughly depressed. The car was clearly running very badly indeed. In just over a week's time we were due to set off on our shake-down run to Istanbul. Our trip to the Lake District had been a disaster and no-one seemed to have any idea of what the problem was. Adrian had agreed to take another look at the car, and I was due back over to Colne a week later. We had spent all this time working on the car and here we were months later, with the car running like a dog, no obvious solution in sight, and a 5000 mile trip planned in two weeks' time.

24th August Life can't stand still. The car was booked into Bielowski's today for its new carpets, but when I got there Mick had forgotten to book me in and looked really surprised when I turned up at the door. Nonetheless, he agreed to do the work, and also thought he could seal the leaks around the hood. I had a great walk back along the canal bank into the centre of Sheffield and caught a bus home to Foolow. What a gentle and civilized way to travel!

Jim Stiles rang to say that John Turner had made the new hydraulic valve in aluminium and Jim would fit it in place for me on Sunday. Later in the afternoon, Adrian rang to say that the car should be run-in very, very slowly indeed and that he was sending me a letter to this effect. I was really starting to feel very uncomfortable about this whole affair; it sounded to me as though somebody was preparing to cover his back!

25th August I took the bus into Sheffield again and strolled along the canal bank to Bielowski's. The car was completely ready with its smart new carpets but, sadly, Mick hadn't had time to cure the leaks around the hood; this was going to have to wait for another time. In any case, at this particular time, it was the least of our worries.

26th August I received my letter from Adrian, and it was exactly what I thought. This was a man who I think could feel problems coming on and was wanting to make sure that he had covered every eventuality in writing. In his letter to me he suggested his concern that I was trying to draw comparisons between the performance of the Chevrolet and the performance of our XK, so I really felt that we were heading in the wrong direction here, but also felt that I should be responding. Many years in business taught me that you should always fully respond to letters – you never know what is around the corner. I have therefore written a long, detailed reply to Adrian correcting some of his inaccuracies and assumptions.

27th August Dropped the car round the Jim's for him to fit the hood mechanism.

28th August Picked the car up and Jim had done a great job, the hood worked perfectly. John's reproduction in solid aluminium of the original bakelite part was a superb piece of engineering. It really was most gratifying to be so well assisted by friends.

29th August Big day today. I took the car over to Adrian's, as agreed. It was absolutely bucketing with rain and water was pouring in around the hood. The car was running really badly on the journey over, and was struggling to climb the slight incline on the motorway just before Colne. There were also some dreadful noises coming from the engine compartment. As soon as I got to Colne, I asked Adrian to come with me in the car and drive up the same incline on the motorway so that I could recreate exactly the poor performance that I had endured on the drive over. It was very clear from the expression on Adrian's face that he realised something was not right, and when I questioned him he mumbled something about the engine sounding very poor indeed.

The arrangement was, however, that I would leave the car with him overnight and he would take a look at some of the issues with the springs, and also fit the new fuel pump. Being so far away from home, I had packed my bike into the car and arranged to set off for a ride around the Lancashire hills. I therefore rode off just after lunch with huge trepidation.

As it transpired, I had a great ride that afternoon, did about 40 miles to the Inn at Whitewell where I had booked in overnight. A couple of beers and the inevitable bag of crisps, followed by an excellent meal saw me in somewhat better spirits.

Chapter 3

CALAMITY!

30th August The day dawned bright and clear, and again I had a terrific ride in the morning. By complete coincidence, I discovered that the Tour of Britain bike race was passing through the area that morning, and I had a fine ride over the Trough of Bowland. I bumped into another group of cyclists and rode across the hills to eventually watch the tour climb over Bradford Fell. It was a terrific antidote to rally car preparation, and completely took my mind off 'matters Chevrolet'. Nonetheless, I had to confront the situation, and at 2.00 pm I rang Adrian, who told me the car would be ready at 4.00 pm.

At the appointed hour, and with impending concern, I free-wheeled into the garage to be greeted by a rather strange scene of there being no-one around at all. Adrian came out of his office and was extremely bullish in his manner. His first words were "I'm afraid you'll not be going to Istanbul on Friday". He then said "You've damaged one of the pistons" and, at the same time, handed me a letter. I was absolutely stunned. On the one hand I had anticipated bad news, but never dreamt it could be quite as bad as this. It was quite difficult to gather my thoughts as so many issues were crowding in on me in such a short period of time. What was wrong with the engine? How were we going to resolve it? What about our long-planned trip to Istanbul in two days time, and not least, how on earth was I going to get back to Foolow? Here I was at 4.30 in the afternoon, stranded in revolting Colne, just with my bike. It was all a bit much to take in. I had to stand back for a moment, draw breath and try to get my thoughts in order. I began by asking Adrian how on earth he could consider that I had damaged the car. What was I actually supposed to have done, after all I had only driven the car a matter of 500 miles from a brand new engine re-build. I had been meticulous in my running in, using extremely low revs and following Adrian's instructions to the letter.

Adrian was extremely cautious in his response. I next took the opportunity to read through the letter that he had handed me. It was quite clear that he had spent some considerable time composing the letter in order to infer that the problems were all of my own making and in no way were Auto Services Colne complicit in the problems that had occurred. The more I read the letter, the more I realised it was completely misleading as it exaggerated a lot of the issues that had happened over the last couple of weeks, and certainly put an incorrect slant on various pieces of previous information that had been discussed between us. The more I read the details of the letter, the more incandescent I became, and I was particularly livid at Adrian's suggestion that I had, in fact, caused the damage. Basically Adrian was suggesting that we had ingested road dust through the oil bath filter into the cylinders and that the resultant dirt had caused the extensive damage - a theory, frankly I could not get my head around.

After a while, we both calmed down sufficiently in order to discuss exactly what had happened. Adrian had stripped the engine down and told me that there was a piston that was extremely badly damaged and that it would take at least 5 to 6 weeks to properly repair. He also made it perfectly clear that I would be fully responsible for the cost of any work that was involved in putting matters right.

At this stage we both agreed to differ on our opinions, and I felt that the only solution was to leave and slowly absorb the information that I had been given, and try to assimilate our position relative to all the known facts.

There was the more immediate problem of how to get home as, by now, it was 6.00 pm. I made a few phone calls and determined that there was a train leaving from Skipton which would get me back to Sheffield via Leeds. I made a quick phone call to Yvonne just to give her a basic idea of what the problems were and, needless to say, she was as stunned as I was. What to do?

Adrian agreed to run me over to Skipton in his car, and on the journey expressed his disappointment as to how things had turned out, and told me that he was an honourable man and that, should the problems turn out to be in any way as a result of his own workmanship, he would unquestionably put the matters right at his own expense. We agreed to be in touch the following day.

I have only a hazy recollection of the train journey back to Sheffield. I was so stunned by events that I could not properly assemble in my mind, not only the engineering issues which I had been told about, but could not yet fully fathom, but also the general implications for the eventual preparation of the car for the Peking to Paris, but more importantly what were we to do about our trip to Istanbul which we were due to start two days later. After all, this wasn't just any old trip, it was a five-week long, fully planned holiday for which we had made all the advance arrangements.

10.00 pm and Yvonne collected me at Sheffield station, and we both collapsed into each other's arms, for once both of us short of words, as we could hardly think of what to say to each other under the circumstances.

One conclusion we did reach on the drive back home, was that we wouldn't let some ridiculous and preposterous situation like this affect our forthcoming holiday. We were lucky enough to have the XK in the garage at home, absolutely on the button and ready to go anywhere. We decided that we would simply switch our plans and head for Istanbul for all of the right reasons – but in the wrong car!

Needless to say, I didn't have a wink of sleep that night, with so many things revolving around in my mind, so at 4.30 a.m. I capitulated, got up and dictated a very long and detailed letter to Auto Services Colne, whilst everything was fresh in my mind.

What a day, what a day. For all of the wrong reasons, I shall remember this day for the rest of my life.

31st August I sent my letter by recorded delivery to Auto Services, rang Dave and Jo and outlined the situation, and went in the garage to polish the Jaguar.

Chapter 4

THE ROAD TO ISTANBUL

We found ourselves on Friday 1st September 2006 setting off on this huge, meticulously planned journey to Istanbul, but in the wrong car! On the one hand, the purpose of the journey had become purposeless, nonetheless it was something we had planned for some months. In particular, we didn't want to let Dave and Jo down, but in any case, we particularly didn't want to miss the opportunity of what might turn out to be a fascinating trip. One of the priorities of the journey was to test out our newly purchased, lightweight, quickly washable clothing to see how it performed after days of hot, sticky, dusty driving. Also there was this big step into the unknown – "The Camping Experience". I had camped 45 years ago, but Yvonne had never spent a night under canvas and I think there was a degree of trepidation. Dave and Jo hadn't camped before either, so it added a different focus to our adventure.

Incidentally, one of the issues that we had confronted some time ago was the purchase of camping equipment. I clearly remember that in Rosie Thomas' book she mentioned that she had taken advice from a friend who recommended that she should buy the best possible sleeping bag available, and I recall that it certainly seemed to pay off for her. With that in mind, we set off to tour the local camping shops to search out suitable gear. We needed sleeping bags, a floormat and a tent. Bearing in mind that we were of the opinion that camping would not become an annual habit, we decided to keep an eye on costs. As ever, with specialised equipment, there seemed to be a gigantic range

The road to Istanbul

of costs and we had to remember that we were only to use the equipment for six nights to sleep by the side of the car, rather than buying the type of equipment needed to bivwac on the side of Everest. Eventually, we narrowed the choice down to Decathlon as they seemed to have a wide range of equipment at sensible prices.

The sleeping bag issue turned out to be easier than we thought. We had been warned off down filling which, whilst it had by far the best insulation properties, was easily susceptible to damp, subject to clumping when wet and would take a long time to get dry. A fairly straightforward choice, therefore, was to buy the best quality man-made fibre filling which, most certainly, turned out to be the right choice. The formats again were relatively simple – it was just a case of trading off bulk against comfort. It's rather obvious when you think about it, the bigger and thicker the mattress used under the sleeping bag, the more it would cushion us against the rocks. In the search for minimal weight and size we ended up with a medium range mat, which we suspected would be of minimal value. We were packing a shovel anyway, so at least we could clear the ground to make it relatively level!

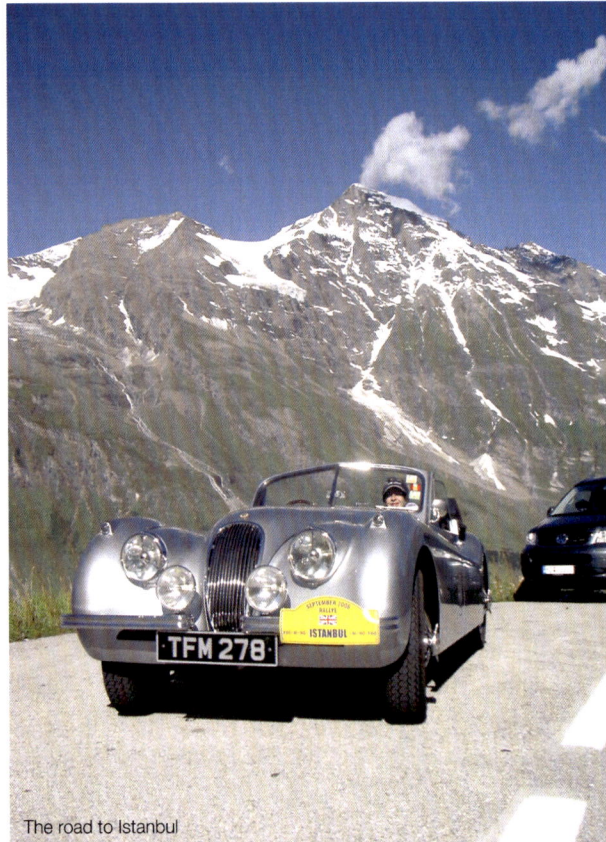

The final choice was to be the tent. Here we were completely spoilt for choice with an enormous range. First thought was, there were two of us, therefore it narrowed it down to a 'two-man' tent! Nonetheless, when we took a close look at these we realised that the minimalist size meant that you put the tent on, rather than climbed into it. We therefore we decided to opt, rather frivolously, for a 3-person tent. Draw no other conclusion from this than we felt we needed a bit more space! By far the cleverist tent on the market was the 'throw up' model. This came in the form of a flat disc about 3 feet in diameter and a couple of inches thick. The plan was that you simply pulled the tent out of the bag and gently threw it into the air. The fully sprung, coiled base uncoiled itself and, lo and behold, the tent would ping into perfect position. We even timed it – at 1.9 seconds. Most impressive. However, and there was a big however, try to get the tent back in the bag. We soon discovered that you needed about one and a half hours and a degree in geometry and gymnastics. It was simply impossible. The salesman in the shop proved that it wasn't impossible by being able to force this uncontrollable, manic, sprung device bag into its bag within 3 or 4 minutes, but then again he was 6'4", had an arm span of 3 metres and a pair of feet with an apparent claw-like grip.

We tried, my how we tried, but simply could not harness the damn thing, furthermore we worked out that if we couldn't train the tent to go back in its bag on the shop floor in Decathlon, we stood very little chance at 5.30 am on a windy morning in the Gobi Desert!

The overall effect of this, however, was that it made our choice much simpler and we tracked down an extremely light tent with carbon fibre poles that magically reduced itself to something the size of a cigarette packet. We practised erecting the tent at home and eventually were able to get down to a time of 4.1/2 minutes to erect it and 9 minutes to demolish it.

We also kitted ourselves out with good quality, super lightweight, easily washable, totally non-iron clothing and completed our camping set with bathtowels which had remarkable qualities. They folded up to the size of a pocket handkerchief, yet when opened had the texture of a hearthrug and the ability to absorb a complete bodyfull of water with no problems.

The morning of Friday 1st September saw the XK packed to its absolute limits with all our equipment for the mammoth trip. It indeed had been quite a logistical exercise as, of course, the XK had only about 25% capacity of the Chevrolet. Our overall plan was to visit the Goodwood Revival with a group of friends for the forthcoming weekend, then generally make our way across Europe with our eventual destination to be Istanbul. However, the morning we were about to leave, the newspapers and radio published horror stories of terrorist activities and unrest in Turkey and, at this early stage both Jo and Yvonne were a trifle sceptical about venturing as far as Istanbul. Dave and I decided to keep our counsel for a few days whilst inching slowly eastwards. We decided that we would make a judgement on the situation a little later.

So, off to Goodwood to meet a large group of friends for a few days, with a stopover at South Lodge just outside Guildford. The first disappointing news we had was that Dave and Jo, who were to join us in the Sunbeam Alpine were experiencing problems with the car cutting out on the journey down to the South of England and, indeed, they didn't arrive until very late that evening having discovered that their newly fitted alternator had failed: It was hardly a vote of confidence that a critical piece of equipment had failed after such a short distance. Saturday morning dawned to see Dave and Jo driving off to a nearby Halfords for new equipment whilst we wandered off to Goodwood.

Dinner on the Saturday evening saw me sitting next to Richard, from whom it will be recalled, I had originally bought the Chevrolet. I regaled him with my tales of woe and he was absolutely incredulous, suggesting that, without question, ingesting road dirt into the engine in such a short time was, in his view, simply an impossibility. Richard, however, being a very positive thinker, suggested that he had a solution which may well help us out in the long term. He felt that the best solution was to remove the car from Adrian Bailey's workshop and take it to his own home. Richard, rather fortuitously, had another Chevy engine of his own which he suggested he would be prepared to completely rebuild himself and, indeed, install in the Chevy. His overall plan was to remove the present, damaged engine so that it could be set on one side for the experts to examine. This scheme had the obvious benefit that we could at least progress the car and continue its preparation, whilst still having the opportunity to review the matter with the original engine. Needless to say, it took very little consideration on our part before we accepted his kind offer with alacrity, and agreed to keep in touch over the next few days. It certainly was the first positive thought that we had had for almost a week now, and it meant we could set off on our journey with some hope for the future.

Departing Goodwood on the Sunday afternoon, we found our way to Portsmouth and the ferry across to Caen. The Monday morning found us rolling happily eastwards, pointing in the general direction of Turkey. We had attempted to anticipate our journey for the first four or five days, and had booked hotels ahead. On our first lunchtime stop on Monday 4th September, I rang Adrian Bailey to find out what the current situation was. To my surprise he told me that he had invited a specialist, called Mike Booth, to investigate the engine and, indeed, he had already taken samples of the sump oil and was sending it away for analysis. Adrian went to great lengths to tell me that it would appear that the problem was caused by dirty oil, and immediately suggested that the oil had become dirty through poor filtration to the carburettor – this seemed to me like attempting to place the blame on Keith at this early stage. Adrian went on to tell me that, having taken the engine apart now, he had discovered that the engine was, in his words, "completely trashed", describing how, not only were the pistons and cylinders badly scored, but the crankshaft and camshaft were also badly damaged. Gosh, plenty of food for thought here. I felt very remote being on a driving holiday and discussing all of this at arm's length. However, there was a more immediate diversion to take my mind off problems associated with the Chevrolet – the XK was playing up, with it stuttering, popping and wheezing and generally not running very smoothly at all. We staggered into Mulhouse quite late in the evening with all sorts of things on our minds.

Tuesday 5th saw us driving around Mulhouse looking for a suitable garage and, eventually, we found someone who was eager to assist. Everything possible was tried and tested. Plugs were replaced, plugleads cleaned and checked, the coil was tested, condenser and rotor arms checked, but still the problem persisted.

Lunchtime came and went, and it wasn't until late in the afternoon that the problem was discovered. A copper vent pipe at the rear of the engine had been rubbing against the accelerator cable and had worn through a small hole on the inside face of the tube in a location that wasn't immediately visible to the naked eye. Needless to say, the mechanic who eventually found it was 'cock a hoop' and, after ten minutes of brazing the problem was solved and we were at long last on our way.

The endless hours of sitting around in the garage in Mulhouse certainly gave us plenty of time to catch up on phone calls. I spoke to Richard who said he could pick up the Chevy straight away but, when I spoke to Adrian, he seemed extremely cagey and was not keen on releasing the car for at least a week. He did, however, give me the phone number of Mike Booth, his independent consultant, and seemed to be quite content for me to telephone him. I duly made the phone call and listened to Mike describing his back ground in the motor industry. Most certainly he seemed quite knowledgeable, although a little pedantic (witness forty-four minutes on the phone). He explained that his findings were, in his view, quite clear inasmuch as the severe damage to the pistons, piston rings and bores was at its worst on cylinders 3 and 4, with less wear on cylinders 2 and 5, and even less wear on cylinders 1 and 6. In his view this seemed to suggest ingestion of some form of contaminant through the air inlet, and indeed, he told me that he was already having an analysis of our oil. I asked what he thought may have caused the contamination, and he seemed to be quite clear that he expected to discover heavy deposits of silica. Not fully understanding what he meant by this, I asked him in what form the silica was, and he explained that this was crushed rock used for road surfacing which would eventually turn to dust and ingest through the filtration system. I asked him if Adrian had told him that the problem had commenced from as early as 180 miles, but he didn't seem to appreciate this, even though I suggested that, in my limited knowledge, it would seem highly unlikely for sufficient general road dirt to pass through an oil bath filter and cause such extensive damage in an amazingly short period of time. During the course of conversation, he happened to mention that there may be some dependence on the amount of oil in the oil bath filter and suggested that he recalled that the level was slightly below the marked level on the filter equipment, even so I suggested that if the oil bath was slightly less than full, it still surely couldn't have in any way affected the nominal amount of road dust that would have passed through it. Nonetheless, he was somewhat non-committal and suggested that nothing more could be done until he heard back from the laboratories with the result of the analysis.

Having got plenty of time on my hands I thought that another call to Richard would be worthwhile, and I spent some considerable time passing on Mike Booth's revelations about the road dirt. Richard, who was standing next to his own mechanic, Mike (2) was apoplectic at the thought that anyone could suggest, authoritatively, that road dust could have wrecked an engine in such a short period of time. Interestingly, Mike 2 came up with a theory that if it was silica, it could well be in the inlet ducts if, indeed, the engine or manifold had been sandblasted. This revelation really did hit home for me. I was wallowing around, with very little knowledge, but awash with utter disbelief about what I was hearing from the so-called experts. Suddenly, this really did seem to be a logical explanation. If the manifold had, indeed, been sandblasted, then sandblasting sand, by the very nature of its function would be very hard. I could imagine that a huge amount of damage could be wrought inside the workings of the engine. Suddenly, it seemed very clear to me – at least we had an eminently plausible explanation.

By late afternoon the XK was purring along, and we continued inching east. However, the hours spent in Mulhouse meant that we had lost a day's travel and most of the evening was spent re-arranging hotel accommodation for the next few days.

6th September and we are travelling through Slovenia. I spoke to Adrian, who told me that he had no report yet from Mike Booth, and this therefore meant that we would be considerably delayed as Mike had nipped off on holiday. The point of my call was, however, to ask him to ensure that I also had samples of the oil both from the oil bath filter and out of the engine. I thought that I should be arranging my own analysis. It was interesting to note that at the end of our conversation Adrian repeated once again that, no matter what the outcome, he would behave honourably (remember this!) I was intrigued with Adrian's final comments that day, he told me that he had always thought that my expectations were too high!!! I suppose he was right really – I had rather expected the engine to last a little longer than this………………

Slovinia, Croatia and Bulgaria came and went. By this time Dave and I had managed to effectively play down the Turkish terrorism threat and had persuaded the girls that Istanbul was a 'must'. Surprisingly little objection was registered and we pressed on day by day, driving between 200 and 300 miles each day. What a fantastic trip, we enjoyed pleasant coffee and lunch stops, had a memorable stopover in Belgrade, and loved Sofia so much that we stayed an extra day to take in this breathtakingly beautiful city.

The cars were going beautifully, with the only concern being the strong smell of petrol from the boot of the Sunbeam. Dave had arranged for a new alumium petrol tank to be fitted immediately before we left, and the bolts securing the sender unit appeared not to be adequately sealed. One and a half hours emptying the boot and three minutes with a spanner seemed to effect a cure.

The only administrative problem we were experiencing en route was the business of obtaining insurance for the individual countries we were passing through. Before we left I had contacted the embassies of all the Eastern European countries to find out what the situation was with regard to obtaining insurance, only to be met on each occasion with a complete blank. We headed on regardless and managed to negotiate separate insurance deals at each border. On the whole of this trip we passed through sixteen different countries and had sixteen different experiences. Each country had its own regulations, sometimes we were able to purchase insurance just for the two or three days it would take to cross through the country, and other occasions we had to bite the bullet and buy a full month's insurance. Nonetheless, the whole exercise was relatively simply – it just required us to hand over substantial amounts of money on a regular basis to heavily armed desperados situated in grimy offices with cracked windows.

As we were now awaiting the analysis of the oil, and Mike Booth was away on holiday, we had a considerable period of time without any contact with the UK and simply enjoyed our touring holiday. We pushed on to Istanbul with

First visit to Turkey

no trouble whatsoever, apart from arriving in the heart of the city in rush-hour with the temperature at 35 degrees! In the very narrowest part of the city, the Sunbeam eventually over-heated and, with fuel vaporisation, cut out in the most inconvenient spot. Yvonne and Jo took this opportunity to abandon us and went off to find their first real Turkish coffee. Many local hands soon pushed the Sunbeam off the road, and after a cooling off period it fired up again and we were able to make the hotel in time for dinner.

Istanbul was quite magnificent. We all felt it was an inspirational choice for our destination, and the city exceeded all of our expectations. It was vibrant, cosmopolitan and a welcome rest for a couple of days. With both cars and occupants well rested, it was time to head back west again, and we soon found ourselves heading towards the Greek coastline. It was in the almost unpronounceable Alexandroupolis we had the most amazing experience.

Having stopped for coffee in the middle of town, we had just set off when Yvonne realised that she had left her sunglasses behind in the café. We suggested to Dave and Jo that they carry on ahead and we would nip back to get the sunglasses and eventually catch them up. Five minutes later, sunglasses successfully retrieved, we were heading out of town, mid afternoon, when suddenly there was a bang at the

rear of the car. I glanced over my side of the car to see a leather-clad motor cyclist sliding past us on the ground. Realising all was not well (!) I pulled up immediately, only for the car to be totally surrounded by Alexandroupolis residents shouting and screaming in somewhat excitable fashion, pointing alternately at both the bedraggled motorcyclist and at a black trail of oil, which stretched way back out of sight up the road. I had no idea of what to make of the situation until someone pointed under the XK, the engine of which was still running, when it suddenly occurred to me that we were the cause of the problem as thick black oil was pumping out all over the road in an ever increasing pool. By this stage the motorcyclist, who was, mercifully, unhurt (albeit a little oily) had staggered to his feet, and was more concerned about the scratches on his bike, had been joined by a member of the local constabulary, who made it clear in no uncertain terms that I had a lot to answer for. Imagine our consternation when it was made clear that Yvonne should stay with the car whilst I was asked to accompany the motorcyclist to the local police station to give our statements. I was not even given the opportunity to telephone for any assistance for the car. Meanwhile, of course, Dave and Jo, not having any knowledge of the situation, were heading off into the setting sun.

Consternation in the police station when it was discovered that nobody at all spoke any English and, remarkably, the police discovered that I had very little Greek. After an hour, an officer who spoke English was summoned from other duties and he questioned me in detail whilst his colleagues wrote out a full statement, which I was eventually asked to sign. Imagine my concern, however, when this report was handed to me and I realised that it was written not only in Greek, but in Cyrillic script. They could have written anything. Nonetheless, it appeared to be prudent to sign or suffer the consequences. The moment I appended my signature to the page, the atmosphere changed, the police had done their job and the motor cyclist and I shook hands with smiles all around. I was duly delivered back to the car to find Yvonne sitting in an adjacent café being comforted by the only other English-speaking person in Alexandroupolis.

Still no word from Dave and Jo – their phone was turned off.

What to do? My first thought was to make a call to the RAC European Assistance in Lyon, and they explained that they would arrange for transport to pick up the car. Our only thoughts were that, at this stage, the XK had completely expired. Sitting by the roadside waiting for the breakdown truck to arrive, we were somewhat surprised to see a small red car pull up, and an overall-clad mechanic climb out and in word perfect Greek asked us what the problem was. Our new-found English speaking café proprietor friend was luckily on hand to translate and explain the situation. At precisely the same moment the breakdown truck arrived and two burly men commenced the job of hauling the XK onto the back of the truck. At this stage it became clear that the mechanic was suggesting that his father, who owned a nearby garage, could possibly help us and, as we had no idea of what else to do, agreed that this was, perhaps, the best possible solution. With the car firmly strapped on the back of the truck, Yvonne and I climbed into the cab and we set off. Imagine our surprise, therefore, when after 50 metres only, the truck turned right into a garage forecourt and it was announced that we were at our destination! Things got even better. The garage proprietor, who had an unpronounceable name about half a metre long, turned out to be a local rally driver and, even better still, had a close friend who owned several XK Jaguars, all of which he had worked on and was familiar with. Five minutes scrutiny under the bonnet and he told me he could fix it by the following morning. From a situation that we thought was completely terminal, we had apparently a very simple solution.

By this time Dave and Jo, realising that we had not caught them, had turned around and miraculously managed to track us down (indeed, Dave paced out the length of the oil trail on the road and announced that we had been blowing out oil for 500 metres! – no wonder the poor motor cyclist had fallen off when he braked too sharply.) The local garage proprietor also pointed us in the direction of a small hotel down the road and, indeed, we had possibly one of the best evenings on the whole trip!

8.30 the following morning, we walked back to the garage to find the car fully completed and the damage (which was a burst aeroquip hose) fully repaired for a total cost of 20 euros.

Onwards we travelled through Northern Greece, Macedonia, Albania, Bosnia and Croatia.

Still, at this stage, we had not tested out the camping equipment. Everything seemed to conspire against us.

XK and Alpine in Albania

Slovinia, Croatia, Bulgaria etc. didn't seem to have campsites when we needed them, our episode in Greece meant we had to stay in a hotel the night we had planned on camping, the girls were less than keen on camping in both Macedonia and Albania, understandably, and once we started to travel up the Dalmatian coastline through Bosnia and Croatia, the weather was very much against us as we had a couple of days of appalling rain. Heading through northern Italy we decided this was to be the night, and established through our guidebook that the town of Bobbio had an adequate campsite. We were all set up for this and, indeed, spent the afternoon coffee stop hilariously discussing how we would manage that night. The plans were scuppered, however, when with 20 kilometres to go, the Sunbeam suddenly cut out and refused to move. The combined mechanical investigative knowledge of Dave and myself could be written on a very, very small piece of paper, nonetheless we were agreed that it could only be an electrical fault; beyond that we were lost and had no idea how to cure the problem. The only solution was to hitch the Sunbeam up to the XK and tow it into Bobbio. The run into Bobbio was up a hill that got progressively steeper and steeper and, at one point, the XK simply ran out of breath and I did not feel that I could tow the Sunbeam any further without causing damage. We slowly ground to a halt and got out to discuss our next move. Remarkably, we discovered that we were standing directly opposite a garage, albeit closed, that specialised in automotive electrics. What luck. The Sunbeam was pushed onto the forecourt and we walked up to the village to take refuge in a small hotel, which provided perfectly adequate accommodation. Yet another camping opportunity lost!

The following morning at 8.00 o'clock, Dave and I were at the door of the garage and, within an hour, the proprietor, an elderly Italian gent, clad in traditional long-coat-type overall, sucked his pencil, diagnosed a faulty condenser and, within minutes, had it replaced and we were on our way.

This was our last run in to Montauroux and, after 4,500 miles, we pulled through gates in the early evening. It was a beautiful evening and we decided that, despite the comforts inside the front door, we would at long last commit ourselves to our first night's camping – in our own garden! The night passed reasonably well, although we learnt one salutary lesson – do not camp on a slope, no matter how slight. Slippery nylon sleeping bags on top of slippery nylon groundsheet tells its own story! Nonetheless, we had achieved our aim of testing out the camping equipment albeit in slightly unconventional terms.

On Wednesday 20th September, I rang Mike Booth, who I remembered had just returned from holiday. He told me that he had the results from Millers Oil and that the oil had three times the maximum permitted amount of silica in the sample, together with a smattering of ferrous, brass and copper filings. All of which were the result of the damage to the cylinders, pistons etc. Mike advised me that he was now preparing his report and that he would categorically be stating that it was the ingestion of silica through the air intake system that had caused the damage. He expressed his view that we should then present this to the installing engineer (Keith) and ask for his opinion. I did, however, advise him that all of the work was done at our own home and that the oil bath filter was installed the very day that the engine was completed and the car had been driven with it on at all times – he had no comment to make about that at all.

Thursday 21st September, I rang Adrian very first thing to ask for his assessment following Mike Booth's report. Adrian's immediate view was that he was now 'comfortable' with the fact that he had not caused the problem and stated that the issues were down to 'others'. The strong inference here, of course, being that Keith was to blame – presumably because he had actually fitted the oil bath filter. Interestingly, at this stage, Adrian confirmed once again that the damage was due to the ingestion of dirty air and said that the level in the oil bath filter was 'disastrously low'. This was very much at variance with what he had said some days previously, when he simply confirmed that the level was lower than the mark on the filter, but had not previously said that it could, in any way, be considered as disastrously low.

Richard was my next call and he very kindly agreed to send Mike 2 the following day to pick up the car with all of its bits and bobs, including the oil samples etc. I spoke to Mike 2 myself and specifically asked him not to say anything to Adrian about what was happening to the car, or indeed where it was going. By complete coincidence, Mike 2 told me that he already knew Adrian and didn't like him, so the chances of any extended conversation were a bit remote. It was during this conversation that Mike 2 mentioned that he had been investigating the situation regarding processes that should be employed when sandblasting an engine. Once an engine has been fully blasted clean, it should normally be soaked for ten hours or so in a hot water bath in order to purge the engine of any residual sand. I suspect that it was this critical process that had not been carried out.

I rang Adrian back straight away, and told him that I wanted to recover the car the following day between 11 and 12 o'clock. Initially, Adrian seemed a trifle stunned that I had made such an immediate decision to remove the car, but I told him that I was keen to take it away in order to consider my options. It really was the first time that I felt properly in control of the affair, as it definitely seemed to 'wrong foot' him. He, however, asked me what I was going to do about 'the invoice' for the investigative work he had done on the car engine. I told him that I had, of course, not had an invoice and was hardly therefore in a position to pay something that I had not had sight of. Impasse.

Friday 22nd September Amazingly, I got a call from Adrian at 8.49 am to say that he had been contemplating the situation at home and announced that he was not prepared to release the car until he had payment of his invoice in full. I told him, of course, that it was somewhat difficult to organise payment, as I hadn't had sight of any invoice and it was rather late notice bearing in mind that Mike 2 was already on his way. We had a long and detailed discussion with words like "feeling vunerable", "trust", "integrity", and "honour" being much in evidence. The eventual outcome was that Adrian agreed that, perhaps, he had been a little impetuous and agreed for the car to be picked up, whilst he would then post off his invoice to Foolow.

Impasse over, and Mike 2 duly picked up the Chevy, in complete silence, and transported it back to Richard's.

Later that morning, walking back down from the boulangerie in Montauroux, I was musing over the issues of the last few days, and suddenly thought about our Aston Martin. This car has twin carburretors, with no filtration whatsoever – just two open barrels pointing out into the countryside. It occurred to me that we have driven the Aston for in excess of 20,000 miles over the last 3 or 4 years, to every corner of Europe, around the dirt roads of Scotlands, ingesting masses of so-called 'road dirt' with never a sign of a problem. Surely that was indicative in some way that road dirt cannot, conceivably, be the cause of our problems.

By complete coincidence later that day, I was speaking to Andy Bell of Ecurie Bertelli about shipping the Aston to Argentina, where we were going to take part in the Mille Millas. Whilst I was on the phone to him, I explained what had happened to the Chevrolet, with all of the consequent arguments and deliberations of the various involved parties. Andy's immediate response, without any prompting whatsoever, was "absolute nonsense, that simply can't happen. It will be sandblasting from the engine block". He then recounted his own story whereby he had picked up a car with a fully re-built, brand new engine, from London some years ago, and drove as far as Newport Pagnell, by which time, after fifty miles, the engine completely failed. The outcome was that it was silica sand residue left inside the engine. In its own way

this was quite good news as it seemed very much to reinforce my own thoughts. We just needed to prove it now.

Saturday 23rd September, and I received a phone call from Richard to say that they have now stripped down what was left of the engine and, without question, in his view, the inlet manifold had been sandblasted. It was, apparently, quite obvious that its pure, grey colour indicated that it had been recently sandblasted, and he had also found some very suspicious deposits on the inside of the cylinders. In the meantime, I had spent several hours on the internet and telephone, and had managed to track down an independent laboratory in Swansea, who would be prepared to test our oils. This, on its own, was quite a

Evening in Avallon

triumph, as most of the major oil companies that I had contacted were simply not prepared to test one-off samples.

The rest of our trip was spent tidying up one or two loose ends. Dave and Jo stayed around for three days or so then headed back north. We then simply cruised, read, swam and generally tried to think about non-Chevrolet related issues.

After a couple of weeks R and R, we gave the XK a fresh, wash down and headed north, back towards Foolow, having had a hugely successful five and a half thousand mile incident-packed trip.

Chapter 5

ONWARDS AND……

Early October saw us back in Foolow, and my first job was to try and get my mind around where we go next. One of my early calls was to Mervyn Jones of the Swansea Tribology Services, who had agreed to do the oil testing for us. I was more than delighted to hear that his tests had conclusively confirmed that it was silica in the engine that had caused the problem, and not road dirt as suggested by Adrian Bailey. What a result! Mervyn's conclusion was that there was no sign of silica in the oil filter at all, he reported finding iron (from the block), aluminium (from the pistons), copper, lead and tin (from the damaged main bearings) and chromium (from the top and scraper piston rings). All now seemed very clear, it was just a question of how to approach the issue. There seemed to be so much money involved that I decided that a trip to my solicitors was the only course of action. My initial discussions were just simply to take some advice, as I was hoping not to involve the complexities of the law – watch this space.

6th October. I drove across to Richard's to look at the car, and Richard offered me a couple of choices – either the new engine, which is already under way, or my original engine rebuilt with new liners. Really, there was no decision to be made on my part, and I chose the new engine, simply because it was much quicker. Mike 2 has all the new parts on order and has said that he will have the engine completely ready by the 20th October. Whilst chatting, Mike also told me that he had done some more investigation into sandblasting/cleaning techniques, and discovered that the normal approach would be to pressure wash the items in hot water and then be left in a hot water bath to soak for 8 hours a day for a minimum of 5 days. Knowing

The trip back North

what I now know about Adrian, I rather think that this has not happened!

10th October. I decided that a meeting with Adrian was perhaps the next move to see if we could establish any common ground, and I suggested meeting a few days hence. Disappointingly, a couple of days later, Adrian rang and cancelled but promised to rearrange the meeting sometime later in the month.

17th October. Remarkably, Adrian rang today but didn't really seem to be too keen to meet up with me; he said he didn't know what could be achieved. I simply told him that as I felt I was very much the injured party, that a conversation could be beneficial certainly to me and, perhaps, to him also. He took me by surprise, however, when he announced that he knew I had already got a new engine being rebuilt – it appeared that Mike 2 clearly hadn't been quite as silent as he might have been!

18th October. Adrian rang again, attempting to resist a meeting. However, I was persistent and, eventually, he agreed to meet up on the 1st November; it was way ahead but nevertheless, I really did feel that it was an opportunity I shouldn't be missing.

20th October. Richard rang to say the car wouldn't be ready for a day or two, but by 25th October all was ready for collection. By dint of bus, taxi and train, I found my way to Monk Fryston and was delighted to find that the Chevy seemed to be running quite smoothly. Rain was pouring down as I headed south for Foolow and I was somewhat disappointed to find that the windscreen wipers are absolutely appalling – they only seem to sweep the windscreen once every twenty minutes or so. Earlier investigation shows that the windscreen wipers worked on a vacuum principle, one wipe per fortnight clearly meant that we must have a leak in the system somewhere – it was a problem that was never adequately solved during our ownership of the car.

29th October saw local friends Jim, John, Rodger and me taking our now annual trip off to the NEC for the Classic Car show. We always like to have a 'project' and, of course, buying anything towards the Peking to Paris trip was an ideal excuse. I managed to root out some spare windscreen wiper blades, a set of wire stone guards for the headlamps and a curious funnel device with a mesh liner which was, apparently, an absolute necessity for filtering out general debris and camels' toenails from the dreadful petrol that we expected to encounter in Mongolia!

1st November 2006 With all the information and revelations that we had gained on our European trip, I had decided it might be beneficial to confront Adrian and, in particular, was keen to be able to see, face-to-face, his reactions when I introduced the fact that I knew that, indeed, the engine had been sandblasted. I felt that perhaps the best chance of setting up a meeting was to suggest we met on neutral ground; I knew for sure that he wouldn't be prepared to come to Foolow and, frankly, his somewhat depressing garage in Colne didn't seem to be the right scenario for a confrontation. On top of which I wanted the meeting to be on my terms rather than his. I therefore suggested to him that we met and had a coffee in a Holiday Inn on the outskirts of Manchester, which was roughly equi-distant between us both. After his initial reservations, we had agreed to meet on 1st November, ostensibly to talk through the affair and see whether we could amicably resolve matters between us. Today was the day.

It felt strangely clandestine to be rendevouzing in this nondescript environment, but we were at least reasonably civilised and enjoyed a cup of undistinguished coffee before we got down to the nub of the matter. I started by asking him how he really did feel that the damage had been caused and he simply stated that it was all in the report that had been prepared by Mike Booth, which made it, in his view, perfectly clear. But I pushed him and asked whether he genuinely believed that normal road dust could have caused the problem, but he wouldn't be drawn at all and simply

repeated time and time again that he had to believe what the report had said. Eventually I told him all that I had done, the discussions with various engineers and consultants, the analysis of the oil, and then I eventually told him that I knew that the engine had been sandblasted and that this was the root cause of the problem. His immediate reaction was to say that HE hadn't sandblasted any part of the engine, but when I came to ask him how the engine was cleaned up from its original black and filthy condition, he simply said that he wasn't prepared to answer that particular question, suggesting that because of the position we were in he didn't want to discuss it any further, but he was quite specific that 'HE' hadn't sandblasted the engine, and the inference I took was that this was a play on words, meaning that HE specifically hadn't done the work on it.

Quite clearly at this stage we were going to get little further. Adrian wasn't prepared to reveal any more information and I wasn't in a position to push him any further, so I simply handed him a pre-prepared letter that indicated that, sadly, we may well end up in court and suggested that he make contact with his insurers immediately.

Before signing off completely, I said to him "so, do you honestly believe that ingestion of road dirt has caused this?" and at that he looked exceedingly embarrassed and uncomfortable and said that whilst he had never heard of anything like this before himself, this was simply what the report said. Clearly, we were going no further on this issue and, indeed, as I write this three-and-a-half years later, the situation is still not resolved, partly because Adrian's insurance company is intransigent to say the least, partly because the solicitors have dragged their heels unbelievably on a case in which they clearly have little interest, and partly because the stupidity of the legal system allows cases like this to drag on endlessly.

At some time in the proceedings, Richard told me that his upholsterer, who completely coincidentally, had done some work from his Yorkshire home for the Colne-based Adrian Bailey, told Richard that he had visited Adrian's garage, commented upon the Chevrolet being there and was told quite categorically by one of the mechanics that it had suffered a problem "due to the sandblasting when we cleaned the engine up". Sadly, I have never been able to use this particular piece of critical evidence, as the upholsterer was owed a considerable amount of money by Adrian and felt that release of this information may well jeopardise any chance he had of recovering his monies.

2nd November My first job today was to start construction of this central control unit, and I was soon absorbed in joinery work.

Later in the day, I came to drop the bonnet into its closed position, only to find that the front corners of the bonnet once again bashed into the front wings, stripping paint off both sides. What a frustration. Upon investigation, I discovered that Mike 2, having had the radiator out to fit the engine, had not put the steel packs back into place. The only solution was to loosen all the radiator fixings around the perimeter, insert my now familiar piece of 3 x 2 timber across the inside face of the wings, and force them apart before dropping the packs into place and re-tightening everything up. At least now we shan't have that problem again!

3rd November. On a wonderfully clear, cold day, I took the car to Bielowski's to have the hood fully waterproofed and the tonneau readjusted.

The following day, I caught a bus into Sheffield as the job was fully completed. I dropped the car off at Halfords for them to fit the radio into position. There was a huge amount of discussion about woofers and tweeters – all of which was a bit beyond me, so I had a couple of relatively simple speakers fitted into our rear storage compartments. A good job really as we never listened to the radio during the trip.

6th November saw me repositioning the air horn. For whatever reason it had suddenly ceased to work, and I decided relocation on the other side of the bulkhead was the best solution. Halfords had suggested that I needed a new radio aerial. There was already one fitted on the car, but it was a 1950s style aerial which, whilst it looked the part, was apparently not compatible with the radio I had bought! I had a frustrating day attempting to fit the aerial, followed by attempting to fit the stone

guards on the headlamps. Inevitably, the clips that came with the stone guards were of insufficient length, and it took a couple of hours to make longer clips – what a fiddling job.

7th November. The next serious job was to put some running-in miles on the car, so I was up bright and early, washed the car before our 'shake-down' run.

Around this time I had established contact with Bob Maynard at Auto Historic in Leek. There were a lot of additional jobs on the car that wanted doing, and jobs like making a new fuel tank etc. were not projects that Keith could handle working from Foolow. Our idea was to make a first visit to Bob at Leek before setting off for Scotland. Fully packed and raring to go, we set off from Foolow at about 8.30 am. After 8 or 9 miles, there was an awful sound emanating from the gearbox. Horror of horrors, what next! We limped to Auto Historic, who checked the gearbox oil to find there was only a pint of oil and some metal bits in the bottom. Clearly, something was amiss. However, we decided we were desperate to get some miles on the car, and took an easy run up the M5 to Dumfries, managing with just first and third gear. We put 250 miles on the car, but it really wasn't running smoothly, so the following day we decided to retreat to Richard's. Interestingly, we achieved an average of 22.4 miles per gallon, which was somewhat better than I had anticipated. Upon arriving at Richard's Mike, 2 was very much of the opinion that second gear was chipped. What to do? A quick phone call to Keith and, ever obligingly, he arrived the following morning at the crack of dawn and, between us, we took out the gearbox. This turned out to be not too long a job. Keith introduced me to Nick Creswell at Glebe Engineering, who are gearbox specialists based in Stoke on Trent, so I nipped the gearbox across to them and waited their diagnosis.

13th November Glebe Engineering rang to say that the gearbox was quite badly damaged because of bits of the gearing had been inserted the wrong way round. They were talking of upwards of £700 and 8 weeks to sort it out. This was just the sort of news we didn't need. To compound the problems, we were just about to leave to meet up with the Aston Martin in Buenos Aires and take part in the Mille

Millas across the Andes.

18th November. On the eve of our departure, I decided to ring 'Chevys of the 40s', in the USA, who had previously been able to help with many of the spare parts we needed. On this occasion, however, we drew a blank – they simply did not have any gearbox parts. However, through a series of their own contacts, I was eventually able to telephone 'Joe Jnr' in Portland, Oregan. He told me that the gearbox came in two parts, one part of which he had, but the other part he was not sure about and would need to strip down a gearbox off a scrap car.

21st November. From Buenos Aires, I eventually managed to track down Joe Jnr again and, Yippee, he has got the extra part and will post it. I telephoned Glebe and Keith and told them what to expect. The way things are going, the phone calls over the last couple of days are going to cost more than the replacement gearbox!

6th December, the gearbox part arrived at last in Stoke on Trent and, by the 7th December, Glebe rang to say that they had, indeed, rebuilt the gearbox and Keith arranged to collect it the following day.

7.30 am on 11th December. Keith and mate, Pete, arrived with the gearbox and managed to fit it within the hour. Disappointingly, the car was still not performing perfectly in second gear, but there seemed to be nothing more to do than persist with it and hope it would 'bed in'. I rang Glebe to express my concern, and they said "Oh, yes, second gear was in poor condition". What a shame they didn't bother to tell me that before they rebuilt the gearbox and sent it back!

Nonetheless, Keith and Pete had a good day fitting the reversing light, full set of windscreen washers, stripping out all of the old brake pipes and raising them within the chassis so that there was no possibility of damage caused by rocks.

Argentina provided some light relief

1000 MILLAS SPORT-BARILOCHE 2006

Within one of Philip Young's rally preparation notes, I had read that the engine needed to be TIED DOWN to the chassis – something I couldn't quite understand. After diligently reading Philip's notes, I discovered to my horror that the suggestion was to counter the effect of the car dropping into a deep ditch where the overall effect of the 'suspension bounce' was that the engine would attempt to force its way upwards off the chassis. The requirement, therefore, was to fasten the engine down with a series of steel cables. What were we letting ourselves in for!

15th December. The car was to go to Auto Historic today – however, the Chevy had different ideas. It originally fired up but then, just as we were about to set off, refused time after time to re-start. It appeared that the starter motor had jammed and I spent a horrible hour and a half under the car with a phone in one hand taking instructions from Keith, and a spanner and hammer in the other hand trying to elicit some action from our dead starter motor - still no success. In desperation, I phoned Richard and, amazingly, he had a spare, albeit he tells me a manual one and not an electric solonoid – whatever that means. There was no option now but to drive over to Richard's. It really was an horrendous 130 mile round trip in bucketing rain and dense traffic. I eventually got home at 10.00 pm but at least we had hope for the following day.

At the crack of dawn the following morning, Keith (the star!) arrived with Karen, and eventually discovered that the starter motor was completely jammed. Three hours later the replacement motor was fitted and it looked as though we were ready to go. Not so. The battery was completely dead and I think I must have caught the radio controls and it had been on overnight. A quick tow down the road and we were firing on all six cylinders.

18th December I took the car over to Auto Historic for Bob to have a really good look at it. As soon as I got there, would you believe it, the starter motor failed yet again. I had no option but to leave the car there, and Yvonne came over to fetch me.

20th December, I went over to Leek again to review exactly what we were going to do to the car. Bob, having had a really good opportunity to look round the car, presented me with a list.

The rear suspension needed attention, as one of the leaf springs appeared to have failed. Bob's critical eye spotted that, in his view, some of the shackle bolts were too long and some were too short.

The brake master cylinder was leaking.

There were two leaks on the fuel tank.

The steering bushes were worn.

All the earth tags and spade fittings need changing to bolts.

Skid plates need fitting.

The rear wheel bearings need checking.

We need rubber sleeves on the steering arms

Extra brackets are required on the brake pipes

Nylon bushes are required for the shackles

The starter motor definitely needs sorting.

OUCH !

I must have looked a weary, bedraggled and unconvincing customer, as they asked me to leave them a cheque for £3,500 before they would start work. I swallowed hard, wrote the cheque – after all we were in it too deeply now.

Christmas and New Year were completely Chevrolet-free. The car was at Auto Historic and I felt it was in very good hands. Our grand plan was to drive to Montauroux early in the New Year to get some well-needed mileage on the clock, run the car in and generally see if all the modifications were satisfactory, so it was with great glee that on 3rd January we went off to Auto Historic to pick up the car. I must say, I was hugely satisfied as most of the work was done.

The steering pins had been completely replaced.
The rear springs had been changed.
The new nylon shackle sleeves had been manufactured and fitted.
New shock absorbers were on order.
All the electric connection spade fittings had been replaced by nut and bolts (apparently spade fittings shake free and don't give a good contact in super rough conditions!)
The leaking fuel tank had been repaired.
The starter motor had been repaired.
The flywheel had been filed (I know not why!)
The rear break cylinders had been replaced.

With high hopes and a spring in my step, I set off for Foolow in bucketing rain. Second gear was still worryingly noisy until driving up past Ramshaw Rocks, halfway home. Suddenly the gearbox noise stopped completely and the car drove like a dream all the way home. The cost of all this latest work to date, was a staggering £6,690, but I had now reached the point where I had given up worrying – the car just had to be right.

Early morning on 4th January, I pulled the car out onto the grass ready to start packing for our French trip when, horror upon horror, the car wouldn't start. At this stage, we were outside, the hood was down and it was pouring with rain. I really thought I had a huge problem on my hands, however, it turned out that the battery was simply drained, possibly caused by the hood mechanism. I made a mental note to ensure that whenever I was operating the hood in future, I would keep the

engine running. I switched the battery, and all was well. Whew! I spent the rest of the day preparing the car for the trip to France, changing the oil, adding anti-freeze and packing ready for the off.

Chapter 6

A NEW YEAR - IN FACT, PEKING-PARIS YEAR, 2007

The start of the year that would be the culmination of all the plans we had been working on. Surely, things would pick up now and our luck would change.

5th January and we are fully packed and off on the road to Hull to catch the ferry to Zeebrugge. Would you believe it, half an hour from Foolow the car slipped out of third gear – that's a new one – it's never done that before! Nonetheless, we soldiered on and, in fact, the car ran extremely well. It was a fine opportunity to settle into driving the car and understand what would be our 'office' for later in the year. Strangely, the car was still slipping out of third gear, sometimes one or twice in five minutes, sometimes not for two or three hours. We decided to ignore this issue and press on.

The weather in France is normally beautiful in January, and this year was no exception; cold evenings but balmy days. The only job I did on the car whilst we were in Montauroux, was to strip off the new steel bumpers and give them an additional coat of paint. Other than that, we had a great opportunity to gently run the car in and returned to Foolow having done 1,783 miles. I had been making an accurate check on the fuel consumption and we recorded an overall consumption of 17.5 mpg – hardly brilliant. Having said that I had discovered that the speedo is, indeed, six percent slow so that meant in real terms that we actually covered 1,896 miles with the equivalent of 18.5 mpg. It's amazing what you can do by manipulating figures. The only scary moment on the whole trip was descending Mont Ventoux when, for some unknown reason, the brakes with continual useage, simply ceased to function, it really was quite unnerving. The Chevrolet is an extremely large car and, when fully laden, probably weighs well in excess of two tons. That's a lot of car to be driven without brakes, and we certainly had an anxious hour or two with the gearbox being much used when necessity called. Strangely, thereafter when just using braking occasionally on normal undulating roads, the problem seemed to go

away, the brakes were hardly brilliant but, nonetheless, seemed adequate. However, the issue on Mont Ventoux was clearly significant and merited some investigation.

Immediately on our return, I phoned Bob Maynard at Auto Historic and on 24th January took the car across to Leek, together with my comprehensive list. Yvonne and I had discussed the various issues with the car on our trip across France, and we had decided that, regardless of cost, we would now turn the car over to Auto Historic and get them to complete the full preparation. Time was running short.

Around this time the Rally Organisers had contacted each entrant and advised them that the car should be capable of travelling 380 miles between petrol fills. With our existing tank having only a maximum capacity of 13.4 gallons, we have decided to re-think and have a new tank made.

Whilst in France, we had noticed that the car was looking strangely lopsided and, upon measuring the height of the bumper at the front of the car, discovered that the offside was two inches lower than the nearside. Clearly, something needed looking at.

Nonetheless, on this dark, snowy night in January, I left Auto Historics with a spring in my step walking back towards Foolow, from where Yvonne was driving to meet me. Somehow, having come to terms with asking Auto Historic to do the remainder of the preparation, lifted a great weight off my shoulders.

The following day I spoke to Nick Shrigley-Fiegal (part owner of Auto Historic) who told me that he had redesigned the fuel tank and could achieve a capacity of 25 gallons. Nick said that they were a little confused by the lopsidedness of the car as the front spring is not broken, as we had suspected. Investigations continue.

30th January. I took a trip down to Leek to see how things were going on with the car, and was delighted to see plenty of things happening. However, the hub seal on the rear wheel has seized, the brakes therefore got oily and over-heated, having the effect that the brake shoes had completely degraded – hence our problems on Mont Ventoux. Nick had ordered some competition brake shoes, which should overcome this problem. Reading down Nick's list, I see that

The flywheel needs skimming

The detent spring on the gearbox was worn and needs brazing

The starter motor is awaiting a new gear reduction

The shock absorbers were expected any day

The driving seats are to be lowered about 1.1/2 inches (my initial seating frame design was a little inaccurate and was having a significant impact on both our hairstyles)

The master cylinder was damaged beyond repair

My role at the end of the day was to order brake seals and back axle seals from Chevy of the 40s. I ordered them on priority, i.e. next day delivery.

Ten days later, and I was extremely frustrated as no parts had yet

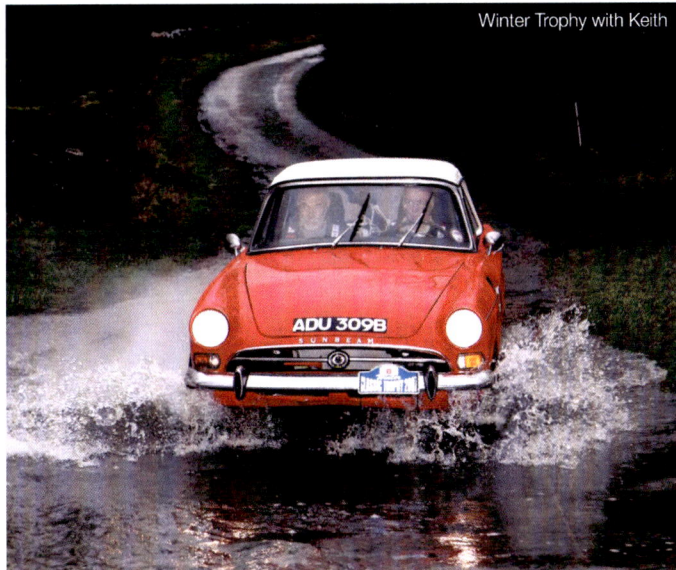

Winter Trophy with Keith

ADU 309B

arrived from the US. Phoned and was told that two parcels had been sent the week previously.

17th February I returned from taking part in the Winter Trophy rally with Keith to discover one parcel had arrived, but not the other. On 20th February, I rang the US again but they didn't have a tracking number and had no idea where the parcels were. There was still nothing by 26th February so I emailed Chevys of the 40s and asked them to send a fresh set.

27th February, Eureeka! I called Parcel Force and the parcel had arrived. I dashed off to Rotherham, 30 miles to the north to collect the parcels and pay the customs duty, then drove back to Leek, 20 miles south to deliver all the bits to Bob and Nick. On opening the parcels, we discover we are short of one rear wheel seal. More phone calls…….

We later discovered that, having taken our address over the phone instead of getting it from their files, Chevy's of the 40s had managed to send the parts to the Ukraine instead of the UK!!

My new alumium fuel tank was ready with a capacity of 28 gallons. That will cost a fortune to fill, methinks! The starter motor still needs to be replaced, as it has been made incorrectly, and I'm told that will be back tomorrow. Bob now advises that, at the rear of the car, we should think of fitting double shock absorbers. We have a distinct advantage here, as Bob, indeed, prepared the Willis Jeep that won the 1997 Peking-Paris rally, so he is very much up to speed with the problems that we might meet. He has come up with an idea to put double shock absorbers on the rear of the car and has already top-mounted these and is in the middle of making new bottom plates for fixing to the chassis. Bob really is an absolute ace, as they have every piece of machinery known to mankind and from a billet of steel he is able to produce whatever is needed for the car. Finally we discussed completion dates and Bob tells me the end of next week will see the job finished.

6th March Bob called to tell me that he was suggesting that we should have a new exhaust with a side exit. What a great idea this is, as it avoids the complexity of winding the exhaust system round the back axle etc. Bob is also going to make an adaptation to the exhaust pipe with a 2 ft. high vertical riser which can be clamped into position for our river crossings!

8th March, a day for good news and bad news. The good news was that the seal had at long last arrived. The bad news was that the 2 inch droop on the front of the car had been traced to the rear spring which had become extremely soggy. There was almost four inches of difference in the bow of the outer spring. What to do. The springs were newly tempered at the beginning of the rebuild and we were supposed to be picking the car up next Wednesday! I immediately phoned GME Springs in Sheffield, and Yvonne shot off to Leek to bring the springs back to Foolow; I then took them on into Sheffield to confront GME. Inevitably, there was yet another problem – they only fire up the furnaces every other day and we have just missed it! Quelle surprise!

Under the circumstances GME agreed to do whatever they could to expedite matters and, in fact, said that they would deliver the springs themselves directly to Leek the following Tuesday. Having sorted all that out I spoke to Mike 3 (one of Auto Historic's mechanics) who told me that the brakes had been sorted and bled, the seals were in place, the differential was back together, the tank was fixed and Bob had gone to fetch the exhaust pipe. All being well, we should be back on for a Wednesday pick-up. What a day!

At least GME Springs did exactly what they said, and managed to deliver at 2.30 in the afternoon. However, Bob told me that he still had quite a few jobs to do and suggested Thursday as the pick-up day. Mike 3 the mechanic had walked out, apparently, and left them all a little short-handed.

The following day, I phoned late afternoon but they were still working on the car and it would now be ready Friday morning. On the Friday I rang again and, at last, good news, everything would be done and ready for 10.00 am the following morning. Then, a horror phone call at 7.30 that evening.

Nick rang to say that they had started the car up for the first time since it came back from France, and the engine sounded dreadful – a horrible noise from the bottom end of the engine. He told me that there was zero oil pressure at the top of the engine but 45 psi at the bottom, which seemed to suggest that the oil ways were blocked. He also said that the oil appeared to be filthy. My first thought was that this was an issue caused by Auto Historic as, of course, the car had come back from France apparently running quite sweetly. Nick was so concerned that he suggested I went down immediately, but this seemed pointless, as I couldn't do anything except, perhaps, survey the devastation. In a daze, I rang Richard to ask if his mechanic, Mike 2, had any ideas, I even rang Nick Shrigley-Fiegal to ask if the disaffected mechanic could have sabotaged the car to vent his frustration about his personal feelings. I immediately felt somewhat embarrassed about such uncharitable thoughts, but I was so exasperated and almost at the end of my tether. Nick, however, was certain that Mike 3 couldn't possibly have tampered with the car at all as, at the time he last worked on the car, there was no battery in the car and no fuel. Where do we go now.

16th March Needless to say, I had a completely sleepless night and was up at 3.00 am. Richard and Mike 2 phoned in the morning and were suggesting that, as the car hadn't been started for six weeks, there may well be oil starvation. Clinging onto this hope, I dashed across to Leek in the afternoon and listened to the engine, which was unbelievably rough. Clearly, something was very wrong indeed. Bob went on to explain that there was no oil in the top end of the engine, so obviously the oilways were blocked. The rocker arms and springs etc. were dirty and oily – Nick says these should be very clean in just 2,000 miles since the last oil change. Bob took the sump off and found that the oil was very black and sludgy with contaminated metal colouring and also a small amount of water. More concerning was that the bearings were worn through to the copper on the surface and edges. Alarmingly, Bob also found a piece of insulation tape washing around in the sump. The other strange thing was that the shims that were used in the bearings are 4 mm longer than the caps – an engineering 'no no' that, according to Bob, "beggers belief". Worse than that, Bob thinks that the crankshaft maybe bent or the block out of alignment.

Mike 2, Richard's mechanic, phoned still suggesting that starting up the engine quickly from a long delay was the problem, until I mentioned, one -that the oilways appear to be blocked with silicone, two – the oil was thick, black and sludgy, three – the piece of insulation tape that had been found in the sump, and four – the extremely worn bearings. I think It was at this stage that he eventually realised that the problem was somewhat more serious than he had imagined.

Bob, ever positive, immediately started work on lifting the engine out and, indeed, had arranged for help to arrive at 8.30 the following morning. He was hoping to get the engine out and stripped down over the weekend and had arranged for someone to check the alignment on Monday morning.

I really could not believe this. We were now on our third engine, and it was such incredibly back luck. I noted in my diary, "when will it all end and, indeed, will anybody believe us!" A very depressing day altogether.

17th March Bob rang to say that he had got the engine out and fully apart by 1.00 pm but the news was not good.

> The piston rings should be about 5,000ths but are 1/16th inch and the gasses are simply getting through the huge gap.

> The hardening has worn through on the camshaft and lumps have been ground away.

> There is a split in the block which has been filled with araldite – allowing water and oil to mix.

So what was wrong with the engine, and what had caused the problems. Once the engine was apart, it was quite clear that the problem had been caused by blocked oilways which weren't allowing the oil to work its way through to the head of the engine – hence zero oil pressure at the head. It appeared that the problem had been caused by the sump having been sealed into place with a squirt of silicone placed around the joint which, when bolted together, had squeezed out of the joint, dropped into the oil in the sump and had then been sucked up into the oilways, causing the blockage. I am sure this was anything but a proper engineering solution, and it just shows that even in the most skilled hands things can go wrong, sometimes with devastating consequences such as this. It was a simple, elementary error, but one with far reaching consequences that no-body would ever have dreamt of.

I knew that the news was not good but really wasn't prepared for the next bit – Bob tells me the only solution is a new engine. This one was beyond redemption.

Here we were, three weeks before the car was due to be shipped to China, and we seemed to be almost back to square one. Where on earth would we find a new engine at this late stage. However, out of the mists of gloom, I suddenly had a brainwave. I was now the proud owner of two Chevrolet engines which had, effectively, been reduced to scrap, but perhaps there was a possibility of making one good engine out of these two duff engines. I had the idea but how plausible was it? My mind started to race but I had too many unanswered problems, so I engaged in a round-robin of phone calls with Richard, Keith and Bob. It was eventually agreed that I could use the block off the original sandblast-damaged engine which could then be machined out for new liners, new pistons could be bought and a new camshaft acquired. Two hours later all of the elements of my idea were in place – we just had to source all the parts and labour and turn the job round as rapidly as possible – we were, after all, going to have to recreate the new engine with sufficient time to fully run it in before our shipping date of 11th April. We were back in business.

The following day things really started to buzz. Richard arranged to deliver the sandblasted block to Leek. Bob rang with a couple of pieces of cracking news, firstly the crankshaft was just fine for alignment and could be re-used, but better than that he had tracked down some original Chevrolet pistons and rings in Shrewsbury and was going to fetch them that afternoon.

Our 'new' block can be sleeved and Bob has arranged for this to be engineered in a couple of days time. The only issue outstanding was that he could not track down the appropriate camshaft. I immediately picked up the phone and rang Chevys of the 40s but, disappointingly, they didn't have any in stock. However, they pointed me to Egge Manufacturing in California who, to my absolute relief had exactly the model we required, plus a set of lifters (whatever they are!) and a gasket set. Needless to say, I was ecstatic and finished my phone call with Chuck by advising him that the next biggest challenge was to get the equipment to us as fast as possible. He promised immediate action.

At the end of this long, long, long day the news was that, all things being equal and all parts arriving on time, we could have the car back next weekend or just after. What a relief. Two days previously we thought our race had been run.

20th March The most amazing thing happened today. 2.30 pm and I got a call from Customs to say that the camshaft had arrived – just 21 hours after I had made my phone call. I could only assume they had strapped it to a rocket – what an amazing service. An hour later it arrived in Leek.

Bob rang later to say he had found a full set of liners and was taking the engine to Joe Bradbury in Cheshire for the engineering work to be commenced.

Two days later all the parts were machined and ready for assembly and by the 26th March Bob rang to say the bottom half of the engine was rebuilt and the new oil filter fitted. The top half of the engine was being rebuilt today, the engine should go in tomorrow and all being well, the car should be ready for collection on Wednesday.

Wednesday dawned and Bob sounded extremely weary. He had encountered all sorts of unexpected problems, one of the engine mountings had broken and the camshaft seals were wrong – it was going to be another day.

28th March. A rather interesting diversion today. Alan, Adrian Bailey's mechanic, arrived at our front door in Foolow, demanding with menaces a cheque in full settlement for the work that Auto Services, Colne had carried out on the engine. I was not in at the time, and Yvonne had to handle this. However, he was sent packing by firm words from Yvonne. In the light of all that had happened he had called at a very critical moment and I expect he got very short shrift. However, I was somewhat concerned at this turn of events as I recall that previously he had told Yvonne that he had occasionally earned a bit on the side by collecting debts. A quick phone call to my solicitor was followed by a letter to Adrian suggesting that he did not persist with this somewhat unconventional approach.

The following day saw another trip to Leek – I am now beginning to be able to drive this stretch of road with my eyes closed! However, the car is still not ready, everything seems to be taking a long time. The new oil filter arrangement that Bob had devised was almost completed but was proving to be extremely complex and the radiator needed to be fitted, etc. etc. Bob told me that the car would definitely be ready the following morning and a pick-up time of 9.00 am was arranged.

Dutifully, I arrived at 9.00 am and the car was standing outside, ready for collection as promised. Bob looked a tad weary for 9.00 am, but all was explained when he told me that, in order to complete the work, he had slaved through the night. The Chevy started immediately and the journey back to Foolow was an absolute joy – we were back on track at last – with engine number 4.

The next couple of days were a feverish blur of activity as I started to finish off all my own last-minute jobs. We had planned a three-day running-in trip to Scotland, and everything needed to be fully completed.

2nd April I washed the car down – almost ready to go, and nipped off for a short spin in the car to check everything was OK, but suddenly heard a strange, tinny rattling noise. Oh no, not again, whatever could this be? I made the inevitable phone call to Bob and at 4.15 pm hit the road to Leek. Once again, after five minutes under the bonnet, Bob discovered that the fixing between the water pump and the fan had broken and without any further ado he set off to make one from scratch – out of a billet of steel he measured, machined, re-measured, checked, drilled, polished and at 10.20 that night finally finished. It really was an amazing effort and a huge tribute to a man who would never give up no matter what the odds. At last, time to go home – but what was this, the hood wouldn't go up and we managed to run the battery down! The Chevy was a big beast to push-start but somehow we managed and I arrived back home at midnight – apparently a much larger, heavier battery is next on the shopping list.

One thing that occurs to me is that the rally is going to be easy-peasy after the car preparation!

3rd April. Up with the lark this morning, ready for our running-in trip to Scotland. The weather was magnificent and was set to hold for several days, and we had booked a really nice hotel in Scotland for a couple of nights. High hopes for some pleasant and easy motoring.

High hopes dashed. The car would not start as the battery was flat. I put it on charge for an hour whilst I had breakfast, but still no go. I prised the battery out of the XK and at least got the Chevy fired up. I made a mental note to take a spare battery and battery charger with us just to be sure.

We had hardly done twenty miles, when the car started to slip out of gear again – but only on the motorways, strangely. There was absolutely no pattern whatsoever. We could be driving along and it would slip out of third gear three or four times in a mile, then it would not happen for twenty to thirty miles. Even stranger, was the fact that it only happened on the motorway, and the moment we turned off onto side roads it stopped happening altogether – explain that! There were one or two other small issues, the car seemed to be not pulling very well at low revs, a bit of anti-freeze was leaking into the passenger compartment, and the nearside front wheel was locking up totally under braking. Other than that we had a faultless 300 mile drive to Balquhidder! The hotel was breathtakingly good and we were really looking forward to a couple of nights here with a long drive up the west coast in between. However, a quick phone call to Bob to report on the issues of the gearbox made us change our minds and, disappointingly, we decided to cut short the trip to get back to Auto Historic. Getting the car right is more important than lapping up the luxuries of Scotland.

4th April. Woke up to a beautiful day once again and a phone call from Bob. He had had a brainwave overnight and remembered that he knew a woman who lived on a farm some ten or twelve miles from Leek and who, rather obscurely, collected scrap American cars. His plan was to whiz over as soon as possible and see if there was a chance of a matching gearbox, and suggested that I crawled under the car to try and find a reference number. Eager to follow up this idea, I jacked the car up, slid underneath and eventually found a series of numbers which I telephoned back to Bob. However,

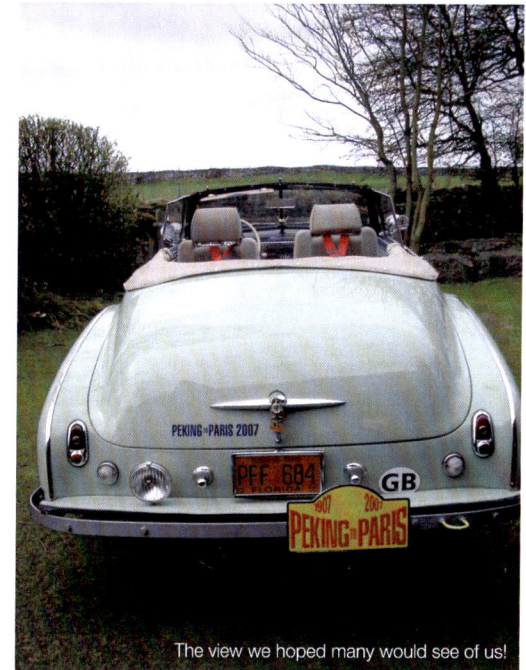
The view we hoped many would see of us!

this procedure brought on another issue, which was strange indeed. I had jacked the car up using the traditional original jack which came with the car. This was an approximately one metre long aluminium bar with huge notches in it. This contraption fastened to the rear bumper and a side handle ratcheted the car up the bar. The huge advantage was that you could get a terrific height on the lift, giving great access under the car. The downside was that I simply could not get the car back down again! The ratchet mechanism had jammed and I simply could not lower the car. The weight of the body was so great that it was overcoming the mechanism. What to do? We were in a wonderful hotel, the main selling point of which was it remoteness! The only solution was to hitch a lift to a nearby farm where I borrowed a trolley jack, relieved the load on the car and, eventually, dropped it to the ground. My immediate plan was for the original jack to hit the dustbin and I made a mental note to take a trolley jack on the rally! Yet again, I consoled myself with the thought that it was far better to find out these problems in Scotland rather than in the Gobi Desert!

We turned round and headed south and arrived back in Leek in the early evening. The good news was that I had been checking the fuel and we managed to get 400 miles on one full tank.

An amazing piece of news when we got back to Auto Historic was that Bob had managed to find a gearbox with the matching number after searching under five or six other engines. He had prised them all apart, taken off the gearbox and taken it to Glebe Engineering in Stoke-on-Trent where a chap called Steve took a look and declared it to be a 'good'n'. What a relief. It appeared to be the correct type. Bob had already cleaned it up and painted it, and it was standing on the bench ready for fitting.

There were now seven days to go before shipping, and I left the car with Bob to

Service the car and adjust the tappets
Change the oil
Sort out the sticking brakes
Adjust the suspension
Cure the anti-freeze leak
Cure the slipping clutch
Check the hood motor fluids, etc.

After our somewhat traumatic day, Bob and Nick were just terrific, so reassuring. We arrived home at almost midnight, feeling at least that Auto Historic had everything under control. Phew!

5th April. WRONG!! I got a call from Bob at lunchtime to say that, after all, the gearbox was not compatible, the new one was half an inch longer than the original and the controls were different. I leapt into the car, picked up Bob and drove over to Stoke-on-Trent to see Steve at Glebe. Within minutes they had both gearboxes apart and, fortuitously, most of the internal parts were compatible. Steve spotted that three particular bits seemed to be quite worn and he felt that he could cobble

Car looking immaculate - almost ready to go

Our secure storage

together one gearbox out of the two that we owned. They agreed to work the evening so that the car could be ready the following day at 11.00 am.

7th April Glebe were as good as their word and the gearbox was picked up yesterday. Friend Jim took me down to Leek at 9.00 am to collect the car and I was surprised to see Bob looking extremely tired and very oily. To my absolute astonishment he told me that, in order to achieve the pick up time, he had worked the night through, yet again. We shook hands and he climbed into his car to drive off home for a well-earned sleep. The Chevy started immediately and ran as sweetly as a sewing machine. I drove home at lunchtime – fingers crossed.

8th April A full day's job cleaning and sorting final items. The car was waxed and polished, everything oiled and greased, windows cleaned, dodgy boot lock sorted and carpets vacuumed.

9th April Worked all day on the car, packing, cataloguing and cross-checking. Everything done by 5.00 pm. But what's this… the car seems to be very low on the back left-hand side. I rang the ever-accommodating Bob and drove off to Leek for 7.00 p.m. The reason was that the springs simply were not coping with the weight of all our luggage and spares. Bob decided that the only solution was to add in additional leaves. Luckily, I had some with me and we both got stuck in and finished at 10.30 pm. Wending my weary way back to Foolow, the bloody gearbox slipped out of gear again. I decided I simply hadn't got the heart to tell anyone. The car is definitely determined to have the very last word.

10th April We finished the last minute packing, did a photo shoot and videoed the car pulling out of the workshop at home. At last we were on our way to the shippers. Due to the phenomenal efforts made by Bob and others we were at least under way.

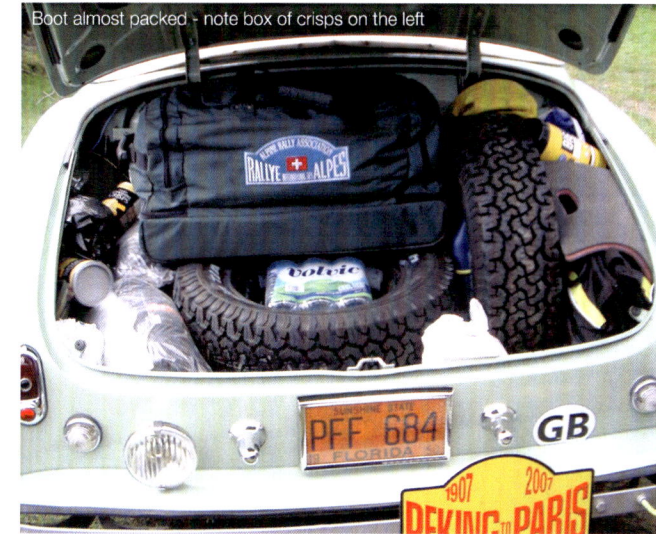

Boot almost packed - note box of crisps on the left

We left home with very mixed emotions, on the one hand grateful that the car was up and running and able to be driven to Bury St. Edmunds, but on the other hand nervously wondering whatever next was going to happen. We wound our way through the back roads across through Chesterfield onto the A1. We had only done a couple of miles down the A1 when, inevitably I suppose, the gearbox slipped out of gear yet again but this time only when the car was decelerating. I worked out in my mind that I would have to devise some system of holding the gear lever into place. My short term solution was to take the belt off my trousers, fasten it under my thigh and hook it over the gearlever. It certainly worked and we made Bury St. Edmonds without any more issues. I made a mental note to pack a spare trouser belt!

Arriving at the hotel early evening, we were able to park the car under cover next to our room. Once having unpacked our luggage, I sat in the car, started it up and activated the hood mechanism. My normal action was to lean my head back to watch the hood moving up towards the headrail of the windscreen. On this occasion, nothing appeared! To my horror, the hood had jammed on one side and the motor was forcing the hood over to one side only, with the inevitable result that it bent two or three of the head rails. This car was not leaving the country without a fight. I engineered a solution by lying on my back in the driver's seat, with my feet in the air, straining and pulling the bent rails back into shape and, after an hour of this unusual posture in the hotel car park, managed to get the hood firmly clamped to the windscreen. It would have to stay like this to Beijing when I would take another look at it.

11th April We were up bright and early and, despite the irritation of the day before, we were in surprisingly high spirits driving off to Cars UK to load up for its journey to China. I think we realised that we had now reached a point where there was absolutely nothing more we could do to prepare the car. We had tried, my how we'd tried and, despite all the odds against us, at least we had secured the car inside its container. Certainly two-and-a-half weeks ago there seemed to be no prospect of achieving this whatsoever. We consoled ourselves that we would at least be on the start line, although at this stage we realistically were thinking there was very little chance of us getting to Paris. I had now limited our ambitions considerably and simply wanted to drive away from the Start at the Great Wall of China with big smiles on our faces. Anything more than that would have to be considered as a bonus.

The following day I rang Glebe Engineering to report the gearbox problem, but Nick Creswell put me somewhat at ease by saying that at least they definitely now knew what the problem was – it was apparently the detent springs and the syncro assembly. A phone call to Chevys of the 40s established that they didn't have such an item, nor did they know where one could be found. At least Nick confirmed that it would not be a problem to hold the gear lever in position, as it would not damage the gearbox. So the trouser belt option is probably the best solution.

Over the next week or so, after having finally come to the conclusion that it was not possible to find any spare parts, Bob decided that he would simply machine one out of some hardened steel. His plan was to make up a new gearbox side plate, obtain a new strengthened detent spring and assemble the whole unit so that I can take it along in my hand baggage. It will be interesting to see what the Customs make of this!

A quick phone call to Peter Banham confirmed that he would be happy to fit the new side plate the moment we tracked down the cars in Beijing.

The remaining weeks until the 'off' were filled with more entertaining and less stressful activities, the finale of which was a wonderful dinner, put on for all we 'Peking-Paris-ers' at nearby Hassop Hall. Our friend, Jim Jackson, had put together a fascinating menu, comprising dishes based mostly on goat, which he thought was extremely amusing, and would get us in readiness for the culinary delights of Mongolia!

And we had a memorable evening with all our close friends, who raised their glasses for a successful rally to us all.

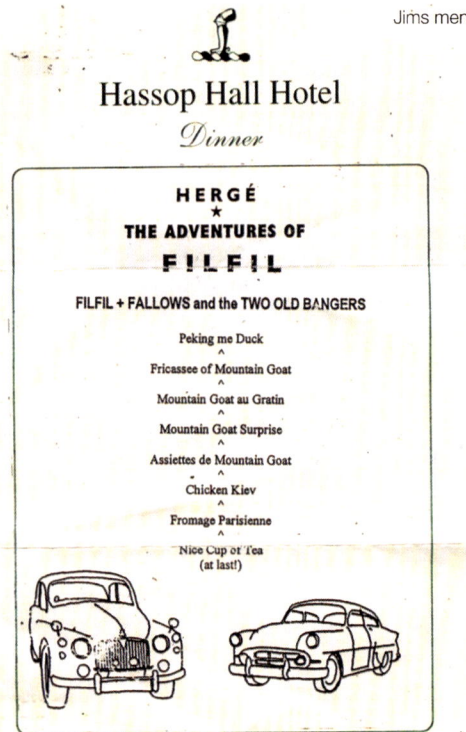

Jims menu

Hassop Hall Hotel
Dinner

HERGÉ
★
THE ADVENTURES OF
FILFIL

FILFIL + FALLOWS and the TWO OLD BANGERS

Peking me Duck
^
Fricassee of Mountain Goat
^
Mountain Goat au Gratin
^
Mountain Goat Surprise
^
Assiettes de Mountain Goat
^
Chicken Kiev
^
Fromage Parisienne
^
Nice Cup of Tea
(at last!)

Chapter 7

YVONNE

So, where is Yvonne in all this? I hear you think! Well, where to start..................

Yvonne

Rallying of any sort is all about team work between driver and navigator and at an early stage, when we were agreed that rallying had become something of a hobby – and as hobbies are supposed to be enjoyable – we determined that we most definitely would not fall out over it, and I must say that in this area we have been hugely successful. Although I say it myself, we are a great team and I think that we generally understand each other's strengths and weaknesses. I suspect I am the driving force to a degree, but Yvonne is hugely supportive in all our activities and, believe me, that really is a great attribute. Peking-Paris was going to be something very special, we were effectively going to be sitting side by side for five weeks continuously and we were both comfortable in the knowledge that this wouldn't pose any problems between us.

When I first mooted the idea, after Yvonne got over the initial shock of the sheer scale of the whole exercise, we both became extremely involved and spent many hours discussing what we were and were not going to achieve.

Being supportive is such a key issue. Obviously, the actual day-to-day activities with the car were very much my remit and as the constant stream of problems slowly started to overwhelm me, it was at that time I definitely needed maximum support, and this is where Yvonne was at her very best. Never with negative thoughts, but always with positive ideas as to how we could overcome the various issues. We developed between us a 'the buggers aren't going to get us down' attitude. Helpfully, she also copes admirably with my mood swings. Generally, I am fairly light-hearted and easy-going but the array of issues and seemingly overwhelming odds which we were confronted with on an almost weekly basis, would test the metal of most people, and certainly on the odd occasion tested mine to the utmost. It is at the end of a long, testing day when things have not gone particularly well that one needs maximum support and succour and I benefited hugely from her 'never-say-die' attitude.

On many occasions I staggered in after late evening hours in the workshop or from some garage or another, and there was always a sustaining meal and an enquiring mind to discuss the problems. Talking about sustenance, it occurs to me that our costs on the rally preparation were significantly increased by the vast amount of baking that Yvonne produced over the 1.1/2 years of car preparation. Yvonne is an avid baker, producing a wide range of cakes and pastries for everyone who came to the house to work on the car. Indeed, I suspect several people were so well fed they made a positive effort to slow down the work on the car in order to increase their cake intake.

One other aspect of the cooking was put to test when Betty Banham, at an early meeting, made suggestions as to what food should be prepared and taken for the rally. Apart from all of the usual suggestions about not eating local salads and being cautious when purchasing food on the roadside, one strong suggestion was to take our own long-lasting cake. We needed something which would last 8 – 10 weeks in total and Yvonne spent several happy hours perfecting the ultimate cake (laced with a substantial amount of alcohol to ensure its preservative qualities in the extreme heat of the desert). I was, of course, a very contented test-bed for these protracted trials!

Keeping up with the paperwork that was being generated was another of Yvonne's primary roles. Documents arrived from the Rally Office with increasing regularity and an extraordinary amount of investigative work and cross-checking was always necessary.

There were two significant issues which needed to be dealt with – the Great Visa Fiasco, followed by the Great Fuel Fiasco.

Initially, the Rally Office had confirmed that the acquisition of all visas would be taken care of by them and covered by the fee for the rally. They agreed to be responsible for all the liaison to ensure that the documentation was completed for all crews. However, at a very late stage, we received a letter indicating that the Rally Office considered it far too complicated for them to carry out this role, particularly as many crews were from such diverse countries as Uruguay, Germany, Australia, America, Argentina, Russia, Malaysia, etc. etc. and I think that, at this rather late date, the Rally office realised that trying to liaise, not only with people of such disparate nationalities, but also co-ordinate collection and distribution of passports to the various countries where we required visas, was simply a step too far. It was, therefore, just two or three months before we were due to leave that the Rally Office dropped on everybody their new proposals. We were all now to obtain our own visas for China, Mongolia and Russia. The Rally Office recognised that they, of course, were creating a considerable amount of work for the competitors and, conversely, lessening the burden of their own work. They announced that, as they had originally calculated that the cost of obtaining visas would be £170 per person and therefore £340 per car, they announced that, rather than refunding this money, they would make an 'allowance' of an equivalent amount for packed sandwiches throughout Mongolia, and a fabulous champagne celebration dinner in Reims on the penultimate night. Needless to say, there was a huge undercurrent of black humour between the competitors, as we tried to picture the level of splendour of the fabulous meal and the exotic sandwiches that would relate to an expenditure of £340! There was somehow an inevitability that this might all end in tears – and it almost did as you will read later.

There was, inevitably, a huge amount of work associated with applying, not only for visas for each of the countries we were passing through, but also the appropriate driving licences. As ever, with every application, there was a request for a ridiculous amount of detail, and it was Yvonne's unenviable task to gather and collate all the details. The good news was that she got all of the information together rapidly and accurately and we were one of the first crews to receive our visas.

The visa issue was rapidly followed by the Great Fuel Fiasco. It will be recalled that at the very outset of the rally, Philip Young had stressed time and time again the absolute necessity to be running cars with low compression engines due to the appalling quality of petrol that we would come across. Much of the original correspondence referred to 70/75 octane petrol, with constant reminders that we should need to fit special fuel filters and carry all sorts of additional equipment to filter out the dust, insects and other debris which we might expect to find. Hardly a week went by when there wasn't a fresh edict from the Rally Office stressing the difficulties we would find en route.

Eventually, with just a week or two before departure, the Rally Office contacted us with their solution. They were going to truck in huge quantities of good quality, high octane petrol which would be available at the end of each day's rallying. However, their solution depended upon everybody buying vouchers for the amount of fuel that they thought they would consume. Furthermore, the organisers made it patently clear that if you did not have sufficient fuel you would simply be left to fend for yourself – a prospect that did not sit too well in contemplation of the somewhat hostile environment we expected to find.

The inevitable outcome was that everybody immediately panicked. Each crew was phoning other crews to try and establish what quantities they were buying and, as everyone felt the need to over-buy rather than under-buy, the amounts we all decided to purchase were increased on a daily basis. No-one wanted to be 'that man who ran out of petrol in the depths of the Mongolian mountains with no possibility of a refill'. The outcome was that everybody purchased vastly exaggerated amount of fuel – all of which had to be paid for up-front. It was Yvonne's job to wrestle with all the figures and arrange for the purchase of said vouchers. The Rally Office's scheme sounded OK but, in the event, the outcome was to become absolutely chaotic.

In the middle of all of this was the rest of the paperwork. We had to produce medical certificates from our doctor, we had to produce lists of old ailments, current ailments and anticipated ailments, details of every medicament we had taken since childhood and agree, hand on heart, to take with us every combination of medicines and treatments that the rally organisers sent out in their schedule. Indeed, it was made perfectly clear that adherence to the scheduled list would be an important component at the pre-rally scrutineering and we would not be allowed to start if we could not satisfy the organisers that every medical 'T' was crossed and 'I' dotted! One of Yvonne's important roles was to assemble the whole medical kit, which was to include essential drugs, antibiotics, dressings, rescusitation mask and emergency blankets. Indeed, it proved to be quite a task as our local GP would not readily comply with some of our requests and the costs for some of the more specialised items became astronomical.

There were a lot of emotions at work here. On the one hand it was an absolute requirement to take all of the equipment, on the other hand it occupied a huge amount of space, but in the background there was also the thought of the significant medical challenges that had so much affected Rosie Thomas in the 1997 rally (she had experienced serious gynaecological problems and the Organisers had told her that she wouldn't be able to continue the Rally unless she could obtain the appropriate drugs. Remarkably, at the very last minute, another competitor was able to help out).

Yvonne decided that simply having all of the equipment was only half of the story and she, therefore, enrolled on a first aid course with the St. John's Ambulance Service.

At least if the Heimlich manoeuvre was necessary, she remarked casually, she would be able to perform it on me.

A game girl

As the time for departure approached, one of the significant jobs was the packing and cataloguing of everything we needed to take, from spare parts and tools, to food and camping gear. Multi-coloured self-seal boxes were bought and numbered, and Yvonne began the task of cataloguing and cross referencing every item so that we not only knew which box everything was in, but also where the box could be found within the car.

All this work proved to be extremely beneficial as, of course, when the Rally actually started from Peking the equipment had been packed away in the car more than two months previously.

One of the more obscure roles that Yvonne undertook was to prepare a note of the pronunciation of the Russian alphabet, and a collection of useful Russian phrases. This turned out not to have much practical use whatsoever, but I do recall one evening in a village garage in Russia, Yvonne spent a happy hour or two with local giggling children reading through our list of 'useful phrases'!

We bought an encapsulator, as we realised that paperwork would not stand up to five weeks in a car door-pocket, and this proved to be an invaluable purchase.

The phrase 'homemaker' took on a different meaning for Yvonne, as one of her roles on the rally was to single-handedly erect the tent on the occasions when I was under the car doing my spanner checks. After two or three practices on the lawn at home, she got the art down to nine minutes erection-time and five minutes demolition-time. The final aspects of Yvonne's role on the Rally were absolutely critical. The ability to find our way via the route book and GPS all the way to Paris, and the requirement to keep within the critical rally timing for the whole of the five weeks. By Yvonne's own admission, mathematics was not her strong subject, but nonetheless over the last year or two, she had mastered the timing to a fairly fine degree and rarely made any errors. She is surprisingly competitive and, indeed, I recall a year or two previously when she stood toe-to-toe with a marshal arguing the point over ten seconds she thought we had dropped on a stage, only to discover that the said marshal was indeed queuing for the toilet and had no idea what she was talking about!

Route finding is the most critical factor of any rally, as all competitors will tell you. You could be the finest rally driver in the world, but if you are doing it up the wrong road, it becomes somewhat irrelevant. The route book on any rally is the navigator's bible, and the first job is for the navigator to get inside the head of the Clerk of the Course and understand the nuances of the route book and how it works. Every rally is different, and the methodology behind them different. When thinking of route books, I am reminded of the very first Scottish Malts Rally that we did. Yvonne was really nervous about how she was going to manage, and I recall the night before the rally start, waking at 2.00 am in a hotel room in Edinburgh to see a light shining from under the bathroom door. I found Yvonne sitting on the edge of the bath reading page by page through the rally book, desperate to absorb all of the information and not make any mistakes. Clearly that exercise was not wasted as we have rarely strayed from the organisers' routes over the years!

Home maker

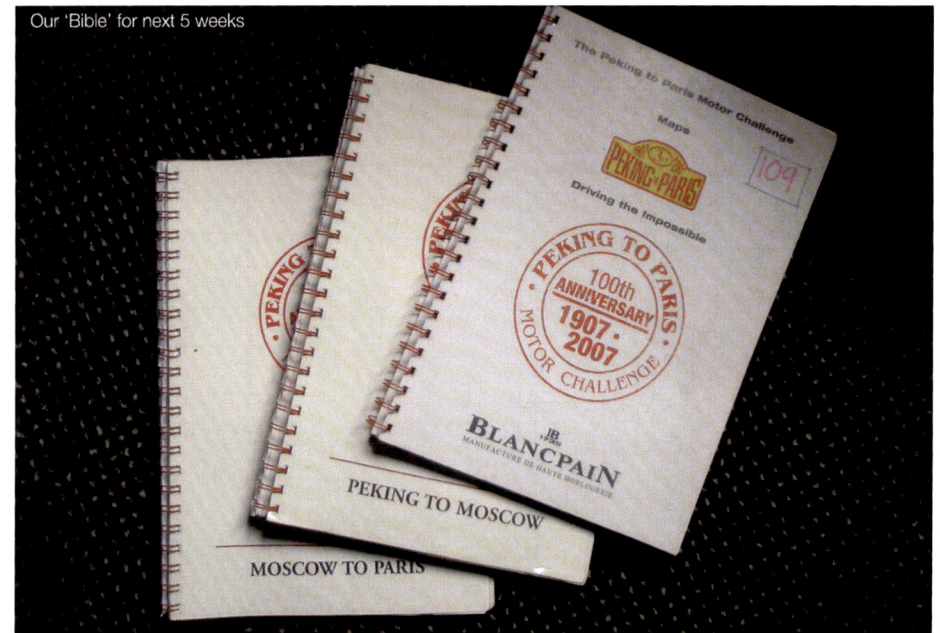
Our 'Bible' for next 5 weeks

It has to be said at this juncture that the Peking-Paris route books were superb, with five weeks rallying condensed into two volumes. There were very few errors at all and it was a fine tribute to the team who had put them together.

The finding of the route on the Peking-Paris was for us to be much more difficult than any other event we had been on. The wilds of Mongolia and the Gobi Desert, with no distinguishing landmarks whatsoever, meant that the navigation throughout was to be based on the use of a GPS, and it is perhaps appropriate here that I take some time to explain how the system worked.

All competitors were advised to buy precisely the same GPS unit, a Garmin 'GPSMAP 76C'. At the start of the rally each competitor had in excess of 700 waypoints downloaded into our hand-held GPS system, and it was the navigator's job to ensure that the car proceeded along the correct route as guided by these waypoints.

As ever, when you reach a 'certain age' the grasp of modern technology takes a little more achieving than when we were young, and the Garmin proved to be a bit of a challenge with its myriad of options. Nonetheless, slowly but surely and with painstaking use of the instruction book, Yvonne overcame all of her initial concerns and became extremely dextrous with masses of information as to distances covered, distances to the finish, temperatures, average speeds and she would occasionally throw in, to keep me alert, height above sea-level!

Each morning when we set off the Garmin registered the next waypoint ahead with a

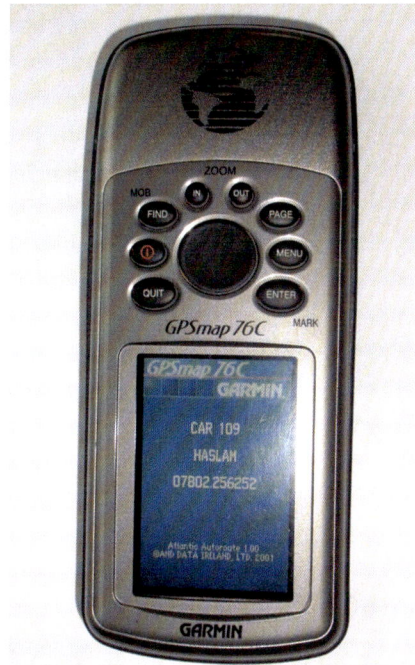

Our Garmin which became such a 'comforter'

swinging needle, which gave us an idea of the direction in which to proceed. Whilst this would appear to be fairly simple, its use in the desert was somewhat complicated by the lack of any road or track. The GPS arrow would point in a certain direction, only for us to be confronted with a rock-strewn mountain, a dried up river bed dropping three feet below ground level, or an area of unpassable scrub ground cover. The only solution was to head for ground which we felt sure was passable and then correct our direction to achieve the necessary waypoint position. As soon as we reached this notional position, the GPS then indicated the following waypoint and we set off with the same exercise again. From our initial concerns about operating the Garmin GPS everyone on the rally realised that it was the most amazing piece of equipment, and we all relied upon it totally. It was so accurate, that in a large town it would actually take us road by road and junction by junction straight to our hotel door – a brilliant plus at the end of a long day's rallying.

So, as you can see, a navigator's role is hugely variable; women are celebrated for their ability to multi-task, and being a crew member on the Peking-Paris took multi-tasking to a different level.

Chapter 8

.....AND SO TO CHINA

At long last the journey was to commence. We shared a taxi with John and Joan across to Manchester airport where we met up with Dave and Jo and Mike and Josie. We had treated ourselves to a business class flight as we had worked out that this was, perhaps, the last vestige of comfort for a week or two! The flight was uneventful and we at long last arrived in the Shangri-La Hotel in Beijing. We had arrived two or three days before the event, in order to take advantage of our first look around Beijing, and over the next couple of days we were continually stumbling across other competitors who were doing the same thing. It was really quite surprising, in a huge city like Beijing, how many times we stumbled across other rallyists all pursuing the same tourist trail.

A wet Tianamen

The first couple of days were a blur of sightseeing. The first day, in absolutely bucketing rain, we took in Tiananmen Square and the Forbidden City. The Square looked even bigger than I had ever anticipated. I suppose it was the complete lack of people in the lashing rain, combined with the reflective surfaces from the rain-washed pavements – it really did appear gigantic. It was not difficult to recall past TV shots of mass displays of troops and weaponry, it was however, slightly disturbing to think that we were standing in the same place where young students were mown down in the relatively recent past.

The rain didn't blunt our tourist aspirations, however, and we manfully took in all of the regular tourist sites, pausing only for various anti-rain purchases such as umbrellas (somewhat over priced at 65p each, we were later advised), rain-proof

jackets and shoes.

The following day the eight of us set off on a long hike around the suburbs, particularly taking in the Yutongs, the traditional old residential areas which were shortly to be bulldozed to make way for an Olympic site. Thinking of the Olympics at this stage, we could hardly believe that sporting events could take place in this environment – the air was visibly thick with a murky brown fog and we were extremely conscious that every inhalation was coating our lungs with the stuff.

Tourism, however, was soon over and our third day in Beijing dawned bright and sunny – fortuitous as we were due to fetch our cars from the warehouse. We all boarded coaches and set off for the outskirts of Beijing, arriving at a newly-constructed warehouse development which housed all of our cars. The air was

David and John inspect the gleaming sunbeam

thick with anticipation, although there were a mixture of emotions from 'delighted' when someone's car started first time to 'depressed' when there wasn't a peep from the engine, or 'horrified' to see peripheral damage caused from the shipping containers. Nevertheless, the cars were soon underway heading back to Beijing.

I immediately tracked down Peter Banham, to whom I had given my spare gearbox bits a day or two before, and was one of the even more 'delighted' contingent to find that not only did the car start up the first time, but that Peter had the opportunity to change around the gearbox components and we were up and running.

The journey back to the hotel was interesting and soon tested out the navigational skills of a few. Beijing has five separate concentric ring roads and tracking one's way around them was not the easiest exercise. Mercifully, our hotel was one of the taller buildings in Beijing and we were able to home in on it with a serious of tacking movements!

Once all the cars were safely tucked into the hotel car park, the serious business of

Safely in the hotel car park

checking and cross-checking everything and ensuring that all was OK, started. Most people were simply buffing and cleaning the cars, but several people seemed to be commencing a complete rebuild in the carpark. Friends like Alberto and Harold, whom we had last seen in Argentina, had imported their car from Buenos Aires and it was widely rumoured that the mechanics were still working on it in the packing case throughout the voyage. Clearly it was dark in there and they hadn't finished their task! The engine was coughing and spluttering, the steering was incredibly vague, the wipers didn't work, and the doors were hanging off. Furthermore, they had not had chance to measure up and fit the sump guard and Alberto, rather unusually, brought the sheet steel sump guard as hand luggage on his flight! Amusingly, to one and all – except Alberto and Harold, the sump guard was completely the wrong shape and despite Peter Banham's very best efforts could not be made to fit. Alberto left the sump guard in his bedroom, which I imagine came as rather a shock to the chambermaids. Peter Banham, to his total frustration, worked for hours preparing their car, and even he could not work his magic on all the defects, and rumour was that Alberto and Harold might not make it very far……..

Later in the day the hot sun managed to force its way through the brown smog, as we queued up interminably for scrutineering. The first cars to confront the scrutineers were checked over in infinite detail, but as the day wore on, the patience wore thinner. It was noticeable that, by the end of the afternoon, cars were given a perfunctory check over before the appropriate signature was appended to the check-card.

By now the tension was building. Wherever you looked there was feverish activity, cars were checked and re-checked, route books being poured over, detailed discussions taking place in every corner of the reception area as to the complexities of the GPS system – indeed, some people were unpacking their GPSs for the very first time! The organisers were making every effort to make crews understand that the critical moment on the rally was when the cars passed out of China into Mongolia and warnings were aplenty that if you felt your car wouldn't make it across Mongolia, you really should contemplate backing out at this stage. There were mumblings that the maintenance crews, having seen the state of some of the cars, were suggesting that as many as thirty cars would not commence the tough journey across Mongolia. On the other hand crews themselves were expressing concern that there were only three support crews. Quite clearly the journey across Mongolia was going to be arduous and with 134 entries would three support crews be adequate?

Another rumour that was rife was that we would all need as much water as we could carry for the forthcoming journey across the Gobi. And, whilst everybody had already packed plenty of water, there were constant raids on all the local supermarkets and crews were seen to be carrying arms-full of extra water back to their cars. We were as guilty as the next and, indeed, arrived in Paris with six full litre bottles which we had originally packed in Foolow!

On the penultimate evening, we were all treated to a superb banquet, courtesy of Blancpain, one of the main sponsors. The atmosphere was electric, brought on by a mixture of building anticipation, vibrant and exciting dancing accompanied by powerful music, and the whole evening capped by quite splendid food. People seemed to be eating as though it would be their last substantial meal for several weeks.

Celebratory speeches were made by guests of honour, dire words of warning were issued, yet again, by the organisers, and the evening was delicately finished off by the Managing Director of Blancpain, who gave us all the opportunity to indulge in a Blancpain Peking to Paris celebratory watch, priced at just £14,500..........

The Last Supper - courtesy of Blancpain

The Rally

Chapter 9

CHINA - Day 1 Great Wall To Datong 363 kms.

Up at 5.00 am. This was it. Hasty breakfast, smart clothes packed away, tyres kicked, and at 6.10 am we rolled out of the hotel carpark for the 60 km drive to the Great Wall of China at Bandaling. On arrival, the welcome in the carpark set the scene. Chinese children dressed in bright, traditional clothing, red and green Chinese dragons, twenty metres or so in length carried by bearers, Chinese lions, stilt-walkers and ancient percussion bands with their pulsating rhythm – even Tony Mason was present dressed in a 'Chairman Mao' suit and, rather obscurely, was mounted on an ancient bicycle?

Cars were lined up in no particular order in the carpark and we set off to walk around, taking in the amazing atmosphere and wonder at the incredible construction of the Great Wall, which stretches over the mountains in both directions as far as the eye can see.

Colourful scenes greet us at the start

The original Great Wall was built in 2000 BC, further to the north than we were. The current wall was built over 150 years later by the Ming Dynasty, with its purpose to keep out the Mongolians. We were aware that driving beyond the Great Wall we were shortly to be heading away from civilisation towards some of the more remote and arid lands of the earth.

At 8.30 am car no. 1, the first of the Italas, driven by David and Karen Eyre inched to the starting line and made its way through a huge crowd that came to wave us farewell. The weather was hot and sticky and the tension was building. At last, it was our turn and, at 9.23 am, we were flagged away,

The Drums

and perhaps my most abiding memory was the throb of those percussion drums beating out their rhythmic message – it's a rhythm I shall be able to bring to mind for ever. As we left the start line the sponsors, Blancpain, handed us a box of two wine glasses!!! What an odd gift to pass on to Rally crews who were about to embark on crossing some of the roughest terrain in the world.

Inching forward through the crowds we eventually found the tarmac of the main road and headed slowly north-west. Dilemma. After two kilometres the Terratrip packed up and I also noticed that the indicator lights didn't appear to be working either. No change there then with the Chevy.

Adam and Jonathan underway at last - with Philip Young riding shotgun!

Over the first mountain range, and the scenery made a dramatic change from the densely populated regions of Beijing, through to the open grasslands of Inner Mongolia. Hardly a mile went by without the site of a broken down truck. Nobody believes in red triangles here, a few rocks strewn around the perimeter of the vehicle was the only warning. The occupants often seen sitting in the cab gazing into thin air (actually, still at this time gazing into thick, brown, sludgy air) apparently waiting for spare parts to arrive from who-knows-where. This was to be a commonplace site for the next week or two.

We had our first stop for a passage check at the Hehelou Restaurant, and as we were an hour early we had the chance to relax a little. Steaming bowls of hot rich goulash-type soup were available, but the tensions of our first day on the road had overwhelmed our appetites and we were both happy to nibble on an apple. We bumped into Dave and Jo just outside the restaurant, and we exchanged first day's tribulations – Dave with a blown fuse on his overdrive and, for us, the gearbox had slipped out of gear a couple of times.

We were soon on an open expressway surrounded by mafia-style police in black, unmarked cars. A long, steady climb for the first mile or two saw us overtaking several cars that had already succumbed to the heat – what a terrible disappointment for them after such a short way. Cars were weaving around, switching lanes all the time, and as cars passed us either to the left or right, an arm holding a camera or mobile phone would stick out of a quickly wound-down window. A cheery wave, and the black window would slide back up, leaving the photographer in anonymity.

The first time this happened, I had expected to be overwhelmed with disappointment, but I gave a resigned shrug and decided that, at this stage, I couldn't give a fig and we would simply soldier on despite the gearbox.

Shortly after lunch, we pulled over to a petrol station and, to Yvonne's great relief, there was a brand new, immaculate toilet block which had recently been built next to the pump. The smile was soon wiped off her face, however, when she opened the door to discover a one foot wide by three foot long hole into an open pit beneath. State of the art toilets had not reached this part of China. Onwards we travelled, passing now through several industrialised Chinese towns and it was clear this was a mining region as the landmarks along the roadside were gigantic mounds of black coal. The swirling black coal dust generated by passing rally cars, mixed interestingly with the still ever present brown smog and produced a kaleidoscope of dark shades. The organisers were easing us gently into rallying, and we had our first scenic

The amazing Hanging Monastary

checkpoint of the event – a visit to the amazing Hanging Monastery at Hunyuan, built 1400 years ago, and clinging precariously onto sheer cliffs above the Jinlong Canyon. The all-timber construction was breathtaking, supported as it was on the rock face by ancient timber poles wedged into the tiniest fissures of the rock face. The red and brown painted buildings contrasted dramatically with the rock face behind. Amazingly, it is open for tourists to wander round at will, providing endless photographic opportunities. Looking back now at this fragile and delicate historical site, I think we were extremely privileged as I really cannot see the structure coping with the endless tramping of tourists for too much longer before the buildings are

closed for viewing only.

The rest of the drive that afternoon was through green, open countryside with verdant valleys and excellent quality roads. The abiding memory was of the brilliant reception we were given all along the road with people waving and cheering, and a policeman at every junction standing to attention and saluting us. They really are going to be arm-weary after a hundred and thirty four cars have passed.

That evening we pulled into Datong, which is a busy commercial city, with a pleasant, comfortable, modern hotel called the Dai Hai. As we drove into the landscaped area in front of the hotel, we were greeted by a brass band enthusiastically playing on the front steps of the building. We had covered 363 kilometres today, and it was a relief to be at long last on our way. A cold beer on the front steps of the hotel, sitting watching the frenzied activity of car-fettling was a pleasant way to finish our day.

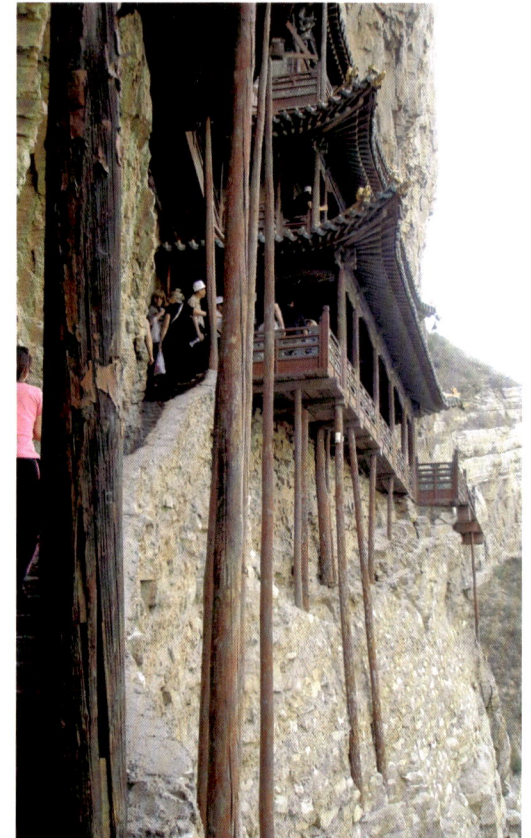

Disappointing news was, however, circulating around the hotel that the 1911 Knox, driven by a couple of Dutchmen, had suffered a major problem with the cylinder coming through the wall of the block, the Knox was last seen on a lorry heading back towards Beijing. What a terrible disappointment the two Dutchmen must be feeling that their wonderful car is out of the rally after such a short period of time.

An easy start today, just 16 kilometres to the Yungang Caves. We are due to check out of here at 10.45 am so there is plenty of time to take a look around this amazing, historical site. The caves are cut into the southern cliffs of Wuzhou Shan, next to the pass leading to Inner Mongolia. The caves contain over 50,000 buddhist statues and stretch for roughly one kilometre east to west; they date back to 400 BC and are hugely impressive. The scale and detail of the carvings is breathtaking, and it is difficult to comprehend how the scale of this huge undertaking was carried out so long ago – the detailing defies the simple tools that must have been used to create these awe inspiring caverns.

The stunning caves at Yungang

After a couple of hours sight-seeing, we were back on the open road, heading through more coal mining areas where everyone we pass was blackened by the coal dust that they live in day in, day out. As we pressed on we slowly left behind the industrialised areas and eventually started to pass through ancient brick built villages, farmland and open rural areas. Initially, the road surfaces were quite good but we soon hit sand and dust. The car that was so pristine just a couple of days ago was now coated in a thick layer of pale grey dust, the consistency of talcum powder.

I'm dying to hand this over to a policeman in the UK

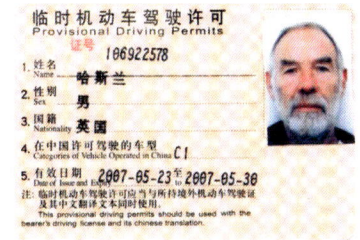

Suddenly, out of the dust we lurched from the rutted road onto immaculate, smooth tarmac. It's the carpark of our passage control which turned out to be a recently constructed hotel, and the place was an absolute oasis, sitting on the side of a lake that stretched into the far distance. We assumed that, perhaps, the hotel had been built to service the forthcoming Olympic Games – maybe water sports on the adjacent lake.

The hotel had everything, saunas, spa, elegant leather furniture, fully stocked bars…………. but, strangely, no food! We had an interesting lunch comprising a cup of coffee and a bowl of dry popcorn. If lunch continues like this for the next five weeks we are going to have significantly improved waistlines!

Sadly, it was soon time to leave this oasis, back onto the dusty road. Initially, the surface wasn't too bad and we were able to drive at a steady 45 to 50 miles per hour. Suddenly, without warning, crash, bang, wallop. What remained of our road had dropped away by almost a foot and in the dusty conditions, with other rally cars both in front and behind, it was simply impossible to see the dip. We seemed to survive the impact but it certainly made us a little more wary for the rest of the journey.

Unexpectedly, we came across a lone policeman standing in the middle of the road, indicating for us to take a right turn. Yvonne was saying that the route was clearly straight on and we stopped to query this with the policeman. However, he was completely insistent that we turn right, so with trepidation we did so. We soon become aware that this definitely was not the rally route and were continually concerned by rally cars passing us in both directions. Some cars returned to the policeman but he was absolutely adamant that we couldn't take the original route. The upshot was, here we were in the middle of rural Inner Mongolia with not the foggiest idea of where we were. As always happens in these circumstances, navigators gathered together and discussed the options, decided to stay together and follow a common route, then did exactly the opposite and headed off in different directions. Mercifully, our little GPS came to our rescue and we were able to pick up a Waypoint somewhere in the far distance, which slowly but surely brought us back to the original route. The wonders of modern technology.

Suddenly, out of the blue, we were greeted by a wonderful stretch of new-tarmac dual carriageway and we ran into the passage control at Hohhot. The welcome into this town was quite astonishing, there were literally hundreds of police out on either side of the road, stationed at every two or three hundred metres. As we drove by each and every one saluted us. We were waved through all the traffic lights at red – what a fabulous welcome. Pulling into the PC (passage control) after the end of this long and dusty run, we bumped into Philip Young who, as a gesture of sympathy gave us his half-drunk can of Sprite – it didn't matter what it was, it slacked the dust. Standing around chatting, there were loads of stories of problems that had happened to people on the run in and, indeed, some people had ignored the policeman and driven straight on, only to find out why the road had been closed. It appears that the original route was significantly worse than the one we had travelled along. Dave and Jo gave a graphic description of following Alberto and Harold's car down a particularly rough stretch of road when, as it hit a particularly large bump, both doors flew open. The well prepared car again!

The run in to our night's stay at Siziwangqi was breathtaking – mile after mile of the pale green grasslands of Inner Mongolia. Endless stretches of majestic beauty. There cannot be anywhere in the world to compete with this stunningly simple landscape. Eventually, we rolled into the camp where tonight we were staying in

Our greeting at Siziwangqi

yurts, otherwise known as gers. Yurts are the traditional dwelling of the Mongolian nomads and are easily transported timber structures covered in felt. As we drove into the camp, the first yurts we passed were quite magnificent structures mounted on huge wheeled platforms. Our Mongolian entourage, however, waved us around the back of the hotel where Yvonne commented that we now appear to be passing through the middle of the staff yurts. Wrong. These were to be our accommodation for the night. Our yurt was simplicity itself – a wooden floor, a latticed inner wall with roof poles clicking into the lattice work, terminating in a central vent in the roof. Entry to the yurt was through a couple of three-foot high doors, beautifully hand painted. The sleeping accommodation comprised of eight thick flock duvets which initially didn't inspire us at all. However, we spread four out on the floor and covered ourselves with the other four and, indeed, had probably one of the best night's sleep of the whole rally.

Dinner that night was excellent – neck of lamb and roasted shoulder of goat, washed down with a more than adequate local beer. The whole rally was then invited to a Mongolian evening with traditional dancing and singing around huge bonfires. This is what we really came to experience.

Home

Up bright and early to a cold, clear, sunny morning, but this morning we have loads of time on our hands as our start time is not until 10.45. This gave us an opportunity to clean up the inside of the car after yesterday's dusty trip, and we also took a guided tour round some of the 'luxury' yurts, which quite a lot of the competitors had been housed in. These came complete with dining rooms, kitchens etc. but we decided that after our excellent night's sleep we really have had a once-in-a-lifetime experience sleeping in a truly traditional yurt in all its simplicity.

Today was a relatively simple day on good quality roads to Erenhot, the border town before we were to leave Northern China. We turned right out of the yurt camp and our next instruction in the route book was 128.85 kms away – almost a straight line through mile after mile of sweeping grasslands. We passed camels, sheep and goats and saw the memorable sight of Mongolian horsemen in their traditional costumes herding huge flocks of sheep. It occurred to us that life in this area of Northern China and Inner Mongolia has probably changed very little since Prince Borghesie passed this way.

One cracking piece of news today is that Peter Banham suggested adjusting the

plug on the back of the Terratrip and it worked! Rather obscurely it jumped 2.7 miles to start with in one go and then was OK, so fingers crossed.

We reached our lunch stop today at Sonid Yougi at 12.15. It was too early to lunch so we didn't eat, in any case lunch seemed to be a big, sticky hotpot in a big, sticky restaurant, so we shared an apple between us and headed on north.

Entrance to Evenhot

The final run in to Erenhot was down a magnificent two-lane highway. This whole region is famed for the finds of fossilized remains of dinosaurs and, indeed, on the outskirts of Erenhot we were greeted by two gigantic bronze dinosaur statues with their necks stretching across the road to form a welcoming arch.

Tonight's accommodation was in a relatively modern, nondescript, multi-storeyed hotel, which was rather unfortunately located opposite the main railway shunting yards producing a cacophony of noise to accompany us throughout the night. This evening the organisers made great efforts to remind everyone that this was the last night in China, and we all should be very sure indeed that our cars were capable of the forthcoming tough days across Mongolia. Indeed, they recommended that a red Model T Ford and a yellow Rolls Royce shouldn't venture any further, as they had both had significant mechanical issues every day so far. Nonetheless, the crews decided to proceed on the understanding that if they had any further problems they were 'on their own' and would have to make their own arrangements to extract themselves from Mongolia.

There was, however, a cracking piece of news tonight, amazingly the Knox had arrived in Erenhot on a truck, and the damaged cylinder, found to be broken at the base of cylinder block, had been chemically glued together and reinforced with steel straps. The crew intends to continue to do the rest of the rally on three cylinders!

Finally, as we turned in, our room phone rang and I was told there was a 'message' for me down on the third floor. The girl's accent was so strong I really struggled to understand the point of the phone call. It wasn't until discussing it over breakfast the following morning, that I discovered that I had, indeed, been offered a massage! Later that night quite a lot of the all-male crews had been seen taking a lift to the third floor……..

View from our bedroom - Suburbs of Evenhot

Chapter 10

Today was the day when, reputedly, it was going to get really tough! We motored for a few kilometres to the Chinese/Mongolian border where we were lined up in the carpark prior to the customs formalities. Each car was given a separate Chinese guard to stand on duty all of the time that we were waiting.

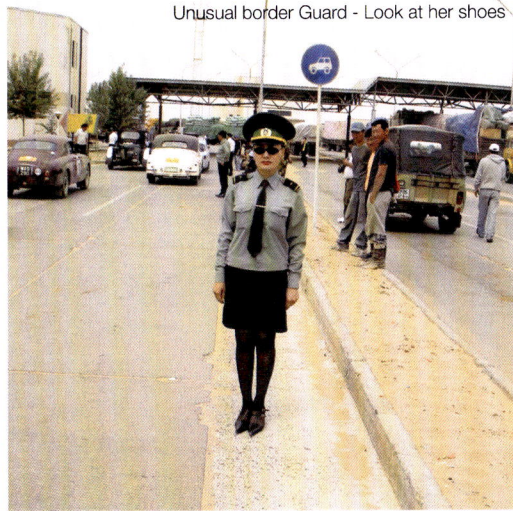

Unusual border Guard - Look at her shoes

And waiting we were! Two hours to get through the border post. Nonetheless, it gave us ample time to savour the last three days' driving through China – memories of the fabulous welcome given to us by people in the towns and villages we'd passed through, the black-windowed police cars silently overtaking us, the stunning transformation from busy, polluted Beijing to the magnificent simplicity of the Inner Mongolian grasslands.

Into the magnificent customs hall we all proceeded, hoping for a civilised and easy exit from China. How wrong were. Immediately, and obscurely, driver and navigator were separated into different queues. The drivers' queue took a mere two hours to get through the border post, but that became fairly pointless as the navigators were nowhere to be seen at the other side. Time was running short for our Passage Control check beyond the Mongolian border, and it wasn't until an hour later that Yvonne eventually appeared from the Passport Office. Into the car she leapt and we flew off trying to be sure that we hit the appointed time – only to find that the organisers, having realised the problem, had allowed everyone an additional hour.

What a transformation, we had driven from the civilised city of Erenhot down a fine tarmac highway, through an archway at the border post, then straight into the desert, with nothing in between. Buildings one side of the border, sand the other.

The rally gathered in a hideous carpark adjacent to a dilapidated fuel station. There was a nervous tension in the air as everyone knew that the next section was going to be exceedingly difficult. Mike O'Shea, in his 1948 Jaguar 3.4 litre saloon, who had experienced continual problems with the low-slung back end of his car, announced that he was planning to avoid the forthcoming desert route and circumnavigate via what he had been advised was a civilised road. The tension and the pressure were relieved slightly when a couple of British cyclists rode into the carpark and got off

Eager anticipation

for a chat. This young couple were riding around the world and it certainly put our exploits into perspective. After half an hour they set off into the wilderness and, as a very fitting tribute, all the cars sounded their horns until the couple rode out of sight.

Wandering around, I came across Harold and Alberto in their 1937 Ford Convertible. Alberto was fast asleep with no cares in the world whilst Harold was questioning just why he was there. Then, with a flash of inspiration, he said "Of course, that Borghese got it right, because when he did it, he came in a new car". Perhaps one of the classic statements of the rally.

Temperatures were rising both inside and outside the cockpits. We were counted down, 5,4,3,2,1 and off we set along a dusty but surfaced road – but for only half a mile. A left turn and there it is stretched ahead of us – the Gobi Desert. Gone were all the landmarks that we used in the route book – turn Left at signpost, turn Right at T-junction, straight on past post office. Now we were using our waypoints (which are latitude and longitude) and following the wavering arrow on our GPS. Out in the open desert there are umpteen options as there are tyre tracks in almost every direction. You chose what you think is the nearest set of tyre tracks to the direction you wish to travel, and proceed until the needle wavers to either left or right.

First view of the Gobi

You then find an alternate track and attempt to keep on following the needle. Initially, the urge is to follow the approximate line of other rally cars, but soon we gave this up to follow our own intuition. Soon we were into the wide open expanses of the Gobi and at times we were completely isolated and alone – not another soul in sight. Momentarily we were distracted when the 1955 Landrover of Nigel Challis and Michael Pink appeared from our right, travelling exactly perpendicular to our own route. They disappeared over the sand to our left and, for a moment or two, there was consternation as to whether who was right and who was wrong! We stay with Yvonne's interpretation which must have been correct, as we didn't see the

Landrover for three more days! (In fact, it broke down in the desert and had to be trucked to Ulaan Baatar).

Two hours into the desert, we came across one of the rally marshall's cars with a chequered flag mounted on the radio arial. This was to be the start of the first time trial section of the rally. The organisers had been extremely reticent about providing any details of these timed sections, and it was always difficult to find out exactly what was expected of us. Now we understood why, there were to be no 'regularities' or 'average speeds' – this was just to be flat out blind. The flag was dropped and off we hared. In many ways it was surreal – we were dashing off to who-knew-where at breakneck speed, only guided by the ever wandering arrow of the GPS. Nonetheless, it was quite exciting. It is extremely rare that we have the chance to drive our cars flat-out with no inhibitions, and here for sure we were never going to come across a speed trap or a 'safety' camera!

Suddenly, haring across a particularly fast stretch of level sand, we hit a dried river gully with a resounding crash. There was a huge clattering noise from under the car and in the rear mirror I saw a piece of unidentifiable metal bounding across the desert. Not knowing what it was, we felt it was imperative we retrieve it so did a huge loop to pick up the offending article. The car seemed to be still going perfectly well, so I hastily threw this unidentified object into the back of the car and continued. It was only later on in the day that I recognised what it was – the first of a long line of smashed shock absorbers that we were to become so familiar with. Clearly, the loss of a shock absorber didn't seem to have any noticeable effect on the car, so we pounded on. As we bounced across the next gully, Yvonne's door flew open and, despite all our efforts, simply wouldn't lock. I had to coast a little to the end of the time trial, whilst Yvonne held the door closed with one hand and managed to hold the route book, pencil and GPS in the other. I noted that we recorded 1 hour 16 minutes 38 seconds for the time trial, but it was extremely difficult to know how that compared with anyone else.

On the fifty mile run in to Saynshand the conditions got worse and worse. The wind was whipping up and sand was blowing everywhere. We came across some pockets of sand where cars were floundering up to their axels. The Chevy was terrific in these conditions, the big all-terrain tyres did their job and we ploughed through axel-deep sand without a problem.

What a day, what a day! We struggled into the final day's control at a fuel station, having dropped about 35 minutes of penalties. Under the circumstances we had endured, we agreed that this was just fine. After a forty-five minute queue for fuel, we then spent an hour trying to locate the camp for the night. By now the wind was getting to a furious level and the sand was blowing in. All our practice erecting the tent at Foolow proved to be beneficial and within ten minutes the tent was erected and we were shipshape. Within five minutes, without warning, the sand storm suddenly blew in and it was almost impossible to see hand in front of face. Yvonne and I wrapped towels around our heads and staggered the 150 metres or so to the showers that had been erected by our amazing support trekking team, the 'Nomads'.

The sandstorm blows in

The Nomads ran two independent teams setting up our campsights, one team leapfrogging the other on alternate days. When we arrived in the camps the mess tents and chuck tents were already set up, a line of toilets had been dug and tented over and an amazing shower combination had been erected. The Nomads carried a gigantic wood-fired boiler which provided hot water to the showers. On our way back to the car, I commented to Yvonne that I had never been so clean. I had been sandblasted from top to toe, then washed clean in a hot shower!

By darkness, the camp site was scene of total devastation, the high winds had blown the chuck tent down altogether, but amazingly the Nomad team were serving an excellent three-course meal out of the back of one of their trucks. The meal was exceptionally good, if a bit sandy. Inside the canteen tent, the wind was screaming around and there was a solitary light bulb swinging wildly from the tent poles. Nonetheless, the atmosphere was quite exceptional. We took our emergency bottle of whisky, Dave and Jo took a bottle of wine and Mike and Josie joined us to celebrate what was one of the toughest day's motoring we had ever experienced.

Whilst we were having a riotous evening in the canteen tent, there was devastation in the desert behind us. John and Joan had had a tottering time being stuck in the sand a couple of times and eventually crawled into the camp at 9.30 pm. They quickly put up the tent, disappeared inside and weren't seen again that night – absolutely whacked. Fifty cars reputedly didn't make it into camp that night. Some cars were stuck in the sand, others completely lost their way, and a huge number were broken down. On top of that the camp site was totally obscured from the nearby village by a small hummock and in the thick, swirling sand many crews simply didn't find the camp site and slept in their cars wherever they stopped – some found they were 150 yards away when the storm cleared in the morning. Needless to say, the support crews were completely overwhelmed and unable to cope. Peter and Betty Banham had been towing Jonathan and Adam in their 1907 Itala and eventually ground to a halt at 4.30 am just a quarter of a mile from the campsite. What a day. We had come for an adventure and, my, weren't we having one.

This morning, surprisingly, we woke up to the gentle patter of rain on the tent. I say surprisingly, because in my mind the words 'desert' and 'rain' don't normally fit into the same sentence!

Fortunately, within a few minutes the rain had stopped and we were able to pack the wet tent away within a matter of minutes. We wandered off to the mess tent where the Nomads had produced the most amazing breakfast. There were cereals, toast, fried eggs, boiled eggs, scrambled eggs, sausages, bacon, tomatoes, jam, honey, coffee – all this in the middle of the Gobi Desert.

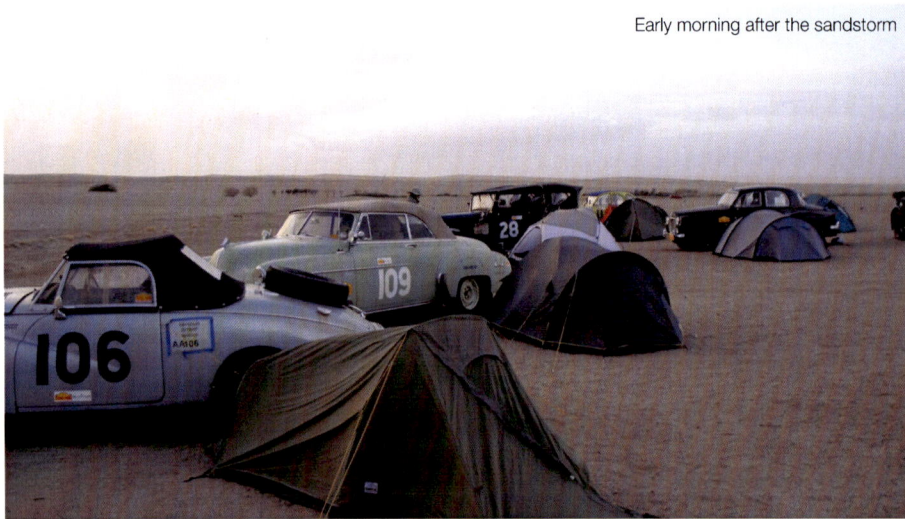
Early morning after the sandstorm

Over breakfast there was much discussion about all the problems everyone had experienced the day before. Steve and Linda Byrne lost all the gears on their Aston Martin DB6, and had to take the gearbox apart to sort out the selectors; they got in at half past midnight. Dave and Jo had the rear anti-roll bar break loose, damaging the wing and the brake pipes. Mike and Josie's shock absorber gave way (much to Mike's delight, as it gave him something to do!). Mike and Sarah O'Shea, it will be

The sorry state of the ambulance

recalled, decided to set off on the tarmac road and avoid the desert route. Frustratingly, they toured the area but never found the tarmac road and were, therefore, obliged to follow the main rally route, getting stuck in the sand many times, and arriving in the camp late at night. The doctor managed to completely overturn the ambulance, which was almost a complete wreck – amazingly he managed to right it and drive it back to the camp. And, finally, John and Joan got stuck in the sand twice, and the glove compartment door fell open!!!

Immediately after breakfast I decided to check over the car. We had plenty of time as the organisers had decided that all the time trials would be cancelled today and, indeed, there would be no timing on the day's rally in order to let all the cars which were stuck in the desert attempt to catch up the rally.   Yvonne was worried about the fact that her passenger door wouldn't close at all and I proposed a simple solution of fastening my trouser belt around her thigh and then around her inner door handle, thereby leaving her both hands with which to manhandle the navigational equipment. For some reason this idea, which I thought was a masterpiece of invention, was dismissed out of hand and I had to resort to proper mechanics. As it transpired the solution was extremely simple, the lock had become jammed up with desert dust and one or two squirts of WD40 solved the problem. A good job really as, with our meagre lunches and lack of coffee stops, I was losing weight by the day and my trousers would have fallen down anyway!

Just as we set off the heavens opened again and we had to stop and put the hood up – yes, that's what I said – put the hood up. We are generally famed for travelling most places with the top down, but with this sudden intense shower of rain I bowed to pressures and we scurried for cover. Within half an hour the sun was out and we were flying through what was probably the most memorable section of the Gobi Desert. There we were on yellow-baked hard sand, racing across the desert at 70 mph. There were no tracks whatsoever, just a line of telegraph poles stretching into the far distance. Rally cars were spread out driving almost anywhere in this no-man's-land and we could see both to the left and right of us cars racing along, sometimes up to six or seven abreast. Occasionally, we would come across a small village in the middle of nowhere – a couple of dozen yurts with the ubiquitous group of horses parked outside and the whole village surrounded by a wooden palisade. We would fly directly towards the village and then attempt to circumnavigate the palisade. All the villagers were out to encourage us on and we wondered quite what they made of this amazing cavalcade of ancient cars passing through their backyards. Surely, they could not have seen anything like this before. Obscurely, we came across a small herd of horses absolutely miles away from anywhere in the middle of the desert. We really couldn't fathom what they were doing there, as there was no visible means of support, no water, no grass. Disappointingly, on an adventure like this, it is not possible to get answers to all of these questions, and I suppose we shall never know how they survive. Later on in the day, it started to pour with rain again, just as we caught up John and Joan in the Rover. John decided he was going to have a race with us which, given the

lashing rain and filthy dust everywhere, got our car nicely dirty, but the stupid vacuum wipers were so absolutely hopeless, we had to fall back a short way in order to create some vision through the screen. I can't imagine what has happened with the wipers – they had never really been much good, but now, when we needed them, they were doing one wipe every 25 minutes!

Miraculously, after 127 miles of open desert, we suddenly came upon a piece of immaculate tarmac road, just 232 kms now to drive on to Ulaan Baatar. Yvonne took the wheel for 100 kms or so, which gave me a bit of relief, but declared she was unhappy with the steering, as it tended to wander from side to side. It occurred to me that I have now driven the car so many miles and become so used to its idiosyncrasies, that I don't give it a second thought.

The final run in to Ulaan Baatar was really evil; we struggled along in a gigantic hot and smoky traffic jam and were very much of the opinion that we had arrived up its backside. The competitors were split up into two or three different hotels, and ours was just outside the city centre. Tomorrow was to be a rest day and our big plan was to search out new front shock absorbers. We repaired to the bar, then off to a local restaurant to recharge our own batteries.

Rest Day? What a misnomer.

The hotel car park was a scene of devastation this morning, with almost every car being worked on. There were a lot of very worried faces; we had only been on the road for five days and there are another thirty to go. We came across Steve and Linda in the Aston, which by now had a seized back axle, and they were looking pretty despondent. Bentley no. 133 had massive problems; the oil tank was split; the radiator had been gouged and the engine mounting brackets had sheared. Walking round the back of the car, we noticed petrol dripping from the tank and, to add to their woes, we discovered that their petrol tank had been split also. Dave had lost the axle straps on the Sunbeam and crushed his brake pipe, and there were many, many more woeful tales of severely damaged cars.

We had been led to believe that Ulaan Baatar was a hotbed of automotive repair shops and spares distributors – to everybody's horror, however, it was discovered to be a Children's Day Festival in the city, and a large percentage of the premises were closed down!

My big job for the day was to have the front shock absorber mounts strengthened. Given the fact that the Chevrolet construction is generally so rugged, the design of the shock absorber supports was so fragile, it beggared belief. The bottoms of the shock absorbers were mounted onto plates with a narrow flange, which hooked inside the main suspension arm. The car had given the shock absorbers such a pounding that they simply 'punched' these support plates out of the flanges. Clearly, a major strengthening exercise was required. However, the main concern was to obtain a new shock absorber. Now when I left home, the shock absorber was, frankly, a fairly foreign object, but I was becoming so familiar with it that I was quite able to hold long and detailed discussions in the bar about their innermost secrets. Needless to say, the shock absorber on the Chevrolet was extremely unusual – it had a threaded pin on either end. For all those people out there who have as little

knowledge of shock absorbers as I had a few months ago, I should explain that some shock absorbers have a pin on one end and a circular flange on the other, whilst many have circular flanges on both ends. Needless to say, threaded pins on both ends have never been heard of in Ulaan Baatar. What to do? Peter Banham had a bright idea; he said "I'm sure the guy in the Rover P4 has just the shock absorbers you need." Who was the guy in the Rover P4 – John, of course. What an amazing situation; here we were standing in a carpark in Ulaan Baatar and the one chap who has exactly the shock absorber I need lives maybe 200 yards away from us back in Foolow. Needless to say, John, magnanimous as ever, very willingly gave over the shock absorber and it was now up to me to arrange to fit it.

The big issue, however, was where to have the brackets made, and I simply could not get any assistance from any of the rally support crews; they were all utterly overwhelmed by queries from every quarter. I could see that everyone was becoming frustrated and fractious, and decided therefore that the only route to success was to sort this out ourselves. Yvonne had the brainwave of talking to the girl on reception, who kindly made several phone calls and told us that she had managed to find two young Mongolian chaps who would be able to help us and would be with us shortly. Shortly proved to be two hours, during which time I lay under the car manufacturing a couple of templates for the complicated brackets that we needed to fabricate. I made the first template out of a piece of paper, carefully folded to the correct angles, then manufactured another template out of a strip of aluminium that I had in my spares. At last, after lunch, our Mongolian mechanics turned up and initially I was little fazed as they looked as though they were barely out of school. However, they then introduced us to their attractive wives and delightful children, all of whom had come along with them as it was the Children's Day Festival, and with no more ado, I was bundled into the back of a mini-bus, together with my templates, and off we drove into the nearby hills. It was a strange situation to be in; nobody spoke any English, of course, and here I was, not having the foggiest idea of where I was in Ulaan Baatar, completely in the hands of these enthusiastic, if youthful, fellows. Turning up at their garage was hardly inspiring either. They flung open the doors of an extremely rough-and-ready shed, to reveal a baked earth floor, an enormous vice, an array of sledgehammers, two or three spanners and an electric drill without a plug. Nonetheless, they set-too with great enthusiasm, found an old piece of steel on a nearby scrap heap and hammered, bashed and bent a couple of brackets that were near perfect. The next job was to drill some locating holes to bolt onto the chassis, and one of them picked up the electric drill – remember it had no plug! My eyes were drawn to the side of the garage where, hanging freely down the wall, was a single cable with two bare ends of wire turned upward. One of the lads bent a couple of hooks on the end of the

with our willing helpers

wire to the electric drill and simply hung them over the mains wire on the wall. Remarkably, the drill worked, and I couldn't help but think what our Health & Safety Officers back in the UK would have made of this.

Unfortunately, they didn't have a drill large enough to make a hole for the centre fixing of the shock absorber but, unfazed, they indicated that it was no problem and we all bundled back into the mini-bus. Five minutes later we pulled up at a roadside, tented structure, where a young man was crouched there with his own personal welding kit. In two minutes, and in exchange for a cigarette, he burned a hole in the centre of each bracket approximately the correct diameter. Back to the hotel, and Yvonne was somewhat relieved to see me return. We'd been away more than two hours; she hadn't seen me leave and had simply no idea that she would ever see me again. In double quick time the brackets were offered up to the chassis, but we then needed to drill some holes to receive the fixing bolts. Yvonne managed to

procure an extension lead which we plugged into a socket in the hotel dining room via an open window and, of course, it came with the sophistication of a proper socket at one end. My ever-smiling colleagues had brought with them the plugless drill and, without batting an eyelid, they bunged the bare wires into the holes in the socket and pushed a nail in each to secure them!

Giving some support

Better was to come – they needed to grind away at a piece of metal and produced an angle grinder which, again, was of the plugless variety. With no hesitation, one of the lads produced a Stanley knife, slit the live cable a metre further up from the socket, exposed the bare wires, gingerly attached the bare wires from the angle grinder and, low and behold, within seconds we were up and running. Eventually, at 7.00 pm, the work was complete. Our Mongolian saviours were all smiles. The two of them had been with us for six hours and, despite all my protestations, would only take the equivalent of £5 for their work. However, Yvonne delved into the back of the car and produced bags of sweets for the children and packets of cigarettes for the men. Hands were shaken, wives were kissed and children picked up and swung around. Its events like today that really make one realise how kind people can be and it was terrific to be in an environment where people wanted to do things for the pleasure of being able to help, rather than being driven by money. Certainly, it is an incident that we shall always remember and, I imagine these Mongolian youngsters will do so, too.

A hot shower; a celebratory drink in the bar, and Yvonne and I retired to The Casablanca restaurant just round the corner for a quiet meal for two, followed by an extremely long, sound sleep.

We hadn't seen much of Ulaan Baatar, but were certainly taking away some very special memories.

This morning we had to be up bright and early and present ourselves at 7.15 in the main square in Ulaan Baatar to be given a send-off by the Mayor of Ulaan Baatar and a splendid local brass band, which seemed to play non-stop for a couple of hours. All of the rally cars were parked up in the main square, and we all had plenty of time to wander round and swap stories about yesterday's exploits.

Rally rumour was rife, and we learnt that Jay Carry's navigator in the 1952 Bentley had abandoned ship and flown home. Jan Voboril in the 1916 Lancia Theta had had a major altercation with his navigator and had thrown him out! Sadly, also this morning, a couple of unnamed rallyists had

The locals seem fascinated by our map

been arrested and had their passports confiscated when they had been found 'peeing' onto the statue of a local dignitary. Eventually, when they had shown some humility and apologised they were later allowed to continue. It really is amazing how stupid some people can be when they are guests in someone else's country.

Our morning was considerably brightened by a young Mongolian married couple, who spoke very good English and seemed to attach themselves to us; they were really enthusiastic about the car. Indeed, after we were flagged away from the start, they followed us for mile after mile in their 4X4, occasionally overtaking and waving

enthusiastically. When we came to the parting of the ways we had the bright idea to hand over to them our Blancpain wine glasses; the chances of them surviving to Paris were unlikely, and we felt that they would provide a lasting memory of the rally to this pleasant young couple.

Leaving busy Ulaan Baatar behind, we were soon driving through grassland landscapes, with just the occasional yurt and flock of sheep. Slowly but surely the road degraded until we were back to the now 'near normal' rough, unsurfaced approximate tracks. Suddenly, Bang! That aweful noise of suspension breakage that was to become so familiar to us. A quick inspection showed that, after all the hard work of yesterday, the brackets had failed. We were to learn that, despite all of the huge enthusiasm of the Mongolian people, sadly their technical skills weren't up to the terrible bashing that we were giving these cars. Something would have to be done tonight.

Have you ever seen such shabby camels?

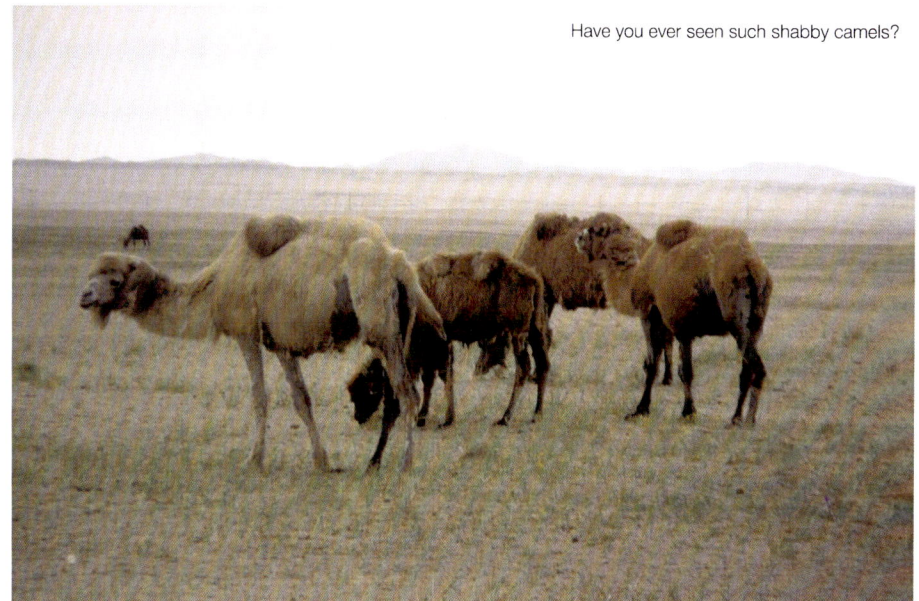

Today the time trials have been reinstated, and we have a couple of extremely tough sections. We decided to drive them at a moderate speed, just ensuring that we stayed within the maximum time limits.

Shortly after lunch the wind got up and, without warning, we were in the middle of an incredible sand storm. It was almost impossible to see the road ahead, and the car was being constantly pummelled by sand from every direction. Inevitably, we had to slow down to almost walking pace but, after half an hour, Yvonne suddenly realised that we were running extremely short on time. Fortuitously, at almost around that time the road changed to excellent tarmac and we left the dust storm behind. We absolutely flew, doing nearly 80 mph for mile after mile and, luckily, arrived at the finish control just 6 minutes inside our maximum time. On our drive in we came across Dave and Jo who were crawling along in the verge of the road. A quick stop and Dave told us that he was having a problem with no brakes – presumably after the hammering it had taken a few days ago; it looks as though they will fall outside their allotted time.

Tonight, we were staying in yurts again and the rally was split into two separate camps. Unfortunately we were in an extremely remote camp situated more than a mile down a very rough track off the main road. The moment we pulled up, my first job was to ascertain what was the problem with the car suspension and how to remedy it. Yvonne went off to find our yurt and I befriended a local lorry driver, who offered to assist. We both crawled under the car and within minutes my helper, who came complete with his own set of spanners, started to undo the large nut on the end of the gudgeon pin (yes, I know it's a gudgeon pin now, but I didn't then!) This

Welding begins

seemed to me to have nothing to do with the problems we were having and I eventually persuaded him to desist. However, unknown to us, this caused a problem that would come back to haunt us in days to come.

Team Mongolia!

It was clear that we needed more welding work to be done, and my helper offered to take me to a colleague in a nearby village. Eventually, we pulled into what was perhaps the crummiest garage and scrap yard I have ever been in. My helper suddenly disappeared and I was left standing there with no-one around. I eventually saw a large, battered garage door and hammered on it and, within seconds, was surrounded by a large group of enthusiastic Mongolians, most of whom were dressed in traditional costume. I was finding it extremely difficult to describe what I required when, out of a nearby yurt, strolled a woman, whom I later discovered was called Teyula. Remarkably, she spoke both English and Russian and immediately took on the role of interpreter. Teyula was 43 she told me but, with the tough existence she was living in this unforgiving outback, looked all of 63. She was absolutely delightful in every way and, within minutes, had organised all the men. They stripped the broken bracket off the car, welded on a new piece complete with a support eye, then made up all of the fixtures and fittings ready to refix the shock absorber. The final piece of equipment we required was a thick rubber washer. In an instant, all of the mechanics set off to scour the nearby scrapyard and miraculously, within five minutes, someone had discovered a refrigerator, the insides of which produced an anti-vibration washer of precisely the dimensions we required. It was a complicated job fixing all the intricate parts together and continuously bits

The village elder oversees

were falling into the sand, but these men were not to be beaten; they guffawed and laughed their way through everything and, eventually, managed to fix the unit securely. Meanwhile, word had clearly got around the village and all the locals came to witness the strange goings-on. The local village madman turned up; he felt the

pulses in my wrist and forehead, reached round my back, felt at my spine and declared I was in good shape. That was quite a relief, actually, as I felt anything but in good shape by this time. Teyula brought out coffee and bread and eventually, at half past nine, the work was finished. In the pitch black now, I found my torch from inside the car and this seemed to fascinate everyone. Presumably there are not many torches in Mongolia. Eventually, everyone withdrew to the yurt and I was handed my bill for the evening's work - £7 in total. I nipped out and brought my whisky bottle and poured a nip each into an assortment of old glasses and rice bowls and we all enthusiastically toasted each other. Judging by the expressions on one or two faces, the whisky was not to everyone's taste but it was a very happy group of people that sat around the central wood burning stove. As I was about to leave, the village elder, who was a gnarled, old man wearing an ankle length purple smock and a gnarled faced that looked as if it had been carved from mahogany, suddenly dug into the depths of his clothing and gave me a little present – his pipe cleaner and tapper-out-er. Teyula gave me some small coins for good luck, and promised to write to me and send me some postcards. We exchanged addresses and with their farewells ringing in my head, I drove back to the camp. When I got back our yurt was deserted, but I tracked down Yvonne who had had supper with John and Joan. I regaled them with my stories of the evening, and devoured my evening meal of a bag of crisps washed down with a good measure of whisky. Wandering back arm-in-arm to our yurt at midnight, we found that our wood burner had been lit and we snuggled down on our wooden campbeds and dozed off with the glow of the fire and the delicious smell of woodsmoke.

MONGOLIA - Day 8 Kharkorin To Bayankhongor 428kms.

Day Dawns in Kharkorin

forget in a long time. Everybody around called to wish me Happy Birthday; John and Joan dropped me off a present of a large bag of crisps and Dave and Jo gave me half a loaf of bread!

Kharkorin was the original capital of Mongolia, and was the first city in Mongolia to build a Buddhist Monastery; it took 300 years to complete and contained between 60 and 100 temples. The Monastery was surrounded by a gigantic wall with inset turrets every 60 to 100 metres. It was outside the Monastery wall that the cars gathered for the morning start – a photogenic gem. The first part of the morning was retracing our steps for a few kilometres, running through the area that yesterday was so devastated by the

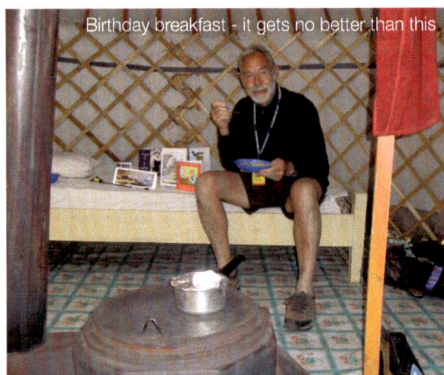

Breathtaking background for our morning start

It's my birthday today! And, I didn't sleep too well in the night worrying about the issues with the car, so was up bright and early at about 5.15 am. It was a stunning morning, very cold but perfectly clear, and the camp site was in the most beautiful setting with the mountains around us on all sides. I rekindled the log fire and soon had flames licking up the chimney. Breakfast was supposed to be

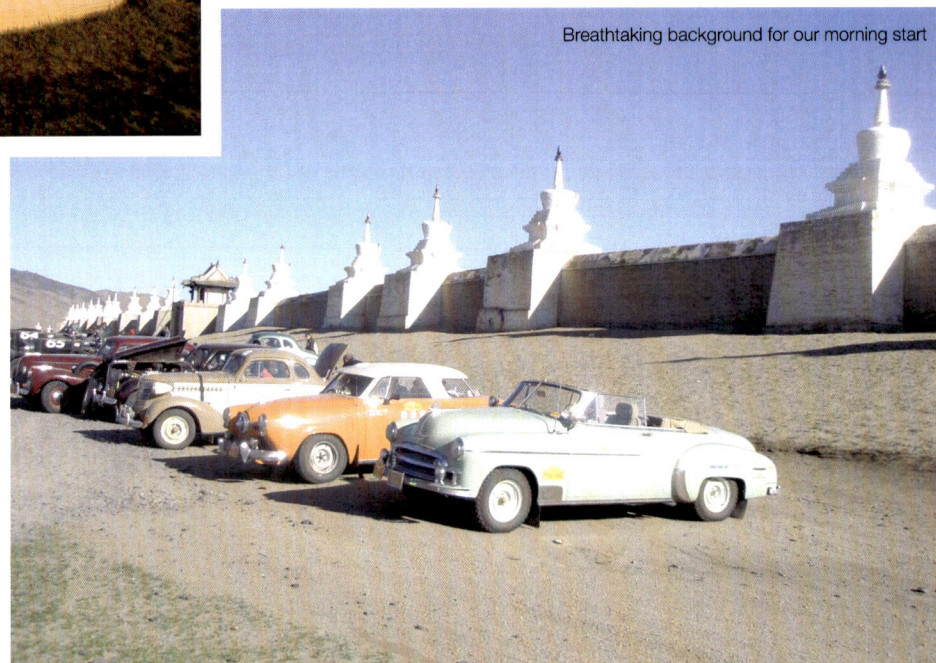

Birthday breakfast - it gets no better than this

in the other yurt camp which was several miles' drive away, so we elected to stay in our yurt and had muesli, an energy bar and a cup of coffee, whilst I opened my birthday cards. Really quite the most memorable setting for a birthday – one I shan't

sand storm. We soon turned off the tarmacadam and headed south, doing a huge loop around a major mountain range. Sadly, as soon as we hit rough ground again, the shock absorber plate gave way once more. Being rather concerned about the suspension generally, I decided to ring Keith in the UK to ask if he could organise for some spare parts to be sent ahead of us. Unfortunately, it was one o-clock in the morning for him, but I left a message on his answer-machine.

The shock absorber continued to rattle around, and I decided it was necessary to remove it, if only to rid us of the awful din it was making. However, after half an hour I simply couldn't remove it because the top fixing had jammed – I gave up eventually, hoping possibly to get some assistance in the evening.

We had a couple of time trials during the day, which were extremely demanding and, again, our absolute priority was to get round reasonably quickly but without excessively pushing the car too hard. At the end of the second time trial, we came across the Sunbeam with Dave standing by the side of it with an extremely forlorn look on his face. The front nearside wheel was leaning at an alarming angle and he was awaiting the service crew to see whether they could assist.

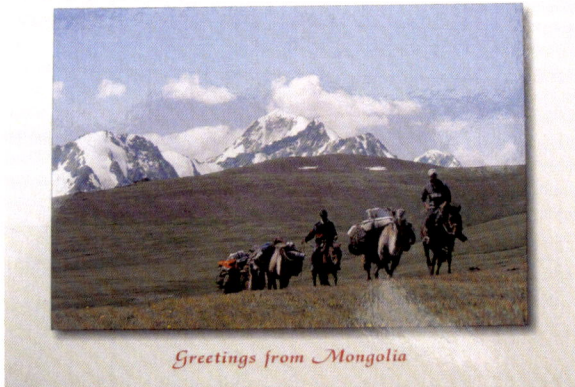

Greetings from Mongolia

Today was a long and exhausting drive over the mountains, totally and utterly unsurfaced with, at times, no signs of any tracks whatsoever. The scenery was breathtaking for the whole day – it was a sight we never tired of. The last run-in to our overnight stop at Bayankhongor, however, was utterly wearying. We had come over a lorry route which, over years of use, had formed a 'washboard' surface; this washboard surface was to be the bane of our

lives; the corrugations that had been formed in the ground were of an extremely even pitch, but no matter what we tried, it was not possible to drive over them without the car being almost shaken to pieces; it was so rough that, at times, we were inching along at 10 – 15 mph, then taking advice from other competitors who said that if we travelled at, say, 50 mph we would skim over the surface, we then tried

Stunning photo by Gerard Brown - it tells everything about how wild it was

Dusty Joan

that – it was just as bad. There was no way to overcome the numbing vibrations. It was around that time that I now realised why Keith had replaced all the bolts on the underside of the car with Nylock nuts.

Eventually, late afternoon, we pulled into a fuel station on the outskirts of Bayankhongor to join the interminable queue for fuel. Shortly after we arrived, John and Joan pulled up with John looking 'a paler shade of grey'. They had been following another car in a plume of dust when they came across an unexpected 90 degree bend in the road. John merrily sailed straight on, over a bank and the car dropped down into a dry river bed. Mercifully, neither of them was hurt and the car seemed to be intact. John drove a short way along the river bed and managed to regain the road. Strong cars these P4s.

The wait in the fuel station turned into a nightmare. It will be recalled that we had purchased petrol coupons beforehand, but what the organisers had not bothered to tell anybody was which octane grade the vouchers represented. The fuel came in two grades of octane, 75 and 85. The people running the fuel station, however, were claiming that our vouchers were only for the poorer quality petrol and the big issue was whether we were to pay 20% extra for the higher quality octane or receive 20% less fuel than the vouchers gave. Inevitably, this situation led to frustration for both the rally crews and the people dispensing the petrol. Something had to give and one of the competitors, rather disgracefully, threatened to punch one of the

The Chevy is surrounded

Nomad crew who was manning the fuel pumps. The outcome of this was that they then refused to serve any more petrol – impasse. Eventually, one of the other rally crews managed to persuade the offender to issue an abject apology at which time petrol started to flow once again.

Nonetheless, we were all having a good time, as all the villagers had turned out to welcome us and people were milling around the cars and chatting all of the time. Several people asked if they could sit in the cars to have photographs taken and we, of course, all willingly obliged, posing with family after family. However, on one occasion Yvonne drifted away to chat to someone else and I also found myself chatting 8 or 10 yards away from the car, when I suddenly saw a family of six open the car door and climb in, uninvited, for their photographic session. I made my way back to car and as soon as I arrived the whole family looked a trifle embarrassed and seemed to evaporate rather rapidly. To my horror, once I climbed into the car, I discovered that our video camera had gone; I was absolutely apoplectic as we had been religiously recording every feature of our journey – our once-in-a-lifetime trip. The local police chief in his very smart uniform was in the middle of the milling crowds with a benign smile on his face, welcoming all the rally cars. Through an interpreter I made him understand exactly what had happened, expressing my concern that, whilst we were very keen to oblige the locals with photographs etc., it was extremely upsetting to find that someone had taken advantage in this way; he shrugged and smiled and seemed to have no interest in my plight, so eventually we left to drive the last 3 or 4 kilometres across the rock-strewn countryside to our camp site destination.

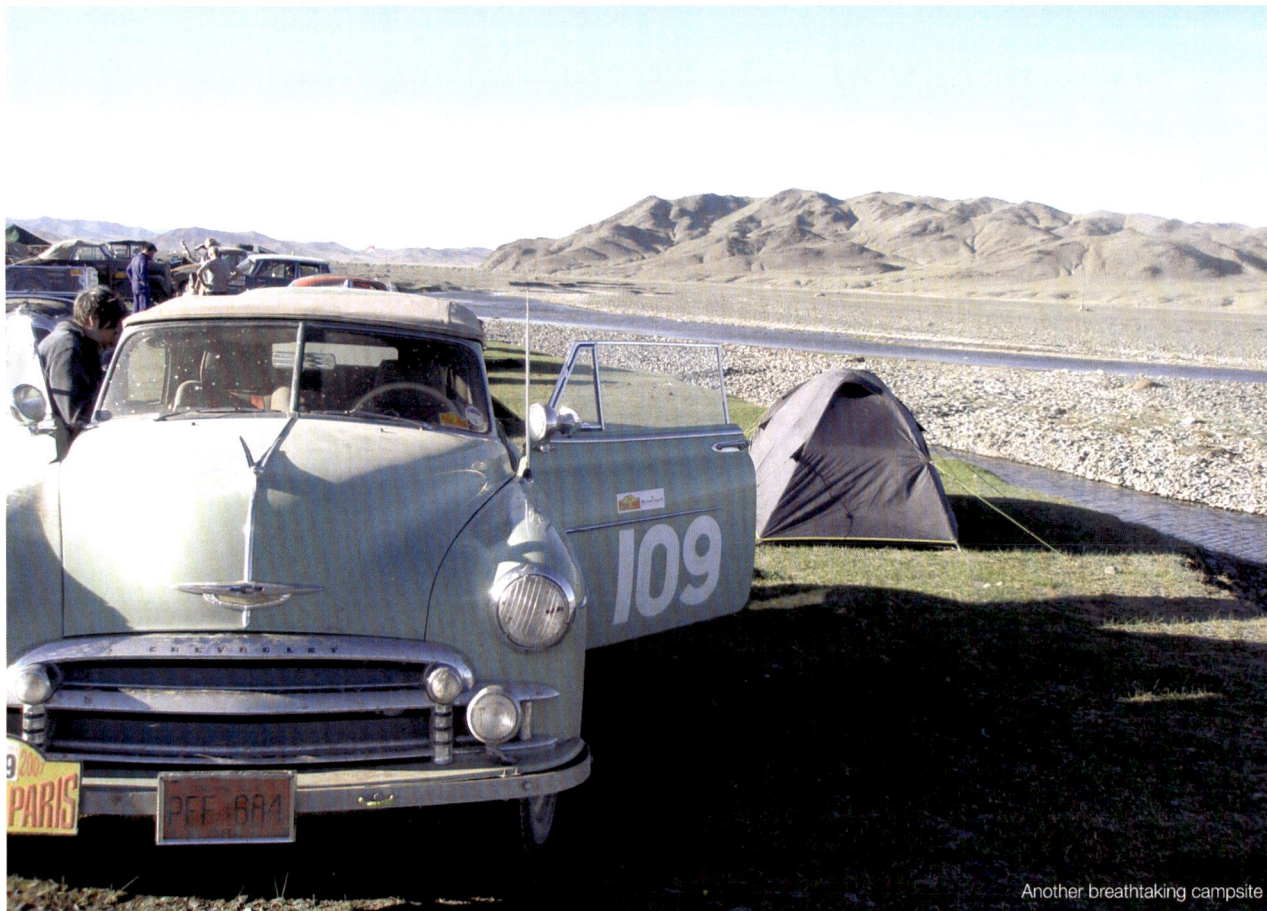
Another breathtaking campsite

The camp site was stunning, being situated by the side of a crystal-clear river on a wide plateau. We managed to get the tent up in double quick time, but both felt a bit low what with the theft of the video camera and the problems with the suspension. Once again, none of the support crews seemed to have sufficient time to assist; on top of that

Dave and Jo hadn't turned up into camp and we had no idea where they were. A shot of whisky, a hot shower and we gathered to have a little party to celebrate my birthday in this beautiful and remote setting. Off to bed quite early at just gone 10.00 pm and I was just drifting off to sleep when Betty Banham called by knocking on our tent door with some good news; firstly she told me that Peter could look at my car at 6.30 in the morning and, secondly, yippee, the police had found my camera. I rapidly dressed and dashed off to the main tent, only to find that my hopes had been raised falsely inasmuch as the police had only found some suspects and wanted me to go to the police station to attempt to identify them. A rough ride, once again, over the rocks to the local police station, only to find that the police had, in fact, taken the seven suspects to the camp site to visit me! An hour later, these seven bedraggled specimens were paraded in front of me but I was adamant that it definitely wasn't any of these young fellows that I had seen in the car. The police took a long and incredibly detailed statement and, eventually, dropped me back to the tent at 1.15 am – not quite what I had planned for my birthday evening.

Up at ten to six, and the first welcome sight, as I zipped open the tent, was the Sunbeam standing just a few yards away – Dave and Jo had eventually made it.

First river crossing

I missed breakfast as I was taking the car over to the Banhams, only to find out that, after all, they were not able to help as more demanding issues had overtaken them. Peter suggested that, as I couldn't get the top nut off the shock absorber, I should chisel it off, but this proved to be impossible as I couldn't hit the chisel within the confines of the mudguard. Eventually, the only solution was to hacksaw it off but,

again, due to the restricted working area, it took me one and a half hours to hacksaw through a 5 mm bolt. At least we wouldn't have the accompaniment of clanging and banging that we had all day yesterday. Yvonne had taken the tent down and packed it away in eleven minutes flat, so we rushed off to find the start. In this rocky, barren wasteland, it was extremely difficult to track down the exact location; mercifully, we rolled up to the line eventually, exactly on our minute.

Dave and Jo had managed to find a welder in Bayankhongor at 7.00 am and Dave was last seen attempting to bolt everything back together as we departed the camp site. Very early on in the day, we had another time trial coming up, and we could see from the road book that there was a river crossing involved. There was a great deal of pandemonium, as nobody could ascertain whether the time trial finished before the water or afterwards. Fortunately, it was before, but immediately after the time trial we came across a large group of cars that had gathered to prepare themselves for crossing this stretch of water that was probably 35 or 40 yards wide. Before we left Foolow, I had manufactured a two foot high upstand connection for the exhaust system, and I rapidly fitted this in place to make sure we didn't inhale any Mongolian river water; fortunately, we cruised through without any problems and I paused at the other side just long enough to photograph other cars, some

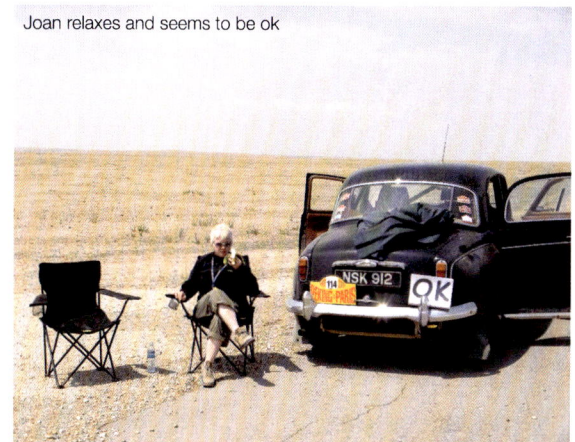
Joan relaxes and seems to be ok

it must have been something to do with the super hard linings that we had fitted.

The rest of the day was more of the outstanding, majestic beauty of the desert scenery. We were running down the bottom of sandy, tuft strewn valleys, whilst the mountains in the distance rose up on either side of the valley and were snow-capped as far as the eye could see. It was sometimes difficult to evaluate the scale of these valleys, and on one occasion we were driving for more than four hours along the valley base before we climbed a rough track to then descend towards the village of Altay. Today was one of the days when we were simply covered in dust from head to foot; the car was full of dust; our clothes were full of dust and, amazingly, somehow it managed to seep into some of the sealed containers we had containing food and medical supplies. The dust was drying out my skin and my hands had become blackened with

of which were successful and some of which were not. A local truck driver had got wind of what was happening and was happily towing cars out of the river. The local exchange rate must have been good as he had a huge beam on his face.

Unnervingly, once we set off, the brakes didn't seem to work at all. I tried the inevitable rapid dabbing of the foot brake to try and dry off the pads but, in fact, it took miles and miles before we had any feeling back in them at all. I worked out that

a mixture of oil and sand, and cracks on my thumbs and forefingers opened up so severely that by this time they were continually bleeding. We came across Richard and Nicola in the Jaguar Mark 2 stuck in the desert, with broken rear springs. We weren't able to be of any help to them as Richard, as always, was fully prepared for such eventualities. However, Richard was able to help us and he gave me a jar of super-dooper hand cream which, at least, eased my problems over the days to come.

Major problems for Richard and Nicola

Clearly, the dry, barren landscape was unable to sustain much in the way of life and, at one stage, we passed numerous horse carcasses for mile after mile. Unusually, in the middle of nowhere, we passed a single yurt looking forelorn and lonesome and totally out of scale in this massive landscape. Obscurely, as we passed by I noticed what appeared to be a satellite dish on a large pole standing to one side; I never quite got my ahead around that one!

After a long, long day we slowly wheeled into the final control, and arrived at the camp site passably early. We got the tent up on the slightly sloping, grassy hillside, and I repaired to the underside of the car for a complete spanner check. Having whipped off the front wheels to adjust the brakes, I spotted that the large nut on the gudgeon pin (yes, that gudgeon pin) seemed to be extremely loose, so I tightened it up as much as possible but, again, it was extremely difficult to get the leverage due to the proximity of the mudguard. Amazingly, sitting in this remote region, I managed to get Keith on the phone to discuss the purchase of our suspension spares. He told us that we were 4th in class and 13th overall, which amused us that we didn't know our position whilst on the rally, but he seemed to have all the information sitting in the comfort of his Staffordshire home!

We heard bad news from Dave and Jo; their welding was completed early in the morning, but within ten miles it broke again. The last news we had was that they were on a truck to somewhere, we know not where.

Later on, as we slowly walked back from another memorable meal in the canteen tent, we were relieved to see Richard and Nicola roll in at 10.30 pm so, at least, they are back with us. During dinner, the organisers announced that, as there had been so many car casualties on the rally and the whole event had become so fragmented, it was necessary to pause so that everyone could catch up. Tomorrow, therefore, was to be a completely time-free day; there was to be no start time, no time trials and no finishing time which, hopefully, would allow the necessary re-grouping.

Weary crews put up tents in Altay

... for mile after mile after mile

MONGOLIA - Day 10 Altay To Khovd 433kms.

After another nourishing 'Nomad' breakfast, we set off at about 7.30 am determined to get as many kilometres under our belts as we could before the heat of the day. The first 15 or 20 kilometres descended a long mountain pass on a dust-ridden road. The car was going well and, indeed, we had now become extremely used to the loping mode the car settled into without its front suspension – who needs shock absorbers! We caught up quite a lot of the pre-War cars who had also set off early, but the nightmare was attempting to overtake them; plumes of grey dust poured from the back wheels of every car and overtaking was a matter of taking your life in your own hands until you were out of these individual dust storms. Inevitably, there was an 'incident' when Jon Kennedy and Garrick Staples, in their 1959 VW Cabriolet drove into a dust storm, only to find that they had ploughed into the back of a Luxemburg La Salle and then spun into the side of a Danish Bentley. Luckily, no-one was hurt, but Jon told me later that he was somewhat stunned by the different attitudes of the two crews. The Luxemburg crew immediately demanded sight of his insurance policy (in the middle of Mongolia?), whilst the Danish driver, Jans Pilo, took a look at his damaged front wing and announced that it was only glass fibre and it would give him the opportunity to replace it with a proper steel one when he returned home! Sadly, this incident had bigger implications for Jon and Garrick; one of them apparently tried to blame the other for the

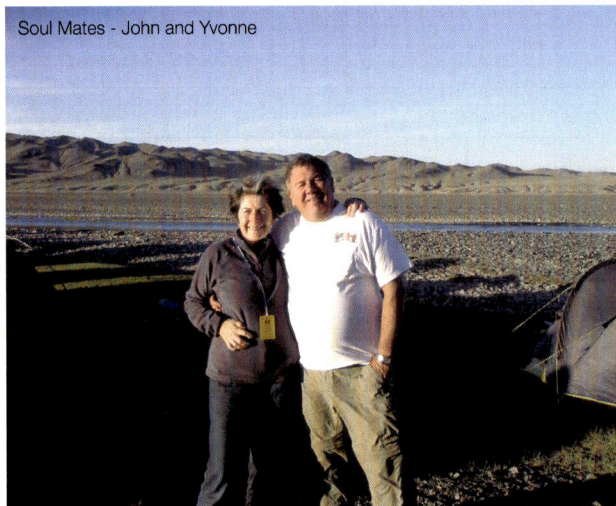

Soul Mates - John and Yvonne

accident and, instead of accepting that 'things happen', chose to fall out, with the result that they never spoke to each other, conversationally, for the rest of the trip. The only words that were spoken were 'left' and 'right' and they followed the route book instructions like this right through to Paris. The moment their car pulled to a halt at either a passage check, a main control or, indeed, a hotel, they both got out and went their separate ways. Jon found the two of us soul-mates (as we were travelling fairly closely together on the road) so whenever Jon was out of the Beetle he wandered across for a chat. Jon, it appears, has the identical Chevrolet Bel Air Convertible at home, albeit in a different colour. He proved to be quite a help whenever we had any problems as, of course, he knew the Chevy inside-out.

Like yesterday, we were travelling through hundreds of kilometres of arid and desolate landscape, mainly at over 2,000 metres altitude. Also, it's another day of the 'washboard' with its endless car-breaking and back-jarring corrugations. All the time we were criss-crossing from one track to another, trying to seek out an area that was less damaging than another. Many times, I found myself trying to levitate over

This just tells you how tough it was

the bumps by clinging onto the steering wheel and lifting my body weight off the seat, kidding myself that this would help in some way or another. Today was absolutely endless; mile after mile after mile where, whilst the scenery was still magnificent, one's mind was constantly worrying about the damage that was being caused to the car. At one stage, Mike and Josie came steaming past us in their Chrysler 75, travelling three or four times our speed – clearly he was following the edict that the faster you drive the

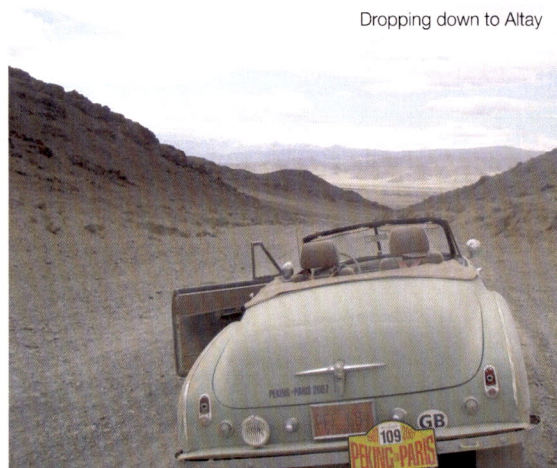
Dropping down to Altay

corrugations, the better it was. It wasn't – five miles further on we came across Mike ruefully looking down at where the shock absorber had smashed off its

supporting bracket. The day seemed never ending; somehow at every waypoint the evening stop seemed to be further away, but eventually we pulled into Khovd to look around for the camp site. In fact, this was more difficult than might have been expected; the Nomads had found a location for the site that they considered was much better than that indicated on our GPS. Eventually, after half an hour's searching, we struggled down a steep, rock strewn hillside to be confronted by what must have been the most wonderful, natural camp site on earth. After the rigours of the day, the jolting and crashing of the car, and the boiling hot temperatures, what lay in front of us was a smooth, silken, bowling green-like stretch of the freshest grass which the pastures of England would be proud of, edged by a wide, crystal clear pouring stream and rimmed with majestic mountains as far as the eye could see. Surprisingly, we were second car in, arriving at 5.00 pm behind the Holden of Mick and Andrew Mykytovich; our early-morning start and persistent driving had

Possibly the most beautiful campsite in the world

paid off, and we were able to have the first choice of the best possible tent location next to the cascading river. Our plan was to relax for the evening and absorb this setting – what must be the best camp site in the world. By now, our tent-raising skills were second to none and, within minutes, our little home for the night was completed. Yvonne wandered off to the Nomads' tent where she discovered that she was able to buy half a dozen cans of beer which we popped into a polythene bag, tied to a rope and dangled in the river ready to slake the thirst of our friends as they arrived. In the early evening setting sun we sat out on the grass at the back of the car, dug out the inevitable bag of crisps and cracked open a beer. Heaven on Earth!

A little later, I decided it would be prudent to do a quick spanner check on the car. A first look revealed that one of the rubber bobbins on the exhaust support brackets had sheared, but this was rapidly replaced. I was having a quick check around on the front off-side wheel when I spotted that the huge nut (yes, that one) had disappeared, and the whole of the front suspension wishbone had flirted off the gudgeon pin. Initially, I was beside myself, but thought that I could perhaps put a

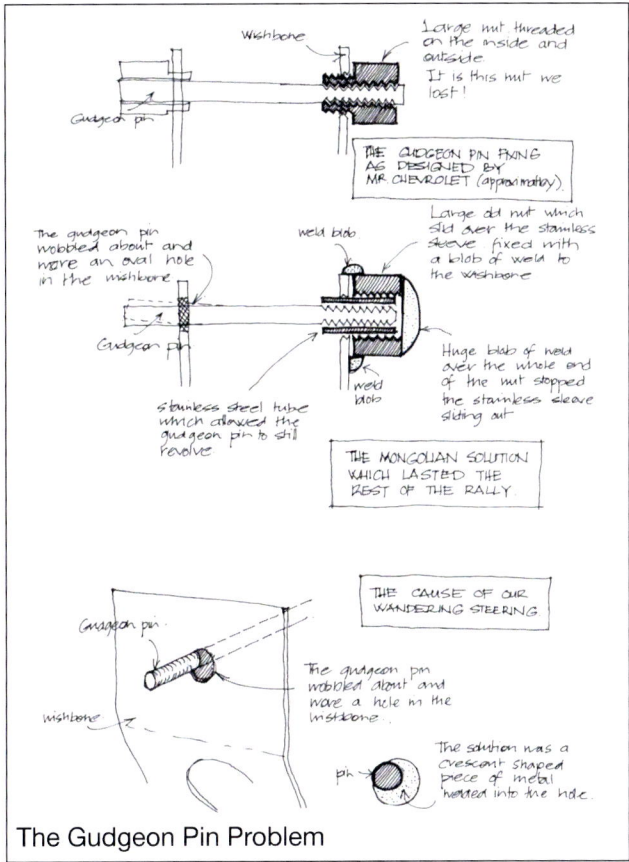

The Gudgeon Pin Problem

big nut on the end and tighten it up. At that stage Andy Vann, in the 1952 orange Studebaker, whom I had marked down as the ultimate mechanic (he was always blackened in oil from head to toe day in day out) told me that it was an extremely special nut indeed, being threaded on the inside face to tighten onto the gudgeon pin and also threaded on the external face where it passed through the wishbone. We were done for! Or were we? Several heads got together and, eventually, someone suggested that it would be possible to use some tubing to slide over the gudgeon pin. At this stage, luck played an enormous part; I dug out my spares and, would you believe it, I found two lengths of stainless steel tubing, one of exactly the right internal diameter to fit over the gudgeon pin, and the other of exactly the right diameter to fit through the hole in the wishbone. Jacking up the suspension arm, and with a lot of prising and gasping, I eventually managed to insert the tubing into the correct locations and decided that all it needed was, in the morning, for me to visit a garage and have the whole assembly block welded together. Finishing that job, I then turned to the engine and decided the check the oil and water. To my horror, I couldn't get the bonnet up and discovered that the bolt holding the

Mike and Josies Chrysler fuelling at Khovd

massively-tensioned spring which activated the bonnet had broken. Eventually, with absolute brute force, two or three of us managed to raise the bonnet but not without the rear corner of the bonnet gouging the top of the wing for three or four inches. On the one hand, it was disappointing to damage the body work but somehow it almost seemed irrelevant given all the issues that had gone on before.

We decided to relax and enjoy the moment having fixed what seemed a short while ago an unfixable problem. A group of us wandered off to the canteen tent to eat but, during dinner, the organisers announced that, contrary to rumours that were running through the rally, tomorrow we would revert to normal rally timing. I panicked and decided that I really ought to have the welding done this evening, so at 9.45 pm I struggled over the rock-strew hillside, back into Khovd village to find a garage. On the way across, I came across

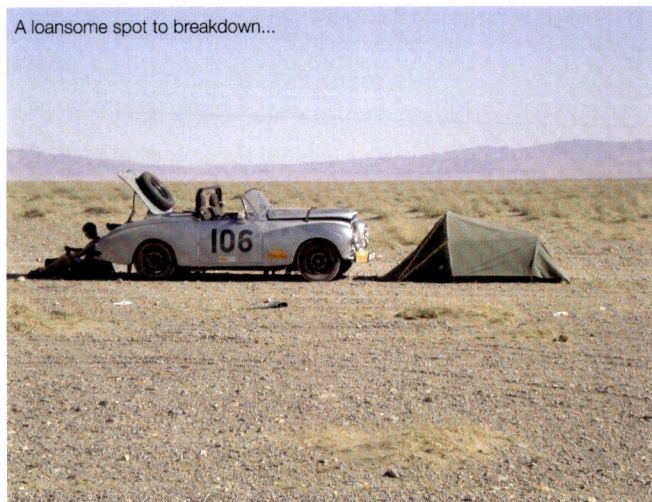

A loansome spot to breakdown...

John and Joan limping in with their tails of woe for the day; to my utter embarrassment I discovered that John had damaged his front shock absorber badly, and who had his only spare. I did. Not only that, but we had 'marmalised' it and dispensed with it several days ago. (As it transpired, the damage to John's shock absorber was not as bad as initially thought, and he was able to retap a new thread onto the pin on the end and refit it. At least, I didn't feel so bad, eventually.)

It's almost impossible to describe how

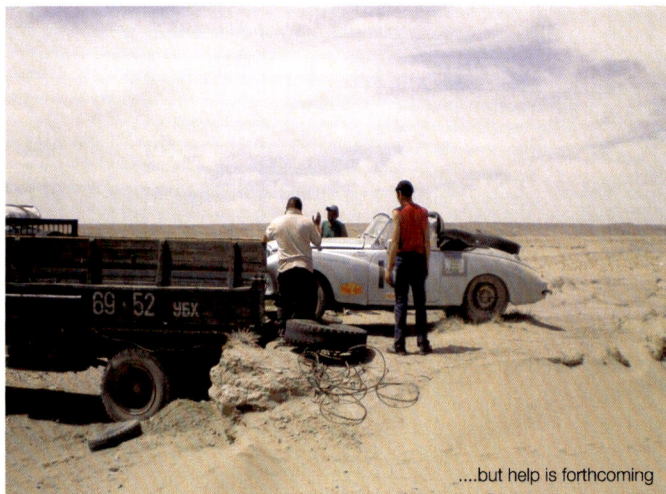

....but help is forthcoming

'Heath Robinson' the Mongolian garages were; mud floors, no light, minimal tools, maximum enthusiasm. Within minutes two or three men were climbing all over the car. They found an enormous nut in the depths of their workshop, inserted it over my jury-rigged stainless tubing, and with gigantic blobs of weld, fused the whole assembly together; it was crude beyond belief, but it was to last us all the way back to Foolow. In passing, I vaguely mentioned the problem with the bonnet. They were unfazed by this and within half an hour had made up a new set of bolts and once again the bonnet were fully operational. Their charges for this work? £4. I gave them the only note I had for 20,000 togrog, which related to about £8 or £9, and immediately had four friends for life.

Struggling back to the camp site just before midnight, I came across a huge ditch that I certainly hadn't come through on the way back up and, inevitably, got completely stuck. Fortunately, at that moment, the Clerk of the Course happened to be driving by and gave me a tow out.

When I got back to Yvonne, I heard all the horror stories of the evening.

By 8.30 pm only 35 cars had arrived out of the full rally complement of 134 cars. There were apparently scenes of devastation half way across Mongolia; all the support teams were completely exhausted and some of them didn't even return that evening. People were coming into the camp site at all times of the night. David and Adele Cohen, in the 1931 Model A Ford, who were in the garage when I left, couldn't find their way back to the camp site and had a nightmare in the rocky terrain, eventually arriving at 1.30 am. A chap in a huge American car had complained that the engine was overheating and the steering seemed to be a little heavy; once the bonnet had been lifted it was discovered that the engine mountings had disappeared, the engine had dropped and stretched the fanbelt which had snapped, and the engine had then sat down tight on top of the steering – no wonder he'd had over-heating and steering problems; I can't imagine what he's going to do. The last thing this evening was that we heard, disappointingly, that Dave and Jo had temporarily abandoned and were being trucked back to Ulaan Baatar.

Day 11 dawned and, upon unzipping the tent, it was welcoming to see the clear blue skies as the backcloth to this stunning campsite. A first look around made us realise how tough yesterday had been – there were very few rally cars in the camp. Only 65 cars made it to Khovd last night and, indeed, we were woken on several occasions hearing cars clattering and banging onto the camp site as though they were having their last gasps. Over breakfast everyone was talking about how tough yesterday had been, and there were tales aplenty of the classic car devastation which had been seen along the whole route. In fact, we heard that over 20 cars were on trucks and slowly make their way to the border and on to Russia, where it was hoped that substantial repairs could be made at our next rest-day stopover at Novosibirsk. Several of the rally organisers were heard making noises about poorly prepared rally cars, but the general consensus amongst the participants was that the route was simply too tough; the majority of contestants had followed all of the organisers' suggestions for car preparation but the fact that only 65 cars had made it to camp last night was a testament to just what conditions had been like.

Again, the general rumour was that timings for the day would be cancelled. However, the organisers had a different idea and, whilst all of the time trials for the day had been cancelled, the Main Control and Passage Control times still remained in place, albeit slightly relaxed. Today, being a relatively short day, the organisers were hoping that most people would limp to the border camp so that the rally could gather itself together as one large unit ready for the Russian border crossing. We heard a cracking piece of news this morning that we were twelfth overall and third in class which for us, given the hardships we had endured, was terrific news. Speaking to Mike, he was also delighted; he is eighth overall and first in class. He is looking a little weary this morning, however, as sorting out the broken suspension bracket took forever in Khovd town last night, and he didn't get back into the camp until 1.50 am!

This morning, as ever, Yvonne's first job was to collect our 'lunch' from the Nomad organisers. It may be recalled that these packed lunches were offered to us as a trade-off for the organisers not having to arrange our visas. The lunches generally proved to be a dismal failure. For a start we had constantly been warned by the organisers about eating anything but very fresh food – and yet what was happening was that we were being given sandwiches of an indeterminate meat which had been carted across the Gobi Desert day after day by our intrepid Nomad camp organisers and left out in the heat of the morning until we collected them. The sandwiches were supplemented by a piece of fruit and a biscuit; on a daily basis we, together with other rally crews, dispensed with our sandwiches once out in the open desert. I suspect there was a trail of very well-fed insects along the whole of our route.

Passing through Khovd town immediately after the start, it could be seen that every garage and workshop was crammed with rally cars; wherever you looked vehicles were being fettled and parts were being welded. My enduring memory of the drive through Khovd was of the flashing sparks from welding equipment as we passed down the main street. Jose and Maria in their MG Magnet were seen in a queue to a garage forecourt and we stopped to wish them good luck – particular as they were

Yvonne de-camping

We appear to have got the hang of river crossings

a member of our 'Dry Martinis' team which, to date, was highly successful.

The moment we left Khovd we slowly started to climb into the mountains, and back to the atrocious road conditions, sand, gravel, potholes, gravel, sand, potholes. Shooting along the huge valley bottom, we swept around a corner to find Pit and Frank in their 1966 Mercedes Saloon (complete with roof mounted 'taxi' sign!) standing in the road waving us down. I could see that Pit had something in his hands but it wasn't until we drew closer that I realised that it was the loose end of a tow rope. They had slid off the road and into a deep basin of sand, from which they couldn't extract themselves. The Mercedes had been flying and Pit and Frank were leading the rally, so it was imperative that they got out of the sand and continued to maintain their position. Rapidly, we connected the tow road to the towing eye on our front bumper and, within minutes, they were back on the road driving away from us as though we were standing still. The Mercedes was particularly well prepared and they rarely seemed to be having any trouble. A glimpse inside the cockpit of the Mercedes was quite interesting as there was a large computer screen mounted on the navigator's dashboard; Frank had managed to download the route onto Google Earth and therefore had a fascinating insight into the terrain they were crossing.

At this stage I should mention Australians, Mike and Anne Wilkinson in their 1951 Riley RMB Saloon. Mike had spent many, many hours preparing the car, and Anne had spent just as many hours decorating the car with Aboriginal symbols. The work had been beautifully done, and it

Bow wave

was useful for us as we could pick out their car from miles away. Mike and Anne were running one car in front of us so, inevitably, we were seeing them on a regular basis. Driving through the desert, both using our GPS systems and both navigators interpreting them slightly differently, we would suddenly see them veer off to either right or left and disappear from sight. Inevitably, some time later, we would see them again as our routes criss-crossed and weaved around following whatever track the GPS needle was pointing to. It was remarkable really that two cars taking part in the same rally should effectively take such significantly different routes, but nonetheless it

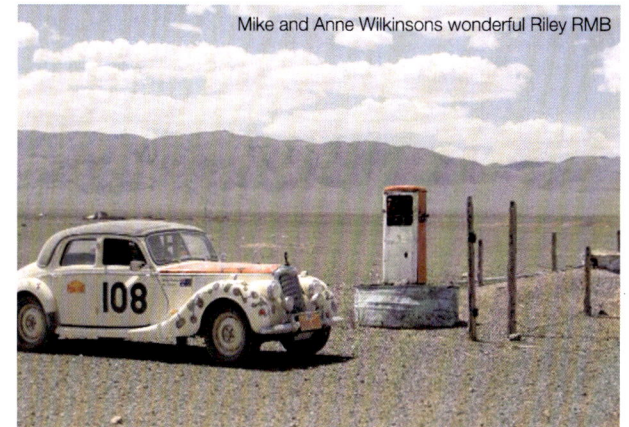

Mike and Anne Wilkinsons wonderful Riley RMB

was fascinating as it ensured that the rally was not in any way processional.

As the day progressed, the scenery started to change. From bone dry rock and sand we suddenly climbed over a mountain range where the ground surface became sweeping hills of pale green grass. The backcloth to the grasslands was snow-capped mountains and, occasionally, we caught a glimpse of an azure blue lake in the distance. Breathtaking scenery which demanded photo stops whenever a new vista appeared.

Go Richard, Go

Today was another day where we encountered a considerable number of river crossings. Coming across a particular stretch of river at high altitude, we followed what we assumed was the main track along to the edge of the river. Taking a deep breath and nudging into the water, we seemed to be going reasonably well when suddenly the front wheels hit a gully on the riverbed, the nose of the car dipped down and, with the suddenness of the jolt, I relaxed pressure on the accelerator with the inevitable conclusion that the engine cut out. As luck would have it a small local truck was nearby with the occupants enjoying probably their best day out in years watching the antics of these ancient cars as they tried to cross this unforgiving landscape. The Mongolian family backed up to the water's edge and indicated that if I could throw them a tow rope they would happily pull us out. Ah, the tow rope – now where had I put that? I remembered that I had left it in the boot in a place that was easy to get at for just these circumstances.

Now, at this stage, I decided that I had to make a stand on behalf of the drivers in the rally, and informed Yvonne that "tow rope and associated matters" were strictly the navigator's responsibility. We had a long and detailed discussion on the matter which must have lasted, oh, two or three seconds. The argument seemed to run on the lines of "do you want to do your own baking for the rest of your life, or what?"

Simon and Liz forge across in the remarkable 2CV

Gingerly opening the door I was relieved to see that the water level was fractionally below door cill level. I was wearing shorts so opted to step out into the river and wade round to the boot. Let me tell you that the river water at an altitude of 2,000 metres is exceedingly cold and, would you believe it, I just could not find the tow rope – it wasn't in the place I had expected it to be and it took what seemed like minutes of trawling through our luggage before I eventually found it. Quickly the rope was secured to our towing eye and, within moments we were back on dry land.

It doesn't look too deep from this angle! However........

At this precise moment a member of the rally organisation appeared from behind a large rock calling " - sorry about that, I mean't to wave to you to cross lower down where its much shallower…."

A squirt of the inevitable WD40, the car shook itself down like an enthusiastic sheepdog and, bidding goodbye to our rescuers, we set off again. This time, I left the tow rope clipped to the towing eye and wound the rope around the bumper – it was to act as an insurance policy as we were never to be stuck again. Glancing back in the mirror as we left the waterside, we saw our Mongolian family climbing back to their viewing point, enjoying the bags of sweets we had given them and eagerly awaiting the next river victim.

The last fifty kilometres was absolute hell, as we slowly banged and clattered our way over the rough, mountainous passes. Inevitably there was a bang and a clatter at one stage when the left side shock absorber eventually succumbed. It was only a short way to the camp site so we elected to cope with the clattering noise until I had the chance to remove it at the camp site. The camp site was, again, beautifully situated under a rim of mountains next to a cascading mountain stream and at the rally's highest altitude of 2,600 metres. It promised to be a chilly evening. Approaching the camp site we managed to get within 300 yards of the Nomads tents but then found crossing this final stretch to be almost impossible. The ground was criss-crossed with a myriad of ditches full of running water; each of these troughs was perhaps 2 ft. wide by 2 ft. deep and it was just impossible to drive across them. There was, of course, a route to the campsite but it was like a medieval Mongolian maze where one was driving up and down, finding dead ends and having to reverse. This last section of our day's journey was all the more frustrating as we were almost at the end of our tether after this long, tough day, and it was so frustrating being able to see the smooth green grass of the camp area, but finding it so difficult to reach.

Nonetheless, the moment we arrived, Yvonne whizzed the tent up in expert fashion whilst I did my spanner check under the car. Apart from the shattered shock absorber, which I removed, the only other damage for the day was that all three rubber support bobbins on the exhaust system had sheared, so I replaced all of

The quite stunning run-in to the Mongolian-Russian border

those using up the last of my spares. Remarkably, given the remoteness of our location up in the mountains, we suddenly were besieged by Mongolian youngsters, some who were dashing around the camp, giggling, shouting and generally trying to comprehend the scene, and teenagers who were picking up and playing with tools as crews were doing their spanner checks. There was a lot of discussion amongst competitors as people were concerned about security and, eventually, the organisers managed to shepherd the children to a 'holding area' at the edge of the campsite. The end of the day saw us have a substantial aperitif and another good dinner, courtesy of the Nomads. As we left the canteen tent, wearing a warm glow, we realised that it was going to be an extremely cold night. It's at such times that we realised that the money expended in buying our 'top-of-the-range' sleeping bag was money well spent – we had a great night's sleep.

Chapter 11

SIBERIA - Day 12 Tsagaannuur To Bijsk 635 kms.

An early start again this morning, with a long distance to travel but, more immediately a major border crossing to navigate. Navigating the velvety Mongolian maize again, we slowly made our way the 14 kilometres to the Mongolian border where, following instructions, all of the cars hade to line up in numerical order. What a shattered collection; a considerable number of cars are on trucks standing by the wayside and many more are continuously being worked on as we stand in this interminable queue. There were stories of devastation yet again from the day before. By midnight last night, only 80 cars had arrived at the camp, with 55 cars still out on the road. Many people chose to put the cars on trucks and there were all sorts of stories about hugely inflated prices to truck cars. Someone was asked for 10,000 Euros to truck the car to the next town, although they eventually managed to negotiate this right down to 1,000 Euros. Some crews drove right through the night and, indeed, as we were having breakfast, four cars crawled into the camp, pausing just briefly enough to join us for breakfast before wearily inching their way towards the border post.

The interminable queue for the Mongolian border

The border was on the edge of the desert – possible one of the most remote border posts in the world. There was a small village with an assortment of old, tumble-down timber cottages, and the whole of the village had turned out to welcome us.

Inevitably, in this lonesome outpost, the whole of the rally was held to ransom by an immaculately dressed Mongolian soldier, who controlled his border crossing with an iron fist and a meticulous attention to detail that would have befitted Checkpoint Charlie. Slowly, oh, so slowly, the line advanced towards the border gate, only eventually to be stopped altogether when the wooden and barbed wire gates were ponderously closed whilst our customs officer retired for 'morning coffee'. For two-and-a-half hours we waited before eventually easing through the Mongolian border and heading across the stretch of no-man's land towards the Russian Customs Post. If this was what it was like getting out of Mongolia, what on earth would we be confronted with at the Russian Border.

Pulling away from the gates on a long, straight gradient, we came across Mike and Anne in the Australian Riley, stuck on the hill with no power whatsoever. Mike had been having continual carburetion problems. We hitched up the tow rope but, sadly, just didn't seem to have the muscle to pull them. There was an awful smell of burning clutch plate, so regrettably we had to abandon them to await attention from the Service Crew. Whilst I was standing by the side of our car disconnecting the tow rope, I took a look at the front and was alarmed to see that the front off-side wheel was leaning at a fairly jaunty angle – clearly something we needed to get fixed in the not-too-distant future.

The Russian Border

17 Kilometres down the road and we espied the Russian Border; an immaculate, modern building looking starkly out of place in this barren landscape, and what's that we see just beyond the border - the sight of delicious, smooth, black tarmac – level and pothole free. Stealing ourselves for a long wait, we inched through the queue, being directed to drive through the antiseptic wash to the border post itself. Apart from the Customs Officers wearing perhaps the silliest military hats we have ever seen, they were efficiency personified; every car was handed a plastic document case with the individual rally number, and within ten minutes we were out on the open road, sampling smooth running for the first time in what felt like weeks. Being a bit short of petrol and knowing we had a huge day in front of us, the first job was to pull up at a petrol station and squeeze 78 litres into the tank. At £1.70 a gallon this was the bargain of a lifetime. Rolling along with a full tank, and Yvonne preparing our mid-morning snack of crackers and pesto spread, I reflected on the last four or five nights' camping. Before the trip, the camping had been a concern – to Yvonne in particular. The outcome was exactly the opposite; the camping was brilliant; the locations without exception, breathtaking; the food was excellent; the showers were a godsend, and the Nomad team looked after us as five-star guests.

Setting off into Siberia, we really didn't know what to expect, but what we found was quite extraordinary; it was just as though we had been dropped into central Europe. It was astounding to come across such an amazing transition between two countries. From barren but beautiful mountain ranges, we were transported into Swiss or Austrian look-a-like surroundings; sweeping hillsides covered in pine forests; snow-capped mountains; wide tumbling and cascading clear rivers. With a hundred

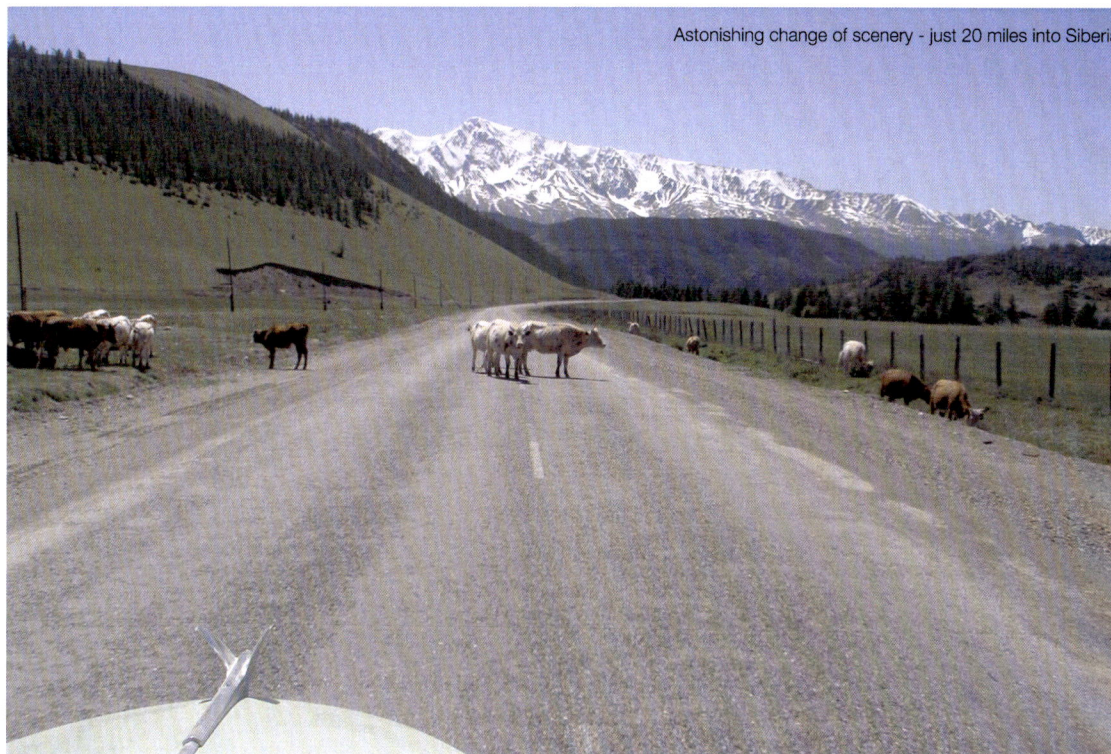
Astonishing change of scenery - just 20 miles into Siberia

miles behind us, we pulled over to a little roadside café and had a very civilised, heavily sweetened coffee, followed by a very uncivilised toilet stop – the inevitable plank over a hole in the ground. In fact, this particular 'loo' was more unusual than most - with matching doors side by side, each with its individual gender symbol. Imagine Yvonne's surprise when, upon cautiously opening one of the doors, she found that there was no dividing wall inside! Over coffee we talked to a couple of competitors in a pre-War car who were bemoaning the fact that they'd had four punctures since the Russian border; they were running on Blockley tyres which had been a nightmare; over twenty punctures since the rally started. They had phoned ahead and, hopefully, a cache of tyres will be flown into Novosibirsk in a couple of days' time.

Bounding down the hill from our coffee stop, I noticed that the car seemed to be wandering around a little, followed by a knocking from the front nearside wheel that was rapidly getting worse. I leapt out to discover that all of the wheel nuts on this wheel were loose; one had snapped off altogether. I immediately headed for the tool kit only to find (as I see from my notes) "….some bugger has stolen the wheelbrace." Maybe that relates to the security problem with the kids last night – we shall never know. I managed to find another spanner that fitted but, to my horror, when tightening them up another of the studs snapped off, so we were now running on three wheel nuts out of five and clearly needed to find a solution. Within 5 kilometres we managed to find a garage in a small village, up a lane just off our route.

The bearded young fellow who ran the garage immediately set-to, but with his primitive equipment it took him almost three hours to drill out the two studs, make two more and then weld them into position. Meanwhile, Yvonne entertained the local children who had

Our Siberian saviour

gathered with her efforts to speak Russian by trying to formulate phrases from the useful phrasebook guide we had brought with us; communication was almost impossible but the garage was ringing with laughter as a good time was had by all. Eventually, at 8.25 in the evening, he finished and charged me the princely sum of £4 – what a star. However, we now have the thick end of 180 miles to do. Once under way, Yvonne started preparing our 'haute cuisine' dinner of crackers with vegetable spread, followed by pieces of the rich fruit cake she had brought with us. Realising that we would be very late in, Yvonne rang the rally organisers who confirmed that our hotel room would still be available. Darkness fell and was accompanied by a light drizzle. Suddenly, it was pitch black and we encountered a problem which we hadn't experienced before not having driven the car too often at night. The ancient laminated windscreen seemed to deflect and distort the oncoming car headlights with the effect that it was incredibly distracting. This 180 miles turned into a horror drive which I hated intensely and I think, as we slowly eased into Bijrsk after midnight, I was more tired than I had ever been in my life, Sadly, for once, our GPS didn't want to play properly when we got into the town, but a friendly policeman in a passing car realised we were lost and escorted us to the city to the car parking site.

Tonight, the cars were to be parked in a central location with all the competitors being bussed off to a variety of hotels. By now, it was 1.00 am and at that time of the night, the last thing we needed was a long coach trip around the outskirts of a harsh industrial city in Eastern Russia in bucketing rain. Worse was to come. We arrived at the Hotel Vostok which, I can honestly say, was the worst accommodation I have ever stayed in in my entire life. Leaving the reception, we climbed up the stairs, each floor level getting significantly worse the higher we got, until we reached our floor. No floor covering, dark brown, battered, shabby bedroom doors, two single beds made out of chipboard, one small paper-thin sheet and evil-looking blankets, only one small black striped handtowel in the bathroom, where the floor covering was peeling up and the open shower tray was so badly cracked, that Yvonne thought it had been vandalised. If we'd had the car nearby we would have brought in our sleeping bags, but the car was 30 minutes' bus drive away, so we crawled wearily into bed at 1.45 am and slipped away into a deep sleep.

Hotel Vostok facilities

A rude awakening. A large Russian women came striding down the corridor, banging on all the doors at 6.00 am to wake us all up. This seemed a real intrusion, given our late arrival last night and the fact that our departure time wasn't until 10.45 this morning. We decided to ignore her and rolled over for an extra hour. We eventually stumbled downstairs at 7.30 am and enjoyed a little scene, which probably reflected a small snapshot of how communism worked many years ago - striving to provide employment for everyone. As we wandered into the breakfast room we were handed a ticket by one young girl, which we then had to hand over to a young man sitting only a couple of metres away, who proceeded to neatly file it away! Breakfast was a surreal experience; we were served an unusual combination of Spam and mashed potatoes, followed by a fine dish comprising a teaspoon-full of tinned peas, half an egg and a blob of mayonnaise, five slices of bread, half a teaspoon-full of jam and a cup of the wateriest coffee ever tasted. Breakfast was served by a selection of young girls, who had clearly spent far longer preparing their dress and make-up than they had preparing breakfast. Their hairstyles were flamboyant, make-up totally extreme with scarlet lipstick, nine-inch deep mini skirts and five inch high stilettos. They all looked as if they had just finished a night-shift in some other nearby local establishment. We were delighted to eventually leave the Vostok behind us; it was the worst hotel of the whole rally and, frankly, made the camping exploits of the last six nights, seem positively luxurious.

After being bussed back to the main secure carpark on this grey, damp morning, I took another look at the front wheel which was starting to lean at a quite alarming angle. I had a word with Peter Banham but he was, yet again, overwhelmed with work and suggested it would be better to leave the problem until tomorrow's rest day in Novosibirsk. So, nothing more to do. We wandered off and had a cup of coffee with Mike and Sarah O'Shea but I couldn't settle as I needed to know how serious the wheel problem was. Eventually, I persuaded Andy Inskip to take a look and in a jiffy he had the wheel off and at least was able to identify the problem. It was our old friend the gudgeon pin which had come loose at the other end of the wishbone and, through the constant vibration, had worn the original circular hole into an elongated oval hole. Andy felt that we were OK to continue for the day and suggested we took it easy. However, we lost twenty minutes setting off, although Yvonne had checked us out on our correct start time. As we were still running on our Gold medal position, we needed to be sure we could catch up some time. Initially, the road out of Bijsk was very much like last night – more holes than tarmac, but soon we were out on the open road and able to make up a bit of time. The road was a strange mixture of good, long sections of decent tarmac then, suddenly with no warning, huge holes that would have swallowed a donkey. With our lack of shock absorbers the car seemed to take a terrible pounding every time one of these holes caught us out. To compound the misery of driving on these horrendous stretches of road, it had now started to rain and our vacuum wipers were, again, playing up, with one sweep whenever they felt like it, in fact it became a game between us trying to guess when the wiper blade would actually move!

This morning there was a rumour of the possibility of foreshortening the journey a little by taking a main road rather than the side roads indicated in the route book. However, we were wise to this and were sure there would be a secret check on the loop road. In any case, I am always of the opinion that if rally organisers choose a given route, why would you not follow it? Inevitably, after 40 or 50 miles we did come across a secret checkpoint and those who chose to take the quicker main road route would have missed this and possibly endangered their medal status.

The drizzle continued all morning until our lunchtime stop, which was a roadside shack in a layby. I was still shattered after yesterday evening's drive and, whilst Yvonne went off down the road with one or two other crews for a sandwich, I opted for a snooze. Just as my eyes were closing, I glanced at the mileometer and noted that it read 6,666.6 miles; I appreciate now that it doesn't seem to have much significance, but strangely it seemed a satisfying statistic as I slowly slipped into a deep sleep.

The afternoon's drive was relatively straightforward; it was through typical Siberian countryside that we were to become extremely familiar with over the next four or five days. The land was almost completely flat and comprised large groups of trees interspersed with huge areas of grassland with sporadic settlements, with surprisingly pretty, although somewhat dilapidated, traditional timber Russian houses. Initially, we wondered why such vast, flat grasslands were not more cultivated, but, of course, eventually realized that we were in Siberia where, with its notorious winters, it clearly was not able to sustain any form of agriculture.

The last 180 mile run into Novosibirsk was on decent roads and passed without incident. However, it did give me some time to think over how I could solve the problem of the oval hole in the wishbone. It occurred to me that I could have a crescent-shaped piece of metal cut which could then be welded around the oval hole to reform it to a circular shape. This was one of the little jobs I had planned for tomorrow's rest day.

Novosibirsk, with a population of 1.5 million people, was huge, uninteresting and full of traffic, but the hotel Sibir was excellent and welcoming. The evening was simplicity itself; a few beers in the bar, an excellent meal – very civilised indeed; we slept like logs.

Yesterday evening the organisers advised us that the local Landrover dealership had offered servicing and workshop facilities for all of the rally cars, so we breakfasted early and were soon scurrying across Novosibirsk behind our taxi, hired to show us the route. Our first disappointment was that we were quite clearly completely ripped off by the taxi driver, who charged us 1,000 roubles (about £20) for our ten minute journey. We later heard during the day that other people had been charged as little as 50 roubles for the identical trip! Our second disappointment was that the scene as we arrived at the garage was one of total mayhem. Clearly, many crews had breakfasted much earlier than us and the carpark was simply log-jammed with rally cars, all trying to fight their way towards the workshop bays, with requirements for various elements of work ranging from ten-minute quick fixes to virtual car rebuilds! To add to the scene that confronted us, I also was very aware that there seemed to be more men in smart suits swanning around than there were men in overalls. The scene rapidly grew quite ugly as people fought for their own interests and there were even stories of fisticuffs happening at the front of the queue. Yvonne and I rapidly decided this definitely was not for us, and made other plans. I nipped around the back of the Landrover dealership with my bagful of broken shock absorber pieces and was more than delighted to discover that Landrover Defender shock absorbers are almost identical. Within a few minutes I had purchased two new shock absorbers for the princely sum of £120 and we soon nosed out of the car park to look for someone else who could help us fit them.

David Cohen in his Model A Ford similarly decided he was appalled by the goings-on in the garage and we set off together. After just half a mile, I spotted a large pair of garage doors which were covered top to bottom in hub caps nailed onto the timber surface; this was the sort of garage I was looking for. We banged on the doors and were immediately surrounded by enthusiastic young mechanics who were just so keen to help. Within what seemed like seconds, the car was jacked up and our problems were discussed in much detail. However, all the mechanics disappeared as rapidly as they had arrived, and I was left with one chap with a mobile phone and a smattering of English. Confusingly, he told me that they couldn't do the work, but that he had a friend with a much bigger and better garage who would be able to help us out. He leapt onto a motor bike and we followed him for ten minutes before bumping and crashing over some railway lines into quite the shabbiest garage; bigger it was, better it wasn't! Nonetheless we were, again, greeted by boundless enthusiasm from everyone in the garage. The two cars they were working on were immediately bundled out of the garage, and the Chevy was soon over the pits with three men working on her. Our new shock absorbers were deftly fixed into position and they cobbled up our old brackets to support the bottom pin. My idea of the crescent-shape infill for the oval hole on the wishbone was sketched rapidly onto the back of a cigarette packet and a hunt around the scrapheap at the back of the garage produced an adequate lump of metal from which they cut a very approximate crescent shape with a welding gun and, within minutes, sparks were flying and it was welded into position. Buoyed by all this activity, I decided that these chaps were too good to miss so whilst they were beavering away, Yvonne and I wandered across the railway tracks and found a motor factor who was able to fix us up with some oil. We had a full oil change and changed the oil filter. I took off the oil bath, washed the thick Gobi desert sand out of the bottom with paraffin and momentarily wondered about sending a sample of this foul, black, soggy mess back to Adrian Bailey as a present with the message "this is what oil bath filters are supposed to do". However, the moment passed, and I didn't do it.

Two and a half hours and £30 later we were finished. Fantastic value for money and all thanks to these enthusiastic, young Russian mechanics who bade us goodbye with a quick wave, then turned to David who had been patiently waiting behind us. We enjoyed the luxury of Chevy cruisin' back to the hotel on our smart, new shock absorbers; we had a civilized sandwich lunch in the hotel and did some housekeeping. Yvonne washed more clothes, checked our emails, updated our blog, whilst I shovelled the worst of the sand out of the car, and generally had a major clean up inside ready for a fresh start tomorrow.

We were on the crest of a wave; the car was sorted, cleaned up inside, all our office work had been completed and we decided to treat ourselves to a meal out, just the two of us. After an aperitif in the bar, we ambled through the pleasant, open shopping areas of Novosibirsk, eventually settling on a small Chinese restaurant that was a little like an upmarket takeaway. Our pleasant evening was topped off with an espresso and a long chat with Jon and David Goodwin in the hotel bar before slipping very satisfied off to bed. A great day today, with a job well done.

Up with the lark today, at 6.00 am. Checked out at 7.00 am and left at 9.45 am. I never quite got my head around why we needed to be up so early but, with a great flush of enthusiasm, I nipped outside before breakfast to wash the car. It was a lovely, crisp morning and I decided it was a real feel-good factor to start with a clean, shiny car.

Breakfasts, now we were in hotels for the rest of the trip, were quite fascinating. Everybody did a lap of the buffet choosing their breakfast items, but then, when breakfast was eaten, all the navigators took a second trip around the buffet picking up delicacies that could be had for lunch later in the day. Initially, people were really quite surreptitious, but as the rally wore on, inhibitions were dropped and people were quite merrily packing bread into large polythene bags and even making sandwiches at the buffet table ready to pack into lunch boxes. Everything disappeared, cereal, fruit, bread, sliced meat, hard-boiled eggs, yoghurts, soft drinks etc. Even flasks were filled with coffee. The hotel management must have thought we were a hungry lot.

This morning I decided to lodge a query with the organisers. For some obscure reason, we were listed as almost six hours behind the front runners on the rally, and I really could not understand how this could be. Whilst we had experienced our problems with suspension etc. in Mongolia, it rarely delayed us too long as we were always up with the front runners and well inside our maximum lateness period each day. The only thing that had happened was that when we were attempting to be fairly careful on the time trials we had dropped a few minutes here and there, but never six hours' worth!

It was a magnificently clear morning as we eased our way through the mid-morning work rush hour traffic . Today was a long day ahead of us but once out of the city the roads opened up and, for once, were of reasonable quality; we simply plodded on all day on a virtual straight road through the heart of Siberia. Identical countryside, patches of trees, patches of open grassland, patches of trees again. No signs of villages, towns,

houses, people or animals. It really was an extraordinary area of countryside; neither beautiful nor memorable – just repetitive, mile after mile after mile. At one stage, tiredness swept over me and we pulled off the road for 40 minutes so that I could have a doze in the car whilst Yvonne had a walk around. The route book seemed to have us arriving in Omsk at 11.00 pm but the organisers had announced that timing was relaxed for the day and we were able to make up time without any penalties for being early. The outcome was that we arrived four hours early, cruising into Omsk at about 7.00pm.

Omsk is a delightful city on the Irtysh river with majestic buildings with gold towers, cathedrals and fine architectural edifices. Once the capital of Siberia, it was the commercial and trading hub of Eastern Europe, until the communist regime took control and moved the capital back to Novosibirsk.

The hotel was just fine – extremely modern at ground level, but the quality of rooms got worse the higher the floors went. We were to learn that this was a common feature of Russian hotels, and when the accommodation was nearer the clouds than the ground, unsubstantiated rally rumour said that it was all to do with the 'deals'

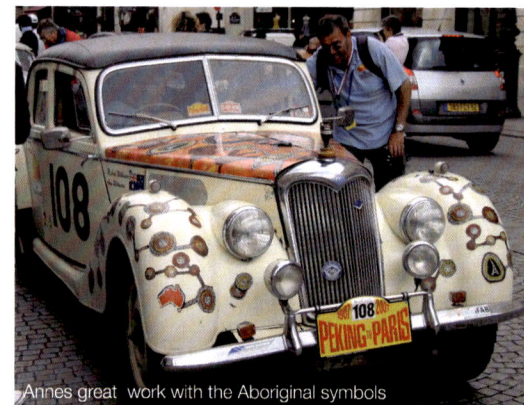
Annes great work with the Aboriginal symbols

Philip Young had struck! Today, needless to say, we were on floor six! Soon installed, we took a walk around town and I was able to find some great hand cream for cracked hands and feet. Indeed it was so good that I have constantly been on the look out for the identical cream in the UK but to no avail. A gentle drink in the bar with team mates Jose and Maria, dinner with John and Joan and we both slept like tops.

Today was to be another long plod through almost identical countryside. The highlight of the mid morning was a checkpoint located in quite the seediest truck stop I have ever seen. However, we were given the good news that there was an extra hour on our timing schedule for the day to make the evening control a little easier. Lunch was, as ever, taken on the move with our hardboiled eggs, crispbreads and banana, and Yvonne was just dusting off the remnants of lunch which somehow had glued itself to my front, when there was that familiar noise of metal grinding along tarmac from my side of the car. Pulling into the roadside, I looked to discover that the bracket holding the bottom of the shock absorber had once more snapped off with the result that the shock absorber was trailing on the ground. Overalls were donned, the toolkit extracted and I set off to remove the offending article. The top of the shock absorber was simply a threaded pin, the top of which was squared off to take a spanner. It was almost impossible to stop the whole shock absorber rotating but I

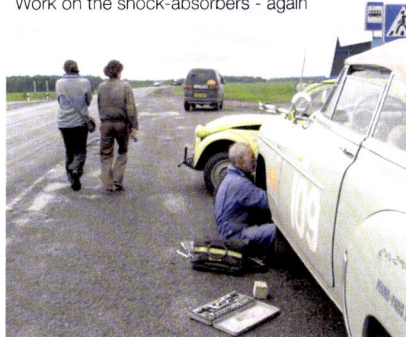
Work on the shock-absorbers - again

eventually discovered that, by locking a pair of mole grips onto this squared off pin, I was able to free the unit and attempt to drop it out through the centre of the coil spring. However, of course, mechanical equipment often never does what it is supposed to do and, because I couldn't collapse the length of the shock absorber, the only move was to jack up the wishbone and collapse the coil spring, thereby giving sufficient space. The issue, however, was that the car was jacked up on our one and only jack and we had no means of raising the wishbone. Heroically, Yvonne flagged down a young Russian couple who indicated that they had a jack, but it took them almost twenty minutes to extract what appeared to be all of their worldly goods from the car boot to eventually produce a poor quality jack that simply bent under the strain of trying to lift the whole front end of the Chevy. Whilst the young

couple were disappointed, he and his wife happily posed draped over the front of the car for photographs before shooting off into the distance. Fortunately, David and Adele Cohen pulled over and produced a car jack that seemed substantially older than their 1931 Ford, nonetheless it worked superbly and, in a jiffy, the wishbone was cranked upwards, the shock absorber slid out of place, and we were back on the road in no time at all. I made a mental note to buy a new bottle jack and throw away the stupid jack that came with the car.

As the day wore on, the weather got greyer and greyer and eventually drizzly rain took us all the way to Tyumen, where we arrived at 7.00 pm well inside our scheduled time. Pulling up to check in outside the wonderful, smart, modern headquarters hotel, Yvonne discovered to her horror that we were, in fact, billeted into another hotel at the other side of town. Inevitably, it was dreadful; it was called the Yutnai, which we re-named the 'Yucknai' for the rest of our stay. We made a note that the room was a significant improvement on the Vostok but, there again, anything would be. The route notes to the hotel were extremely complex, but we appeared to be the only rally car to find it without getting lost; everyone else arrived damp, dispirited and highly irritated. As ever, the evening improved enormously and, whilst we needed a route map to find the restaurant, a couple of drinks in the bar and an excellent meal with Mike and Josie and John and Joan, suddenly made the day feel a whole lot better.

Way behind us Jo is having a tough time in the desert

We managed nine and a half hours sleep last night, despite the most amazing duvet which started just under our armpits and finished just below our knees. Nonetheless, endurance rallying certainly guarantees being ready for a good night's sleep. It was a grey, miserable and damp morning, and the dining room presented us with a similarly grey, miserable and damp breakfast, which we toyed with for a few minutes, before deciding to give best and head back to the smart headquarters hotel; this proved to be an excellent decision and there was ample time to partake of a first class breakfast with all the lucky souls who had stayed there last night.

Today was a relatively relaxed day, and we were standing outside when Jose noticed that every time I dabbed the accelerator, the distributer was slightly rotating, and I had a moment or two whittling until Andy Inskip, who happened to be passing by, said he reckoned that's how it should be anyway. Apparently, it's on a vacuum arrangement with a vacuum adjuster! This all sounded like 'double-Dutch' to me, but if this was how it was supposed to be, that was OK with me. Nonetheless, the car seems to be spluttering and popping a bit this morning, and I think tonight it will need fresh plugs and points changing and I made a mental note to ensure that was my first job.

This was another day of long, flat plains with lush pastures and, again, very little civilisation to be seen. The first 50 kilometres of road were quite smooth, but then the road started to break up dramatically and we were weaving our way around extremely muddy stretches and rough pot holes which seemed to stretch for mile after mile. Noticeably, the truck traffic was picking up and it was necessary to weave around these trucks whenever we could, otherwise we would not stand a chance of making our schedule for the day.

Eventually, Yekaterinburg arrived on the horizon with a blur of magnificent gold minarets, and we were cruising along the elegant dual carriageway to the secure car park in front of the sports centre, where we were welcomed by the local car club which gave us a great reception.

On the run-in to Yekaterinberg, there was a really concerning accident, serving to make us all realise that you can never let your guard down. It will be recalled that Jan Voboril had thrown his navigator out of his car in Ulaan Baatar, claiming utter incompetence. From UB onwards, Jan had, amazingly,

Jan Voborils Lancia Theta

driven the rest of the event on his own. Whenever he reached the outskirts of a township, when navigation proved awkward, Jan's technique was to pull over on the roadside, await another rally car, and simply follow on.

Here, on the outskirts of Yekaterinberg, he had picked up Mike and Sarah's Jaguar as his lead car. All was well, until near the centre of town, crossing a substantial main road, Mike saw a gap in the traffic and darted through it. Jan's 1916 Lancia Theta was a bit low on 'darting', with the effect that, when he reached the said gap – a tram had filled it! The resounding crash damaged, not only the tram but, a passing Mercedes too. Unsurprisingly, Jan's front suspension and steering became somewhat re-designed, and there was great misery as it looked as though this might be the end of Jan's trip. Mercifully no-one was hurt, but the traffic system in downtown Yekaterinberg took some time to return to normal.

Within the last mile or two, I had heard grinding noises coming from under the car and, upon pulling up at the finish, I was horrified to discover how low the car was sitting on the road. I swung my leg out of the driving seat and the car park surface arrived much earlier than it should have done. I glanced around the back of the car and spotted that the mud flaps, which were normally a couple of inches clear of the road, were in fact trailing three inches onto the tarmac. A quick look under the car revealed the problem immediately – both rear leaf springs had snapped. I decided the first thing to do was to get Yvonne and our luggage to the hotel in the centre of Yekaterinburg. There was a rest day tomorrow and it was an opportunity for Yvonne to unpack some gear and wash our clothing. My low spirits were momentarily lifted when we arrived at the hotel, which was a superb, modern edifice in the centre of Yekaterinburg, and our room was first class.

Explaining my problem to the receptionist, who spoke particularly good English, she immediately tracked down a garage, ordered a taxi for me and explained to the driver what his role was. I followed the taxi driver 8 or 10 kilometres out of town, where he eventually pulled up outside the local Lada main dealership. This was not what I had been expecting as, by now, I had come to the conclusion that small garages run by independent owners were the best bet. I paid the taxi driver and was standing outside wondering what to do next, when amazingly a chap in a smart suit stepped out of the reception and spoke to me in faultless English asking what he could do to help. Vladimir, as I later learned, was a Professor of Science from Yekaterinburg University, who was at the garage waiting for his car to be serviced. He had been there since 11.00 am and it was now 5.00 pm (so no different from UK garages, then!) They seemed to have a much higher patience level in Russia than we do in England. Vladimir introduced me to the service manager, who appeared to be a typical Russian character with a completely deadpan expression. Vladimir explained to him what I wanted and I kept my eyes glued to the service manager's face to see if I could detect from his expression whether he was going to help or not. With my heart in my mouth, I asked Vladimir whether they would be able to help, and was much relieved when he said "but of course, no problems at all". They would do everything I needed. Immediately, the service manager called up two or three of his staff, cars were wheeled out of one of the bays, and the Chevy was soon set upon by an enthusiastic team of four chaps. They immediately stripped off the rear springs and were much relieved to discover that I was carrying spares of not only the long outer spring but also the additional spare leaf. The existing springs were removed, completely taken apart, new clamps made and eventually refitted back to the car. Meanwhile, two other chaps came along and started to weld up our front shock absorber plates once again, whilst two more fellows came along, did a complete spanner check under the car and pumped grease into every known orifice. When the car was started up one of the mechanics realised that the engine sounded a little rough, so two or three of them spent half an hour changing the plugs and tuning the engine. It was getting quite late by now – almost 9.30 pm – and Vladimir was still with me. He simply enjoyed the experience of being able to speak English and he and I formed a close bond, drank umpteen cups of coffee together and eventually exchanged email addresses before he picked up his car at 10.00 pm and left. Clearly, the Department of Science wasn't busy that day. When I wandered back into the workshop bay, to my surprise the car had disappeared, but I found it just round the corner, being soaped, washed, leathered and cleaned inside. Finally, all the tyre pressures were checked before the full ensemble of mechanics gathered together for a ten-minute photo session. I took photos of them, they took photos of me, they all took photos of each other and I was given a hat as a reminder of my time at the garage. The bill for my six-hour stay and use of ten mechanics was 2,000 rubels, about £40. Finally, they announced that they would drive me back to the hotel because it was a long way back and I realised that I had no idea of the route. One of the mechanics got in the car with me and the rest piled into a small truck whereupon we drove at about 60 mph back into the centre of Yekaterinburg. The mechanic travelling with me, Ivan, couldn't seem to take his eyes off the keyring in the car. Fastened to the keyring was a small Leatherman's multi-tool that Keith had given me as a keepsake before we left. As we all bade fond goodbyes on the pavement, Ivan asked me if it would be possible to have the Leathermans. On one hand, I was disappointed to lose it, but given the terrific help they had all given I felt it was the least I could do. What an amazingly memorable night, Vladimir, Ivan et al, we shall always remember you. 11.00 pm and Yvonne and I had a quick bite, a hot coffee and slipped off to the luxury of our room knowing that once again the car was sorted.

At last the term "rest day" had some meaning for us. After the marathon session on the car last night, we were determined to play the role of tourists for a day and take in some of the sights in Yekaterinburg. Nonetheless, I could not resist the temptation to nip down into the car park and see how well the tuning of the Chevy had worked out. Low and behold, it started first push, which was a great feeling; I removed the key determined to have the rest of the day as a car-free-zone.

Jonathan and Adams Itala sucumbs - again

We had a long, luxurious breakfast with Mike and Sarah O'Shea and spent a bit of time catching up with rally news. It was great to hear that David Spurling and his son, Jonathan, in their 1953 Morgan Plus 4 had at long last caught up with the rally, after spending three days totally lost in the desert section; having run desperately short of water, they were eventually tracked down by one of the back-up crews and,

following a bit of trucking and some spirited driving, were now back with us. Also Albert Eberhard in his 1926 yellow Rolls-Royce Silver Ghost, had rejoined us, although he has had a torrid time and most of the repairs he had carried out have been less than successful. Judging by Albert's tempestuous rant at the hotel receptionist last night for something trivial like having the wrong coloured duvet on his bed (!) he has presumably worked out that he has several more significant problems to overcome before he makes Paris.

Many other cars had been picked up in the desert and, clearly, many thousands of roubles had changed hands to welcoming Russian truck drivers, as a significant number of crews took the opportunity to short-cut some of the journey in an effort to get to Yekaterinburg where local garages were full to bursting. Jose and Marie in their MG Magnette and Denis and Jill in their wonderful yellow 1927 Rolls Royce had both constantly been plagued with fuel starvation problems and, having overheard my eulogies about the Lada garage, immediately rented a taxi and set off to experience the same success that we had. I only hoped that Vladimir wasn't still there waiting for his car to be serviced!

During our languorous breakfast, John and Joan wandered in. They were staying around the corner at the rally headquarters and, obviously, the breakfast there wasn't quite as sumptuous as ours. They did, however, bring with them exceedingly disappointing news; the organisers, in their wisdom, had cancelled one of the timed days, five days ago, in Mongolia. At that time, it had been announced that they were going to rigorously maintain the daily timing but eliminate the time trials. As it transpired one or two people, who didn't have English as their first language, didn't fully understand, and the outcome was that the organisers had cancelled the whole day. The effect of which was that we had dropped four places from 7th to 11th, which was an incredible disappointment. Needless to say, conversation around the breakfast table became very frenzied, as we worked out that five percent of rally crews who didn't seem to understand the instructions, had affected 95% of us who did, and who drove 'flat out' for hour after hour to meet our times. This really was a blow to our morale, so several teams wandered over to rally HQ and lodged complaints with Kim Bannister, the Clerk of the Course. We seemed to get absolutely nowhere with our arguments but, I suspected, this issue might run and run.

Yekaterinburg is a huge cosmopolitan city with a population of 1.3 million, and is the economic and cultural capital of the Urals region. The Urals have vast mineral wealth and this is, clearly, evident from the economic boom in the city, with many designer shops and trendy bars. Yekaterinburg is probably most famously known for its bloody history, with the execution of Tsar Nicholas II and his family in 1918; the site of the massacre was in the basement of a local merchant's house. Today, the site is marked with an iron cross and an enormous Byzantine-style church, topped with a glittering array of gold-leaf covered domes named, chillingly, the Church of the Blood.

Yvonne and I spent a quiet day wandering the tree-planted boulevards of the city, walking down the banks of the majestic, fast-flowing river, before eventually deciding we really would like a civilised afternoon coffee. Heading back towards the shopping areas we happened upon a particularly extravagant building which, once we had entered, was reminiscent of Harrods or Harvey Nichols; it comprised a huge arcade full of designer shops selling expensive and trendy clothing, together with a magnificent patisserie. Eerily, the whole place was empty, with the exception of the coffee shop which was humming. We never fathomed this particular development as it seemed somewhat of a contrast, certainly with our anticipation of what we would find in the heart of Russia.

A memorable, traditional, Russian meal in a very fine, traditional, restaurant with Richard and Nicola completed our rest day.

Czars resting place

A great piece of news this morning; the service crews have been working non-stop on Jan's Lancia Theta, and here he is on the start line.

8.40 am, and we're off, on a warm, dry day. Our joys of yesterday were a trifle short-lived, however, as negotiating the ferociously potholed road, the front shock absorber came adrift almost immediately. We had done about 35 miles. However, I'm becoming quite adept at shock absorber removal and, within minutes, the shocker was whipped off and hurled into the boot. As we wander along this

The skyline was left behind

shocking roads, Yvonne and I chat and decide that, strangely, the shock absorbers don't seem to make too much difference so, maybe, we'll run without them for a while and save decisions on what has to be done until a little later.

The driving was enjoyable when sections of the road were in decent condition but, unfortunately, most of the roads were terrible and we spent most of the time trying to avoid one pothole after another. This area certainly lived up to its reputation for atrocious roads; it was effectively one hole joining up with another and again I spent most of the day clinging onto the steering wheel trying to levitate with the misguided idea that, by not sitting firmly in the driving seat I am, in some obscure way, lessening the impact! Work that one out, clearly the hot sun is getting to me.

However, the hot sun eased, the clouds rolled in and shortly the rain commenced; not particularly heavy, but persistent. So, we decided to pause, put the hood up and

enjoy a bit of comfort and warmth for a few miles. We pulled up and, with the engine ticking over, I pulled the knob that activates the hood. There was a strange clicking noise from the frame as though somehow the metal framework has become overlapped with itself within the folds of the hood. Eventually, with Yvonne standing on the seat, pushing and prising, we managed to erect the hood but, to our dismay found that a metal rail had pulled away from the main framework and torn a corner of the hood. We sat and looked at each other thinking, yet again, how the car seemed to be jinxed. The moment we solve one problem, another problem immediately arises, and we never seem to run, even for half a day, without something else to occupy our minds.

As the day got darker and danker, our route took us off the open plains into the town of Kungar, en route for the Kungar Ice Caves. This grey, foreboding town was extremely unwelcoming – the pot holes got deeper and were filled with glutinous black mud which, eventually, wrapped itself around our windscreen. Our smart, new

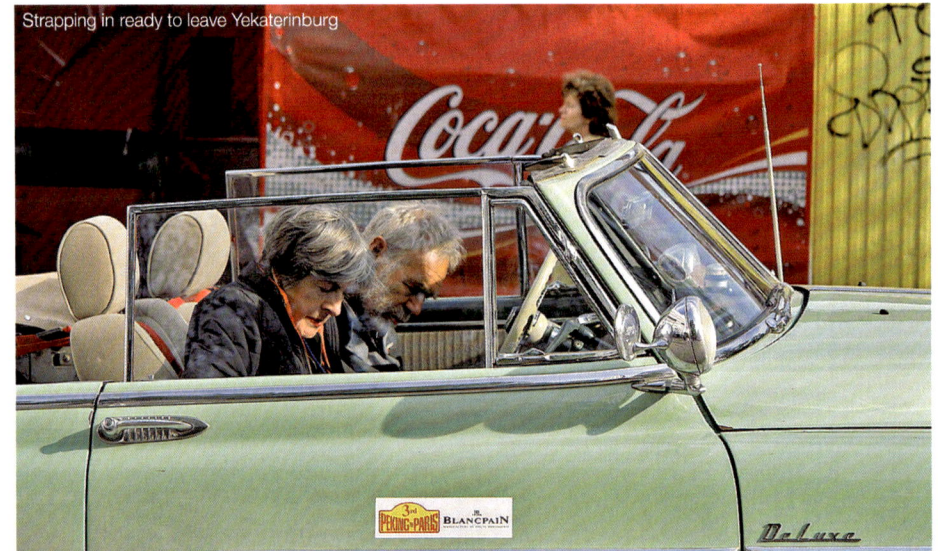
Strapping in ready to leave Yekaterinburg

windscreen washers squirted a drizzle of water like an early morning mist over the windscreen and the slow-moving windscreen wipers simply churned this into a gelatinous sludge. The only way to progress was to stop every 500 yards and attempt to shovel off sufficient of this filth to provide an aperture through which to peer into the gloom. The Kungar Caves were well off the beaten track and the road simply got narrower and worse, until we were limited to limping along at 5 to 10 MPH. Eventually, we oozed into the car park to the Ice Caves, only to find that they had closed for lunch and wouldn't open for another 90 minutes. Despite the attraction of trudging underground through muddy tunnels, looking at stalactites, we decided to save this experience for another day and elected, with umpteen other cars, to soldier on.

A regular sight en route

The run in to Perm was uninspiring, to say the least; the rain had stopped, however, and the hood was down as we drove into the back of an enormous traffic jam as the one million Perm residents all seemed to be heading in the same direction as the hotel we were heading to.

Our road book described the Hotel Ural as "an enormous place of varying quality", so we arrived with a degree of scepticism wondering what we might find. The hotel was a gigantic, Soviet style concrete edifice with a vast marble columned reception area, which made it look more like a mausoleum than a hotel. We knew the signs weren't good when we were told our room was on the eighth floor (the old adage again – the higher the floor, the worse the conditions). Arriving on a landing the size of a tennis court, we were confronted by a corridor that appeared to be quarter of a mile long, and I said to Yvonne "pity the poor devil who is staying right at the end of this". Yes, of course, you are right – it was us…. Ours was the very last room. In fact, it wasn't as bad as we had expected, we had a suite with its own sitting room, although clearly the décor, curtains and carpets hadn't been changed since it was built in the 1940s.

During the early evening, I spotted a note on the rally notice board asking if anyone had any 'silver' gaffer tape. Knowing that I had a spare roll, I sought out Roy Stephenson in his 1960 Aston Martin DB4 and gave him the roll. He told me that he needed it for fixing down his bonnet panel but, amusingly, seemed more delighted that the silver colour exactly matched his paintwork. Attention to detail, or what!

The dining room was, obscurely, located in the cellar of the hotel but, in fact, it was quite atmospheric sitting in these vast vaulted cellars soaking up rally 'babble'. We had a great meal with Mike and Sarah O'Shea and Mike and I satisfyingly finished off the evening with several malt whiskeys whilst we discussed the renovation of Mike's new acquisition, his 7-litre Cooper Masarati. In many ways the conversation was quite surreal, bearing in mind what we were driving and where we were situated.

SIBERIA - Day 20 Perm To Kazan 688kms.

Awoke this morning to a lovely, lovely morning; bright blue skies and a gentle, whispering breeze. The car seemed to be looking a little flat on its rear springs, so we decided that we must jettison some weight, and we went for the high quality, high weight equipment. We were carrying a second spare all-terrain tyre which weighed a ton! I toured around all the rally cars asking if anyone wanted a tyre but, sadly, in the short time available, found no takers and had to leave it propped up outside the

hotel. Hopefully, some lucky soul would have come across this and taken advantage of it. We decided to abandon our old, but totally useless, Chevrolet jack, but the most important decision was leaving behind Yvonne's hairspray, I tried to insist we kept it but she was absolutely determined……..

Hairspray et al

Each morning, after packing up from our night's stay, whilst I was making final checks on the car, Yvonne would take the route book and time card and head for the Main Control, which was, almost always, in the reception area of the headquarters' hotel. She would try to arrive there between 20 and 30 minutes before our start time to allow sufficient time to find out if there had been any changes to the route or any other vital information that we needed to know for that day's journey. She had to check out exactly on our 'minute' to avoid penalty, and it became a pleasant rendezvous for the navigators whose start times were close together. They would sit or stand and chat about the weather, their aches and pains, bruises and strains, how bad the food had been the night before and whether or not they had managed to get their overnight washing dry. They also watched out for each other. Its surprising how, when you have, say, ten minutes to spare and are chatting merrily,

suddenly the time vanishes and you're right on your minute, so each navigator would look around to make sure that whoever wanted the minute before us didn't miss it, and would call that person up if she or he was missing. Yvonne found it quite reassuring at each Main Control to see the same, familiar faces and everyone bonded so well. Most of the navigators in our time group were women, but one of the men was Andrew Mykytovych, who is a real gentle giant; Yvonne thought that, at first, he felt outnumbered by the females, but he soon got used to the company when he started chatting to fellow-Aussie, Anne Wilkinson!   Once Yvonne had lodged her time and had her card signed, she would literally run out of reception to find me, hopefully, sitting in the car with the engine running. From that point on every second was timed and there was no opportunity to stop and chat with anyone until the next Main Control.

Before today's start, there was a huge, festering concern over the timing in Mongolia. Everyone was moaning about what was considered to be a poor decision made by the organisers and a petition has been started. Kim Bannister had been approached and asked if he would convene a meeting to explain the situation. One of the facts that was galling so many people was that the crews of the two identical 4.1/2 litre Bentleys, together with a Mercedes, had been seen trucking their cars, covered in tarpaulins. The cars were rolled off the trucks just before the daily finishing line and driven across the line to be clocked in and were still in contention for gold medals. Inevitably, tempers were fraying as people simply could not come to terms with someone trucking a car and being on a gold medal whilst the rest of us had endured so many hardships to comply with rally timing. This one would surely run and run until there was some equitable solution, although the general consensus was that the rally organisers would struggle to change decisions which have already been made. We shall see.

Today was a huge day, almost 700 kilometres, and we were confronted by a mixture of half-decent and absolutely shocking roads. We were soon in the thick of the truck traffic and it was necessary to constantly pull out and overtake them. Strangely, all these manoeuvres carried out at relatively high speed with trucks coming in both directions were done with a degree of conviviality; rally cars zig-zagging through the traffic this way and that, whilst the lorry drivers maintained a relatively consistent pace but gently swinging off onto the verges whenever there was a requirement to prevent a disaster. Everything was done in a calm and orderly fashion – we didn't know whether it was like this normally or whether the lorry drivers were fascinated by our rally cars.

Mid afternoon, having got through the worst of the appalling roads there was suddenly a loud clang from under the car and, once again, that well known sound when metal meets tarmac. Having pulled off the road, I discovered to my horror that one pair of the rear shock absorbers on the left-hand of the car had ripped away from

Typical Russian housing

their fixings and were trailing on the road. I tried to remove the shock absorbers, which proved to be almost impossible, whilst Yvonne rang the service crews to ask for some assistance. However, once again the service crews were stretched to their limit and we simply couldn't make contact. I decided that the only way to attempt to remove the shock absorbers would be to take off the back wheel, but that turned out to be a nightmare of its own. The wheel would not release between the brake drum and the rim of the rear wing; eventually, the only solution was to let the tyre down, and even then I still couldn't remove the rear wheel at all. I decided on another approach – to leave the shock absorbers where they were fastened to the springs and successfully lashed them to the rear axle with a coil of wire we were carrying.

It was quite a shock opening up the boot to see a piece of metal 4" wide x 10" long

simply ripped out of the boot floor.

After a filthy one-and-a-half hours we were back on the road, and I have to say that, whilst the roads were by now of quite reasonable condition, I could barely tell any difference in driving. As we drove along we smiled to each other as we started to sing "Four Wheels on my Wagon, and We're Still Rolling Along" because that is what seemed to be happening; we were down to shock absorbers on only one corner of the car.

Finally, at 8.15 pm we rolled into the secure carpark and I was absolutely whacked, and could hardly hold my head up. The moment the handbrake was applied, a young Russian chap approached the car; full of enthusiasm for the rally, he immediately pulled out a scrapbook of his own cars and was desperate to talk to me about what he had and hadn't done with his cars. It was really an extremely difficult moment. On the one hand, this fellow was so enthusiastic and clearly had not seen anything like the array of cars in front of him but, equally, we had just driven 700 kilometres and were desperate for sustenance and a bed. Nonetheless we felt it was important to show your best face and I smiled knowingly at his stories until, after fifteen minutes, we gently managed to prise ourselves away.

Fortunately, tonight our hotel really was five-star quality. We had an enormous room and spent a quarter of an hour washing thick black filth out of our hair before retiring for a meal. After dinner I wandered outside and 'phoned Keith who was attempting the complex business of arranging for shock absorbers to be posted from the west coast of America onwards to Moscow. However, we were hopeful.

Rather obscurely we were to put our clocks back by two hours tonight, but couldn't quite understand why two hours, as time zones seem to change by one hour at a time. However, apparently we have crossed an extremely narrow band of one hour time change during the day so the organisers found it easier to do it all in one go. We are now just three hours ahead of BST – the finish is beckoning.

The benefit of the extra two hours in bed was somewhat nullified when the alarm woke us at 4.20 am instead of 6.20 am – yes, you've guessed it, we adjusted the wrist and rally watches but not the alarm! This gave me two hours of extra worrying time to think through a little issue I had noticed as we pulled into Kazan last night. Strangely, the handbrake and gear lever seemed to be excessively hot, certainly hotter than they had ever been before, so I deduced that, possibly, the heat was being generated in the gearbox for whatever reason. This was one of the problems I struggled with when my total lack of mechanical knowledge didn't allow me to think through mechanical issues with any certainty; the upshot being that my mind simply thrashed around in every possible direction without coming to any positive conclusion. An hour of whittling forced me to rise at about 5.30 am and wander off to the carpark to see if I could catch one of the backup crews who might be able to throw some light on the issue. Upon arrival at the foul, disused demolition sight which doubled as our security carpark, I found, inevitably, that all the support mechanics were frantically busy attempting to work on several cars at once. Andy Inskip, helpful as ever, promised me ten minutes of his time later on, so I busied myself under the car checking the strapping-up of the shock absorbers and, indeed, put a nylon strap around as a double safeguard. True to his word, half an hour later Andy rolled under the car to join me and quickly deduced that yes, I was right for once, the gearbox oil was low. He loaned me a syringe, a bottle of gearbox oil, and gave me five minutes' instruction on how to proceed before shooting off to attend to the ever-increasing line of folk who were equally desperate for his attention.

I can honestly say that, rolling around in this brick and mud-strewn morass at 6.15 on a damp morning in an industrial town in mid-Siberia, attempting to defy the laws of gravity by squirting gooey gearbox oil in an upwards direction, was possibly one of the low points of the whole trip. Here I was, frozen stiff, fed-up and with thick, sticky oil making its way slowly down towards my armpits; this was not what I had pictured when we commenced this exotic adventure. However, I soon pulled myself

around with the consolation that it was a job well done and this was soon rewarded with the knowledge that the gear lever and handbrake stayed cool for the rest of the day. The only nagging concern was, where on earth had all that gearbox oil gone to?

Traffic Jam

Kazan and its early morning traffic jams were soon left behind as we set off on another day of almost 400 kilometres, inching yet further westwards. The roads generally now seemed to be improving slightly, but then, suddenly, without any warning there would be a diabolical stretch of several miles with huge suspension-rattling craters, and the ever increasing concern that yet another piece of suspension might let go. Nonetheless, the journey was reasonably civilised and we came across more and more villages and cities as we were approximately following the Volga

River and it could clearly be seen that we were heading towards the industrial heartland of Russia, with major cities scattered on the distant horizon.

Something to occupy the time

Niz Novgorod, formery Gorkey, is a beautiful city on the Volga, and we eased into the checkpoint at an early 4.15 pm. Yvonne hadn't been feeling too good during the day, so whilst she went to the room to rest for a while, I quickly checked the car over and topped up the oil, then wandered across the square past the imposing statue of Stalin to take a brief walk along the banks of the Volga. By the time I got back, Yvonne had revived somewhat and we had dinner with Jose and Maria, Richard and Nicola and John and Joan. During dinner the hotel management had decided that we needed some entertainment to cheer us up and installed a woman singer who, together with her three-piece accompaniment, sang so loudly, and badly, that she effectively ended any form of conversation for the night. To make it worse, a large Australian contingent made a bit of a mockery by applauding ecstatically every time she finished a song, the upshot being that she kept on singing for what seemed an eternity.

During dinner there had been a steady rumour that ten crews had been invited to a meeting in the hotel to discuss some unsavoury issues about which there had been a bubbling undercurrent for the last week or so. As it transpired, so many people were concerned about these various situations that, in the end, in excess of fifty people turned up to cram into the tiny meeting room, and Kim Bannister, the Clerk of the Course, initially looked somewhat overwhelmed when confronted by this phalanx of rally crews, by now well fuelled with wine and ready to tackle these issues head on. The first issue was the organisers' decision to summarily cancel the timings for Day 11. The point made by various crews was that the organisers had described to us all exactly what was required for the day, and we all went out and did what was required. It was, perhaps, the toughest and most car-breaking drive of the rally to achieve our times, and those of us who had been successful thought that to rescind it was simply unacceptable. This issue was eloquently summarised by a long speech from Roy Williams, which definitely had the effect of persuading Kim Bannister to agree at least to reconsider the matter.

The second issue was the covert trucking of three cars which had been spotted on trucks taking different routes on several days. The cars had been covered with tarpaulins so that the numbers couldn't be seen but, of course, inevitably, word had got around. Of course, everyone who had worked particularly hard at driving the whole distance of the event each day was particularly upset and, indeed, one Dutchman described how he had had a problem with his steering, been told by the service crew that there was no assistance available, had limped into camp at 3.00 am the following morning, having lost his gold medal status, to find that the three cars had been trucked for some of the toughest sections of the rally, yet were still on gold medal position, which was patently unreasonable.

The third issue related to the fact that the teams of two of the cars being trucked, had pre-booked servicing along the route and had been flying in their own mechanics to service the cars, all of which was supposed to be prohibited in the rules. This was all going down very badly with those people who had made huge sacrifices themselves to maintain their own cars and, indeed, it just didn't seem to be within the spirit of the event.

One of the burning questions on peoples' lips was how on earth could this situation arise within the framework of the Rally Regulations? Kim went to some trouble, however, to explain that the regulations indicated that cars must leave the start under their own steam and arrive at the finish under their own steam but that there was the facility, at the organisers' discretion, for cars to be trucked. This was obviously designed to allow for a competitor who had a relatively small, but unfixable, problem to keep up with the rally and not drop out of Gold Medal contention. Quite clearly, however, what the three cars in question had done was hardly in the spirit of the event.

My own feelings were that if one chose to enter an event of this magnitude, one should do so with the full intent to follow the regulations and the route throughout. Why on earth would anyone chose not to drive certain sections of the rally and, in the event, sections that, whilst they were incredibly tough, proved to be quite the most memorable in retrospect.

Joseph Stalin overlooks our rally cars in Niz Novgorod

Kim seemed to absorb all of these concerns and, whilst he was clearly uncomfortable about having to review these issues within the framework of the rally, he recognised the degree of unrest and agreed that the organisers would review matters. It was certainly an interesting hour's discussion and emotions were running very high. It will be interesting to see what the outcome is.

Later in the evening we were in the bar with Mike and Sarah O'Shea when Sarah mentioned that, as part of her job, she alternated her time between working a week in London and a week in Moscow. Hearing about our troubles with the suspension, she suggested I should speak to Galena, her PA in Moscow, and indeed, almost instantly had her on the 'phone for me. Galena agreed to look for a Chevrolet dealership which could perhaps do some work on our car. Not quite the normal run-of-the-mill servicing that the Russian Chevrolet dealership carries out I suspect.

There was a degree of anticipation today as reaching Moscow would be a significant landmark. So, full of enthusiasm on a bright, Spring morning, we left Niz Novgorod at 8.40 am with a fairly easy drive on good dual carriageways today. As might be expected, the roads were mainly excellent as we headed into the capital city. For once, we scorched along at 70 mph and eased into Moscow through light traffic to arrive at the hotel at an early 2.00 pm. On the run-in I telephoned ahead to Galena who told me that she had made all the necessary arrangements and gave us the details of the address to track down the Chevrolet garage. The Cosmos Hotel where the rally was booked in, turned out to be a horrendous 3,600-room shabby, tourist hotel, amazingly inefficiently run by incompetent and belligerent staff whose main pupose in life seemed to be to deal with all of the incoming tourists as slowly as possible, and they were clearly involved in some sort of competition to see who could be the most miserable. Our conclusion was that they achieved an almighty 'draw'.

Once we had dumped our luggage in the room, we retired to the patisserie or its Russian equivalent to devour enormous pieces of cream cake and coffee – civilisation beckons.

Later, the concierge hailed a taxi for us and we followed him in our car to the Chevrolet garage. Here we were to experience the first of many Russian scams. The taxi fare was 1,100 rubles to the garage, yet later on the taxi called

The view from 'infamous' Cosmos

by the garage for our return trip cost us only 500 rubles! Our arrival at the garage caused a degree of interest as the mechanics were not quite used to working on 1950s cars. I had written out a list of work that required doing, the main feature of which was to weld back the floor panel in the boot so that the rear shock absorbers were operational. I also decided that the car needed a change of oil, plugs and the brakes checking out. The workshop manager spoke a little English and told us to have a cup of coffee in the reception and join him in the workshop fifteen minutes later. Any concerns about whether they had understood our requirements were quickly forgotten as we discovered that the car had been washed, and was up on a ramp with four or five mechanics working on it.

Back in the hotel, we sat and had a drink in the bar with Jon Kennedy and his wife, Midge, who had flown over from Orange County. Jon was overjoyed to have someone to talk to; the long lonely, silent hours in the Volkswagon with the ever-silent Garrick must have been a real strain.

There were some terrific stories being told about cars arriving one way or another in Moscow. The three-litre Itala has had a modern Volga engine with five-speed gearbox installed and has caught us up after a long train journey. The other great story related to one car which was stuck up on the back of a truck so that when they reached the outskirts of Moscow there was no way of getting it down onto the road. Undeterred the truck driver went onto a building site, found a man with a JCB who built an earth-ramp behind the lorry, reversed the car off, then scattered the earth ramp. People are very inventive when needs must.

The other great news is that we heard from Dave and Jo today; they have had some amazing experiences catching up with the rally and they are due to join us tomorrow in Moscow.

Today was a free day in Moscow, and after an early breakfast with Robert and Jane Aubrey, we opted for the Metro to find our way into the Kremlin. Rather oddly, the stations didn't seem to have any names on them at all, which was extraordinary, but an elderly Russian lady took us under her wing once she understood where we were trying to get to. She had to get off a few stops before us so commandeered another passenger to look after us and make sure we got off at the right station. We surfaced near the entrance to the Kremlin on a beautiful sunny day and sat and had an ice cream outside the Kremlin walls. This seemed to be such a contrast; we didn't really know what to expect of the Kremlin as our only descriptions were from 1950s films depicting the Cold War where all the scenes were of dark alleys on misty, grey evenings, and over-dressed shifty characters glancing behind to see if they were being followed! Somehow, having an ice cream in this colourful setting seemed luxuriously decadent.

Kremlin skyline

Clearly my knowledge of modern history wasn't up to scratch, as I had always presumed that the Kremlin was a large, dank building housing the Polit Bureau and the KGB. Nothing prepared me for the sheer extravagance and size that we found when we entered one of the fortified gates, indeed the Kremlin is almost a complete city on its own with offices, elegant apartment buildings, stunning churches with glittering gold-leaved minarets, palaces, government buildings, all set in beautifully landscaped and manicured gardens; a complete eye-opener which kept us engrossed for several hours.

Later, wandering into Red Square we were somewhat surprised by the relatively small scale. Tyannamen Square in Beijing had stunned us by its enormity, but Red Square seemed quite homely in contrast. On the opposite side to the Kremlin stood Gum the magnificent and cosmopolitan department store, housing names such as Cartier and

Not quite what we expected to see on the Russian billboards

Christian Dior. For me, however, perhaps the most fascinating sight was the building next door to Gum, which was identical in architectural style, but in the middle of a major renovation. In order to ensure that the building works didn't in any way detract from the magnificence of Red Square, the scaffolding to the building site was clad with stretched canvas onto which the entire details of the building façade had been 'hand-painted' in amazing detail. The Gum superstore and its sister building were certainly a reflection of how things in Russia have changed over the last ten to fifteen years, and certainly bore no relevance whatsoever to those black and white films I recall.

Lunch was taken in the shade of huge umbrellas on the fringe of Red Square and, for once, we were happy to pay tourist rates for lunch simply to enjoy this amazing setting. Clearly, lots of other rally participants felt the same and there were more than a dozen other crews enjoying lunch, all making the most of our rest day. Following

lunch, our walk took us past the quite stunning multi-coloured St. Basil's Cathedral and eventually, following the river, we walked back to the Chevrolet garage. The car was completely finished and twenty minutes later we were back in the hotel. We took a walk around the Russian Exhibition Centre, past the gigantic, iconic sculpture of the launch of Russia's first space rocket and on the way back the first people we saw were Dave and Jo. It was great to meet up again as we had not seen them since Ulaan Baatar and clearly had lots of stories to exchange. We booked a table at a well-known traditional Russian restaurant, Indus, for the evening and spent several happy hours recounting experiences.

The much photgraphed St. Basils

Their story was extraordinary. After being trucked for two days back to Ulaan Baatar (and when I say trucked I mean the car on the back of the truck with an inch to spare back and front, and Dave and Jo sitting inside the car as there was no room in the cab for them!). They then had to wait for two or three days in Ulaan Baatar before the spare steering components were shipped in from the UK. A group of Australian guys who were working on a nearby reservoir construction helped with installing the parts and eventually, nine days after we had

So thats why its called Red Square

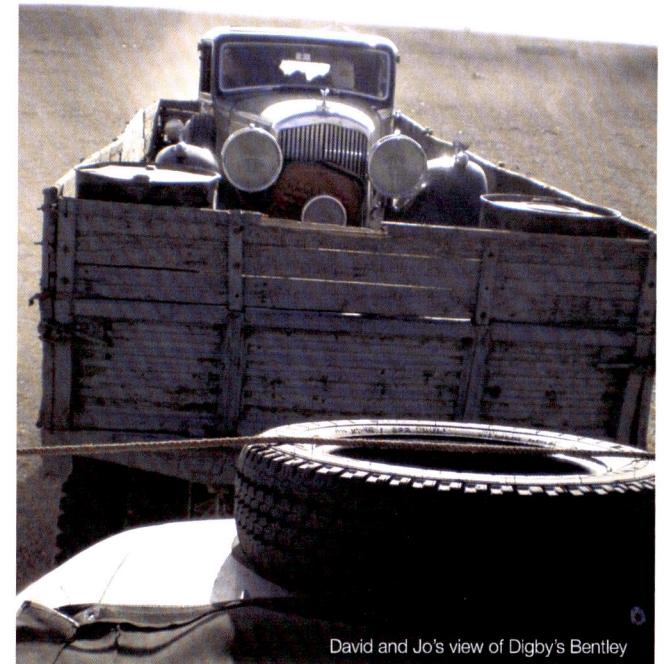

left them behind, Dave and Jo set off in company with Digby and Neville in their 1939 Derby Bentley, to attempt to catch up with the rally. Their plan was to head north from Ulaan Baatar thereby missing out the dreaded Gobi Desert section in an attempt to find more civilised roads through northern Siberia. Somewhere in Siberia they discovered that the car was leaning badly to one side and to their horror found that the rear chassis outriggers, which supported the rear springs and shock absorbers, had almost parted from the chassis. They were directed up a track to the next village where they were assured that welding facilities were available. No-one mentioned that the next village was 90 kms away! Repairs were carried out and they then had 90 kms to drive back to meet up with their original road, and thereafter they drove long, long days, sometimes well into the night and, indeed, the final day into Moscow they had driven for 16.1/2 hours covering 1,160 kms in the day!

Digby and Neville, who had separated from Dave and Jo at the time of the suspension problem, headed on a more southerly route hoping to short-cut through the Ukraine. Sadly, they were thwarted as they had no visas and were turned back, having to retrace several hundred kilometres. Remarkably, they arrived in Moscow with an hour of Dave and Jo!

David and Jo's view of Digby's Bentley

Today was been designated a 'free transport' day to St. Petersburg. There is an enormous distance to cover but no timing at all. We decided to make an early start, so rose at 5.00 am and drove out of the hotel not having had breakfast at 5.50 am. We left absolute bedlam behind. The ever officious hotel staff evidently excelled themselves. Many crews had decided to use the hotel laundry service and had paid extra for 'express' service. Clearly the word express does not properly translate into Russian as the laundry didn't reappear; there were umpteen stories of threats, fights and even the police being called as people attempted to retrieve their laundry before leaving. Mercifully, Yvonne was in charge of our laundry services and our pre-rally choice of lightweight-dry-in-no-time-at-all clothing proved to be a huge success, particularly on this occasion where we were able to avoid the laundry fracas. Breakfast was energy bars taken on the move as we experienced the absolute comfort of smooth, wide tarmac roads but, more particularly the absolute luxury of driving with shock absorbers on all four corners of the car for the first time in almost three weeks!

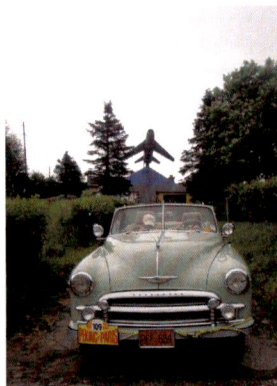

The long drive seemed to be going well enough until suddenly two policemen leapt into the road and waved us down. We had heard many stories of the police pulling over rally cars and extorting huge sums of money for 'fake' speeding charges. Was this to be our turn? As it turned out, no. The police were pulling us over on behalf of a television crew who interviewed us for a local TV network. I'm not too sure how much of our English interview they would have understood, but they seemed very happy with their filming.

One of the mighty Austin 7's we came across

Today kilometres slipped by very rapidly, as we rolled into the fringes of St. Petersburg at 3.00 pm it looked as though as long last we would have a leisurely afternoon's relaxation. Sadly, St. Petersburg's late afternoon traffic put an end to this hope as it took us a further two hours to inch our way through the hot, sticky streets to our hotel. There was a lovely moment, however, as we crossed one of the main river bridges when a girl ran across to tell us that she was one of a crew of two Austin Sevens which had set off some two to three months before us on their own independent Peking-Paris exploits. The two Austin Sevens were parked at our hotel, and the sight of these cars, which were only about the third the length of our Chevy made us appreciate what an amazing journey they had undertaken.

Pulling up to the front door of the hotel we were again reminded of Russian hotel hospitality, when the doorman, who looked as though he was straight out of one of my 1950s films, shouted…. "You, driver, move car immediately." Not the friendliest of welcomes.

Early evening saw us in the bar when Jose approached me to suggest we had a team meal that night in the hotel restaurant. It transpired that it was Jose's birthday and team 'Dry Martinis' had, I believe, a memorable evening although, I am told, that I had somewhat more to drink than usual (not having a high alcohol tolerance, I usually limit myself to a couple of drinks) and really don't remember too much of the last hour…….

Breathtaking view of the Hermitage on the drive in

St Petersburg waterside

looking at the fabulous buildings but making a conscious decision not to go in (as I always feel it is better to leave some things undone to give an ideal opportunity to make a return visit some day), took a wonderful boat trip around the Venetian-styled canals of St. Petersburg, walked the Summer Palace gardens, wandered round the Cathedral and watched buskers rendering breathtaking operatic arias (somewhat different to the buskers I recall in the centre of Sheffield!)

This evening Yvonne had gathered together the eight of us who had flown out from the UK together, we two, Dave and Jo, John and Joan, Mike and Josie, and made a booking at a restaurant called Russian Kitch, which proved to be hugely successful. Lovely atmosphere, great jazz, excellent food – a memorable evening.

Strangely, this morning I seemed to have a thick head, but half an hour working on the car, checking the oil and water, topping up the gearbox oil, and checking the plugs brought me round fairly rapidly. Dave was having a problem now with gearbox oil, which he was losing at an alarming rate. I gave him a long length of plastic tubing and a small funnel which helped with filling, as prior to that he had been attempting to squirt oil into the gearbox with one of Jo's perfume dispensers!

Immediately after breakfast we set off with John and Joan to take in the sights of St. Petersburg. Our taxi driver into town tried the standard Russian technique of quadrupling the taxi fair but after I had grabbed him round the collar and jokingly subjected him to a few mock wrestling moves, he agreed to halve the price which means that eventually we only paid double the normal fare! We did all the tourist things – a wander through the courtyard to the Hermitage Museum, wondrously

Motley crew at Russian Kitch

There was a huge amount of expectation today as the rally was due to pass out of Russia and into the Baltic States. Somehow, this heralded the final run-in to Paris through countries that would begin to become more familiar. Also for the next three or four days the time trials were to start again. It was not possible for the organisers to include time trials in the Russian sector; on the one hand due to the significant distances we had to travel each day, but also I believe it had been extremely difficult for the organisers to persuade the authorities to cope with what was effectively 'racing' on open roads.

Our time out this morning was 7.07 am and it was a bright and pleasant morning as we struggled through the inevitable, interminable traffic jams on the way out of a major city. Soon, however, we were out into open country with picturesque small villages and lush green countryside. Our spirits were soon dampened by a combination of a section of the inevitable Russian rough potholed road which, combined with lashing rain, made the first 100 kilometres rather dismal.

On the run in to the Russian border we started to see various rally cars pulled in on the roadside by the local police and, strangely, the nearer to the border we got, the more cars we saw. The organisers had appointed Alex and a team of his fellow Russian 'fixers' to arrange our exit out of Russia and generally smooth the way. It was understood that a considerable amount of money had passed into Alex's offshore bank account to 'smooth' formalities. Miraculously, however, at a very late stage it was discovered that Alex and his motley crew had, inevitably, disappeared under somewhat sinister circumstances. A pattern of corruption and confusion started to build up in the run-in to the border and the local police were stopping as many cars as they possibly could and simply demanding money, with substantial menaces. People were being forced into paying with any currency they could lay their hands on, with the constant threat of having passports and driving licences and even cars confiscated. The last ten miles to the border post were just bedlam

as indignant rally crews were on the one hand attempting to fight their corner but on the other hand realising they were in a complete no-win situation. We must have been exceedingly lucky as we zigzagged our way to the border and were not pulled up. Jon and David Goodwin in their Aston Martin DB4 were seen as prime candidates for substantial fines with their 'James Bond' connection (which was in fact mentioned by the police). Indeed, they were stopped on two separate occasions two hundred yards apart! Andy Vann in the Studebaker apparently became extremely agitated and belligerent but was eventually forced to calm down and pay up under threat of instant arrest.

Worse was to come at the border where the delays were unbelievable. We firstly queued for one-and-a-half hours at one kiosk only to be turned back when we finally reached the window and made to stand in yet another queue. The Russian girl on duty had a sticking plaster on her index finger and was simply typing out reams of information using her single middle finger. It took nearly forty minutes to complete each individual form – and remember, there were somewhere in excess of a hundred cars due through. We were one of the lucky ones and managed to get through the border in three hours. Behind us we heard stories of crews taking, eight, nine and eleven hours to get through – and this was just to get OUT of the country.

A ten minute drive across 'no-mans-land' into Estonia and here on the border in order to cut down on costs and stop speeding drivers, they had simply dug the biggest, deepest holes across the road that even made the Russian potholes look acceptable. Inching gingerly across these chasms we were eventually met by a smiling guard on the entry into Estonia, which was a wonderful welcome into what proved to be an instant change to what we perceived to be European culture. Behind us we left Russia, with a mixture of emotions. We had met delightful mechanics who had done everything they possibly could to aid us through extremely difficult circumstances, people had worked long, hard hours and wanted little in

return for their endeavours, people seemed genuinely delighted to welcome the rally wherever we passed, but there was also the slight bad taste of the corruption – the relatively lightweight issues of being double, treble and quadruple-charged for taxi fares but more seriously the hugely distasteful issues which many people had experienced with the corrupt police force.

However, here in Estonia we were in what felt like familiar countryside. The sun came out, the roads were smooth, silken tarmac and, of even greater importance to Yvonne, the Cyrillic lettering on the signposts was left behind us, and navigation would become a little easier.

Soon we were turned off the main roads and into the forests to tackle our first time trial. 5,4,3,2,1 go and we were off, rattling our way through a multitude of criss-crossing forest tracks, superbly marshalled by members of the local motor clubs. I had not driven flat out on gravel before at any speed and initially found the experience disconcerting, as it was not easy to recognise how far the car would slip and slide as we sped along. On the one hand trying to make headway as fast as possible but on the other hand trying to ensure we stayed safe and sound. Flying around one right-hand bend, I hugged the corner far too tightly and whacked an overhanging branch, there was a huge bang and flying glass - but no time to stop and examine the damage - must clock in at the finish first. By the second time trial of the day we were feeling a little more confident and starting to enjoy the quite unusual sensation of being able to drive flat out unfettered by speed limits.

Leaving the last time trial we seemed to take a wrong turn somewhere and missed a road section. Suddenly we appeared to have far too much time to achieve the distance to the next passage check. Being concerned about arriving too early, we reversed into a field and munched through some cereal bars trying to use up our unexplained time. Eventually, we pulled into the time check to find that everyone was already there as the timing in the route book had been incorrect, and everyone wondered where we had got to!

Eventually, in the late afternoon, we drove into the centre of Tallin, a stunning city with a beautiful traditional town square surrounded by bars, restaurants, and the façades of the beautiful churches. Rally cars were soon lined up in the square, being surrounded by local residents who were fascinated. Most crews decamped to the bars

Warm welcome in Tallin

surrounding the square and exchanged stories of their exploits of the day. Mike and Josie were particularly concerned as they had inadvertently done two laps of one of the tests and thought that they had jeopardized their excellent second in class position. As it transpired, as we were driving the tests we were not aware of the dramas that had unfolded behind us with the incredible delays at the Russian border and, in fact, eventually all of the overall timing for the day was completely cancelled.

Wandering off into our delightful, Scandinavian style hotel we once again met up with team 'Dry Martini' for yet another team dinner. Richard and Nicola had visited Tallin previously and, before the rally, had taken the opportunity of booking in to the fine 'Bocca' Restaurant. After our meal, we wandered gently back through the ancient streets of old Tallin on this balmy evening, full of good spirits, looking forward to the following day.

As a contrast, having nipped into the garage to collect something from the car, I bumped into Dave who was having major problems with oil spilling out of the gearbox, a rear seal apparently having failed, and Dave appeared to be really 'down' as he laboured on his car until 11.30 pm.

Thirst quencher

Chapter 13

THE BALTICS – Day 27 Tallin To Riga 406kms

It was almost a shame to be leaving beautiful Tallin on this sunny, June morning, so we mentally made a note that this is definitely a town we will return to in the future to take in the local sights and further explore the narrow, winding streets of the Old Town. At least we shall know an excellent restaurant next time we come!

Soon out of Tallin on excellent, tarmac roads, we were then into a whole variety of driving tests and time trials; all designed to test car, driver and navigator in different ways. The first test was on a motorcross circuit that swept around a quarry basin through heavy, sandy sections. Two laps had to be completed, so we were,

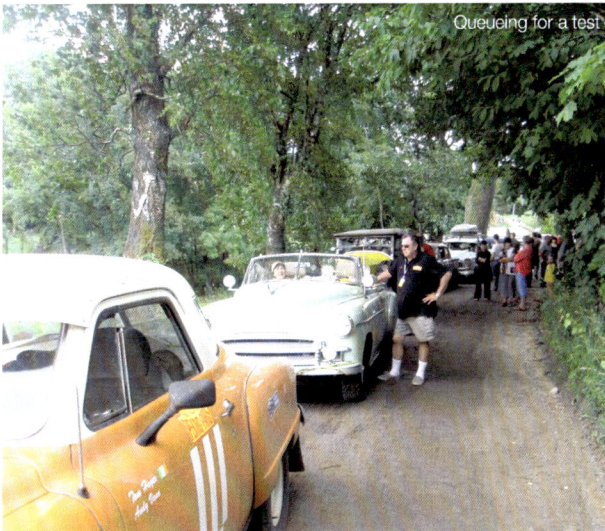
Queueing for a test

inevitably, in a situation where we were catching up other cars, and it became almost impossible to see following another car in the clouds of dust and sand – shades of Mongolia!

Next up was an Estonian tarmac/gravel race track, the navigational complexity of which 'threw' one or two competitors, who ended up doing additional laps. Yvonne expertly guided us round the circuit and, indeed, we were within the fastest ten of the competing cars.

Soon we were passing into Latvia which, for us with our British passports, was just a formality.

After this we were on to single, gravel tracks through the forests and fields, past farmhouses etc, but by now I was getting the hang of driving on these 'ball-bearing' surfaces and we had an excellent run.

Now, to test out the navigators, the organisers had tightened up the times, a situation we realised after stopping to fill up with fuel, only to discover that we were desperately tight for the next passage control, 55 kilometres away – all on gravel roads. Pushing on as hard as I could, I was horrified after, about 20 kilometres, to hear that one of the front shock absorbers had yet again smashed its way through the supporting bracket. What a disappointment, I had rather thought we had put

Another day another country

Really going for it
What a great photo Gerard

suspension issues behind us. What to do? A hasty stop and a crawl under the car confirmed my worst fears, but there was simply no time to spare and, being conscious of the need to retain our gold medal position, we elected to drive on. The scraping of shock absorber against gravel made the most terrible noise but, slowly but surely, the effect lessened. I think it was a combination of us getting used to the noise, and the fact that the shock absorber was slowly wearing away on the gravel. With only minutes to spare we made the start of the time trial and, casting care aside, flew round the circuit and achieved an adequate time. Yet again, we needed to find a solution for the shock absorbers.

As we drove along towards the night's stop in Riga, we tried to list all the little things that had gone wrong with the car since we set off on this trip. We had gears slipping out occasionally (and they still do), the trip failed, the bobbins on the exhaust had snapped twice, the hood mechanism pinged off and tore the hood, the bracket that supports the motor that drives the hood mechanism had split away, the front steering wishbone needed welding on two occasions, both doors had been a struggle to close (and open), although that was mainly due to the dust. The wipers had barely worked since day one, the rear shock absorbers ripped a piece out of the floor, the rear springs had snapped, we had lost both front shock absorbers innumerable times – replaced them with new ones and lost those as well. We counted, in fact, that it was the sixth 'go' with the front shock absorbers at one time or another. We had two of the wheel studs snap, the bonnet hinge broke and ended up scratching the wing and then, of course, we took out the headlight out in one of the tests. Finally, the indicators stopped working, the gearbox started to lose fluid and the temperature gauge had broken a long time ago. "Three wheels on my wagon…………." etc. etc. etc.

After a long, fast run into Riga we eventually ground to a halt circumnavigating an enormous traffic island in the centre of Riga. We had already inched our way past the hotel on our way to find the carpark, so as we sat in 35 degree temperatures in standing traffic, Yvonne elected to walk back to the hotel to check-in whilst I sat in the car for 1.1/4 hours driving four sides of the square.

Once into the underground carpark, I whipped off the decimated shock absorber in no time at all, borrowed an oil syringe off Mick Mykitovich, topped up the gearbox, checked the oil, checked the oil-bath filter, washed the windscreen and we were ready to go for the following morning.

After a shower, I went to reception to meet up with Yvonne, who had gone off to find out the exchange rate for the local currency. Misunderstanding what she had heard from the receptionist, she told me the exchange rate with the result that, instead of exchanging £20 for sufficient drinks for the evening, in the event I extracted £500 from the ATM machine and likely cleaned it out! Inevitably, the story passed round the bar in no time at all and I became the banker for the evening, loaning out Latvian litas by the handful. I can't have done any worse than the bankers of 2009, but we certainly had a hilarious and memorable evening as a result.

Nicola and Yvonne

This morning the start was at the Riga Motor Circuit, just a few kilometres away from our overnight stay. Just sufficient time before the first test, we had the opportunity to look around the motor museum which had, possibly, the finest collection of Auto Unions in the world. Sadly, not enough time to absorb everything – perhaps a note for yet another visit in the future.

Onto the Riga Motor Circuit, and we had the opportunity for two 'flat out' laps on this quite stunning woodland and lakeside track. Off at minute intervals, we were chasing the 1958 Holden of Bohodar (Mick) Mykitovich, whom we managed to catch and overtake towards the end of the first lap. Feeling full of enthusiasm I attacked the right-angled right-hand bend at the end of the long back straight, only to find out that I was a little too enthusiastic and managed to execute a couple of 360 degree turns, ending up pointing the wrong way down the track. Hastily selecting reverse, we managed to swing round and set off in the right direction before Mick and Andrew caught us up. I often wondered if they ever knew how they came to re-catch us so rapidly!

A minor disaster at the finish where Yvonne mixed up the instructions and we roared past the exit turn, only to pull up twenty yards down the road and rapidly reversed before making the correct exit from the circuit. Poor Yvonne was absolutely devastated; we had effectively failed a test but, worse than that, she was concerned that our gold medal was lost and was absolutely inconsolable.

However, there were more pressing matters – further complicated tests to navigate around, which rather took her mind off it. ("No, it didn't!" she tells me.) On the second test of the day, approaching a fast right-hand bend, we suddenly saw Nicola Wainwright, the navigator from the 1960 Sunbeam Rapier Saloon, frantically waving us down by the roadside. Piling on the brakes as we swept round the corner, we came across the Sunbeam which had plunged off the road on the left-hand side

and nose dived into the ditch. Pam was standing by the roadside grinning from ear to ear, so at least they were both OK. Pam had been driving the tests furiously every day and it had always seemed just a matter of time before a ditch beckoned.

Once again the organisers were tightening up the road sections between tests, and we had in excess of fifty kilometres to do on extremely rough roads and, indeed, dropped a full minute over that section before arriving at the next test. The local township had sponsored this last test of the day, and the start line was particularly festive with masses of people out watching. After being interviewed for the local television station, we were handed cans of Red Bull before a flat-out straight line, tarmac test into the next town. It was extremely gripping and I swear that we were

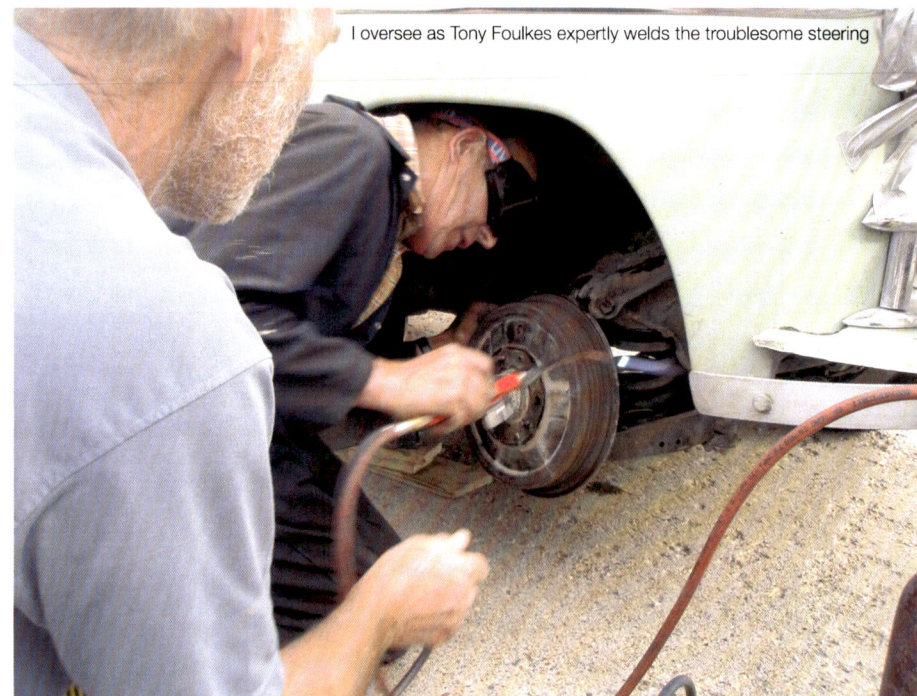

I oversee as Tony Foulkes expertly welds the troublesome steering

airborne at one stage! Eventually, in late afternoon, we pulled into Vilnius and, by that time, Yvonne was still feeling a little low, being convinced that we had blown our gold medal chances on the Riga Motor Circuit. I, on the other hand, was concerned about the damage to the steering arm. The hole through which the gudgeon pin passed had become severely elongated with the effect that, not only was the wheel leaning inwards rather dramatically, but also the steering was becoming extremely sloppy.

The hotel on the outskirts of Vilnius was five-star quality, and whilst Yvonne enjoyed a "to hell with it, who cares" two-person cocktail party with Jo, I nipped down to the carpark to see what could be done with the steering. Andy Inskip gave me a piece of metal and I managed to hacksaw it and file it into a shape that would fit inside the elongated oval hole. It was a new-moon crescent-shaped piece of metal that, hopefully if welded into position, would hold the gudgeon pin firmly in place. Tony Faulkes was tracked down and, eventually, he gas-welded my 'moon' into place and made a really good, sound, solid job of it.

Dave, meantime, had discovered more problems with the cracked chassis member and had taken the Sunbeam off into town for some serious welding. Yvonne and I took Jo down to dinner, which turned out to be a great celebration; the day's results had been published and, amazingly, we were still on Gold. All that had happened was that we were given a maximum time on the driving test and simply dropped a few minutes overall; this really didn't matter on the whole, as we had still maintained our position. All that worry for nothing!

Vilnius car park

127

John and David Goodwin at the start of a fast tarmac test

Liz and Simon Chance line up

Another day, another country. Today we were bound for Poland. The day started with a fairly gentle run through beautiful countryside, but the main activities of the day for us were five separate tests, all demanding in different ways, based mainly on gravel and sand surfaces. The first test, we flew round with no trouble at all, but on the second test we were powering around a corner, only to find Richard and Nicola in the Mark II Jaguar having slid off the road. Luckily, a local farmer was nearby and, within ten minutes, they were back on route, although scoring a maximum on the test. Pit and Frank in the Mercedes taxi, who were running just in front of Richard and Nicola on the overall standings, also had a major 'off' where they went straight on at a right-angle bend into a cornfield and down into a 7 ft. deep ditch. Fortunately for Pit, a large number of spectators had gathered on the corner and ten enormous Polish chaps physically 'bumped' the car back onto the track and Pit dropped just four minutes.

After the first two tests there was a long open road section through countryside very reminiscent of middle England on a beautiful Spring day. After about 150 kilometres,

we came up behind the 'Blue Roo' – Mick and Andy Mykitovich, when suddenly their car lurched to an almost immediate stop in front of us; I only just had a moment or two to swing out to avoid a collision. Clearly, there was something wrong, so I ran back to speak to Mick, who was looking really disconsolate, and could only think that his 'diff' had locked up. Stopping long enough to make sure that Mick and Andy had made contact with the service crew, we motored off to the next test, knowing just how down Mick and Andrew must feel; they were currently running on a gold medal and were fourth in class.

The next test was a complex circuit on rough tracks around the perimeter of a village, which was to be driven twice as independent tests. There was a strange timing arrangement, which I never quite understood, where at one time or another two cars seemed to start at once. Just as we were about to be flagged off, Xavier del Marmol, in his 1937 Chevrolet convertible, pulled alongside and suggested I should let him go first as he was clearly the faster driver and I may hold him up! Naturally, as a hot-blooded male, I was mortally offended by this suggestion but, being British, agreed to give way and let him start first. What a sensible decision this proved to be, as Xavier shot off into the distance, never to be seen again! We recorded 4 mins 59 secs on our first test, but I was more than delighted to reduce this to 4 mins 40 secs on the second run.

The last hundred kilometres run into Mikolajki was just delightful, through the Polish lake district, but the welcome in Mikolajki was more than we could ever have dreamt of. The local township had turned the town square into a huge reception with banners across the road; people thronged in all the cafes around the perimeter. Each car was enthusiastically greeted by a larger-than-life MC from the local car club, smiling from ear to ear through his 'Father Christmas' beard, he welcomed all the cars individually and announced details of the car and crew to the spectators,

Memorable welcome in Mikolajki

calling "Bravo, bravo" as we inched over the line. Music was playing, the atmosphere was bubbling on this summer's evening, so we parked the car and wandered back into the square and sat around in a café with other competitors watching rally cars coming in for an hour or two. At the back of the café was a large poster on the wall advertising the arrival of the Peking-Paris rally, the centrepiece of which was a large photograph of Richard's Jaguar Mark II. (However, one of the cars pictured on this

poster was our XK120 !) I really could not understand how this strange situation had occurred, but upon later scrutiny we realised that all the photographs had been taken from the Beijing-Burford gathering of a year ago. Still it was strange to see our own car featured on a poster in the middle of Poland.

The disappointing news as we rolled into the hotel car park was to see the 'Blue Roo' Holden on the back of a low loader, with confirmation that the Holden had run a bearing on the pinion on the differential. The teeth on the pinion had been damaged and Mick was very pessimistic about having it repaired. Most disappointingly for them, they have lost their gold medal and dropped several places in the overall ranking.

The Chevy just needed its daily top up of gearbox oil, before I then wandered over to help Dave cut a hole in the floor of the Sunbeam so that he could insert the tube and funnel into his own leaking gearbox. The funnel was securely taped to the dashboard so that Jo could continually pour in oil and top up the gearbox whilst they were running.

Checking the overall standings at the end of this long day of tests, we were pleased to see we had now gone up to sixth overall, although unfortunately we had benefited from Mick and Andy's bad fortune. Initially, Richard and Nicola thought they had dropped down to silver after their 'off' into the forest, but that appeared not to have happened, they dropped to third place behind Jon and Garrick in the VW Beetle, but were only 43 seconds behind with three tests to do the following day.

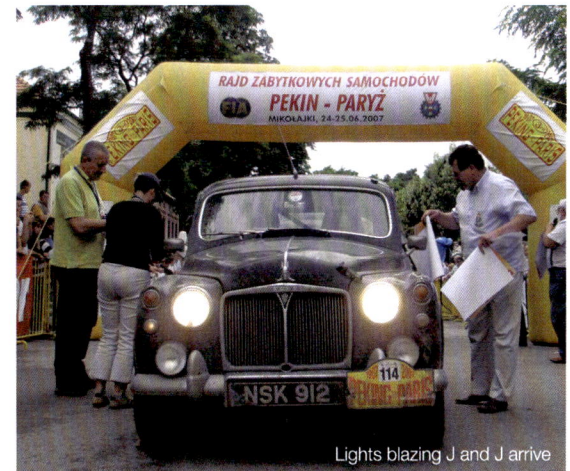
Lights blazing J and J arrive

The first face I saw in the car park this morning was a very serious-looking Richard, surrounded by a huge pile of debris that he had extracted from the car. Today was a big day for him – the last chance to pick up the 43 seconds on Jon Kennedy and Garrick to take them back into second place. Richard was desperately keen to lighten his car and his early morning job was to offload as much of his weight as possible into other cars. There was a degree of irony here, inasmuch as we had spent ages throwing away our own overweight items to limit the damage on the suspension, but here we were now carrying theirs - tools, plastic windscreen, oil and all sorts of unrecognisable spares – but at least it was in a good cause!

The other battle being fought today was that of Mike and Anne Wilkinson in their 1951 Riley RMB and the seriously fast 1951 Studebaker coupe of Tom Hayes and Andy Vanne. Mike and Anne were more than three minutes clear in the current standings, but the furiously driven Studebaker was clearly going to be chasing them down very hard today.

My own concerns lay in our front offside wheel, which was by now assuming a very rakish angle. We were very much on the last leg to Paris now, and definitely didn't want to fail at the last hurdle, so I resolved to try to secure the wheel on our rest day tomorrow in Gdansk.

Our own position was relatively safe, so we resolved to drive today's three tests relatively gently on the understanding that we really had nothing to gain but everything to lose should we make an error.

The early morning part of the drive towards the Baltic Sea was through the same beautiful lakeland countryside that we finished in yesterday and, with the sun beaming down on us and the self-satisfied expressions on our faces, we wandered off to the first test. This was through a serious of muddy farmland tracks and, at one

The Chevy looks worse for wear after a day in the forests.

stage, in a shallow dip in the terrain, we hit a gigantic muddy puddle, with the effect that muddy water and lumps of soil sprayed over the whole of the car and we seemed to be chewing gravel for the rest of the day!

All of the tests went really well and we achieved our aim of moderate, but safe, times. There was an extremely pleasant moment when, at the end of the last test, Kim Bannister and Bob came across and offered us their congratulations. As this was the last test, our position on the rally was pretty much fixed as long as we were just able to make Main Controls within the time windows.

And the news from the other intriguing battles. Clearly, Richard lightening his car had worked, and he was now almost two minutes in front of Jon and Garrick. Tom Hayes and Andy Vanne had also put in a prodigious effort and overhauled Mike and Anne by just one second. This is almost unbelievable, we have driven half way around the world, tens of thousands of kilometres over some of the worst terrain in the world, and here we are with just four days to go with one second separating these two competitors – how close can it get.

Robert Abrey takes it easy

At the stop for lunch we heard one or two interesting stories of cars that had been switched and changed on the rally. The lovely yellow and black Type 44 Bugatti of Daniel Brookes didn't make it through Mongolia, and he had reappeared recently in a replacement red Bugatti (sadly, to break down two days from Paris, and fail to finish). Dutchman, Durk Lindenbergh, in his 1929 6.5 litre Bentley had succumbed in Mongolia but, luckily, happened to have another one (!) which he shipped out to Tallin, and he finished in that one.

Mercifully, today was to be a relatively short day as the run-in to Gdansk was on a horrible, horrible road with masses of traffic everywhere and a significant accident that held up the whole rally for one-and-a-half hours. Tonight's hotel was in Sopot, about eight or nine miles north of Gdansk; we met Dave and Jo for a drink or two, in fact I managed to consume more than my usual two halves and needed an hour's sleep to get over it. The hotel put on an excellent buffet dinner with a barbeque out on the terrace, and there was a definite buzz of excitement as everyone talked enthusiastically about the run into Paris. Significantly, the Gdansk motor club had sent a team of 'fixers' across to the hotel, and they were busy talking to the owners of some of the battered and broken cars. Rumour had it that they were hoping to

track down a whole new back axle arrangement for Mick and Andrew, and Dave learnt to his delight that his new gear box bearings had been flown in. Tomorrow was clearly going to be a busy day.

There is always a traffic jam somewhere in the world

Pulling back the curtains this morning, we were greeted by lashing rain and almost zero visibility. After a quick breakfast, Yvonne and I set off for InterAuto garage, which Andy Vanne had recommended having already had his car sorted yesterday afternoon. Rolling into the garage good and early proved to be a huge success, as the garage owners had heard that the rally was in town and had, indeed, cancelled all their usual appointments to concentrate on working on the rally cars.

The car was immediately fallen on by two or three mechanics, whose main problem was to sort out the increasingly inclined wheel. The whole of the front wishbone was rapidly removed, heated, bent straight then reinforced with thick walled tubing. The mechanics, however, were not happy as they were unable to fathom a system to bolt the whole assembly back together again. My interest was somewhat different from their quest for a mechanical solution, and I told them I was completely happy if they simply welded the whole unit back into place. Clearly, this was not the sort of repair they were used to carrying out, but for us it was an absolutely guaranteed solution, and would certainly get us to Paris – and hopefully, back to Foolow.

Flushed with success as, upon reassembly, the wheel was now almost completely vertical, I got them to change the plugs, the oil and the filter, and I was mightily impressed with the sophisticated equipment on view after the simple technology of Mongolia and Siberia. A suction pump sucked the oil out of the engine into an oil drum without the need for removing the sump plug, and a compressed air grease gun flew round the grease nipples in seconds. After three hours' work, I was ready to leave but, within minutes of leaving the garage, I realised something was wrong as the car was running really 'lumpily'. Back at the garage a quick look through the handbook showed that the plug gap should be 0.35, but I dug out the old plugs he had removed and they were set on 0.7. All the plugs came out to be opened up again, which seemed to solve the problem. Strange but true. I cannot think why the handbook was so inaccurate.

Back to the hotel just in time to meet up with Yvonne, who had lunched with John and Joan. A rapid change of clothing, and we took a taxi into the centre of Gdansk. In my mind, the only association I had ever had with Gdansk was of Leck Walenska speaking to the massed dock workers in front of gloomy, grey shipyards. The Gdansk that unfolded in front of us was so different; stunningly beautiful and not unlike the streets of Amsterdam, where all the buildings were gable end onto the road with a huge variety of intricate brickwork detailing. Coffee was taken in a pleasant spot on a tree-shaded street and we celebrated with apple pie, complete with ice cream, fresh cream, nuts, raisins and whipping cream!

Gdansk had been very badly bombed in the Second World War by the Russians. The Germans had annexed Poland and the Russians attempted to bomb them out of there and simply devastated the town. However, it has been rebuilt brick by brick, building by building as a complete authentication of the original city. Without doubt, we thought, Gdansk will be the next destination for European tourists with its beautifully restored city centre and wide, sandy beaches fronting onto the Baltic sea. The day rounded off with an excellent meal with John and Joan at Rosmarind restaurant, described as "detached house, with superb Italian cooking" – and it was just that.

Gdansk was a huge suprise with its fine buildings

Today is to be a long, tough drive, one of the longest drives of the rally; so I was up early, started up the car and, to my horror, it sounded 'fluffy' and 'wheezy', and I decided it definitely needed a coat-of-looking-at before we set off. Andy Inskip was soon under the bonnet and, within moments, discovered that the inlet manifold gasket was leaking, which he

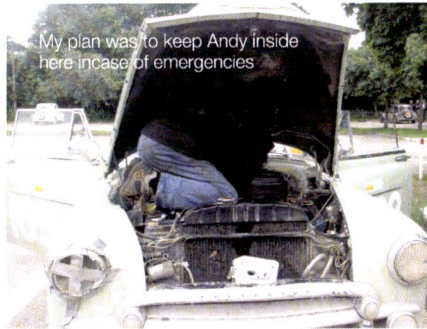
My plan was to keep Andy inside here incase of emergencies

said definitely needed attention as it could damage the valves by sucking in too much air. We were carrying all the right spares, so Andy said it would be a half-hour's job and set off with enthusiasm. Two hours later, he had finished. The job had proved to be somewhat more ticklish than he had anticipated. At one stage, I wandered back to the car to find him on his knees completely under the bonnet within the engine compartment. I had a cunning plan to keep him there to assist with any running repairs until the end of the rally, but he desisted with the excuse that it was a trifle cramped and, in any case, he hadn't had his breakfast yet.

Yvonne, meanwhile, had checked out on our correct minute so that we didn't incur a penalty and we set off to drive over 200 miles to the next time control. It was damp, drizzly and, to make matters worse, as we crossed over into Germany, the road suddenly became intolerably poor. The road was certainly overall tarmac, but one got the impression that it had been laid by independent road workers each concentrating on his own bit, but not necessarily checking out what his mates had been doing. The outcome was that the surface varied in both texture and level every yard of the way for over a hundred miles. Our initial reaction was that surely the roads of Germany were noted for being superb, however, we eventually realised that we were travelling through what was, of course, East Germany and the slick road

layers of West Germany hadn't yet reached this far.

We reached our time control well in hand, but we were greeted by a horror story which must have plunged the hearts of Tom and Andy in the Studebaker to the absolute depths. They had arrived at the checkpoint and, inadvertently, clocked out 50 minutes early – and received a 50 minute penalty. That, it is to be recalled, on the back of leading Mike and Anne Wilkinson by just one second two days earlier. What dreadful, bad fortune at this late stage.

Slowly, the roads got better and better although the constant splattering rain meant that, unusually, we had the hood up for most of the day. At the request of the Mayor of Potsdam, who wanted to give us a bookmark, a pencil sharpener and a flag, we had to divert through the centre of the city which, inevitably, got the whole of the rally stuck in desperate traffic and pouring rain. I suppose one can understand the enthusiasm of the townspeople to see the cars, but really towards the end of a long, tough day like today, it was the last thing we wanted. At 7.00 pm we drove into the underground carpark of the smart, crisp Dorrint Hotel.

As ever, today's stories were exchanged in the bar and, whilst top of the list by far were Tom and Andy's 50 minute penalty, Dave and Jo came very much a close second. The gearbox seals that had been flown in hadn't fitted despite several hours work by Peter Banham, with the result that Dave and Jo, in order to be sure that the gearbox didn't run dry, continuously poured oil down their funnel into the gearbox and used 25 litres (yes, that's 25 litres) during the day. Oh, for shares in an oil company!

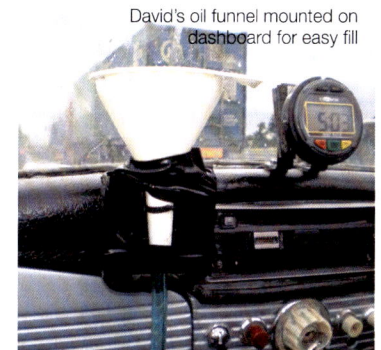
David's oil funnel mounted on dashboard for easy fill

First job this morning, following Andy's advice, is to nip up the studs on the manifold, and I couldn't believe how much they had loosened. Clearly, the rough roads of yesterday morning had taken their toll and Andy's advice was clearly very valuable.

Today's drive was to be through northern Germany heading towards Koblensk and the drive was typified by mile after mile of lush forests and beautiful valleys – not that too much could be seen through the pouring rain that we endured for 250 kilometres. Anticipating the weather, I had applied a couple of coats of Rain X on the windscreen, which worked perfectly well when driving quickly as the water simply rolled off the screen, but didn't work at all when travelling at slow speeds; it was like driving through a waterfall and my eyes were strained with trying to peer through the continuous curtain of water. Whoever dreamt up the idea of vacuum operated wipers clearly should have concentrated his efforts on something more worthwhile! Today was an interminable drive, but the finale was breathtaking, as we crested the final rise to take in the panoramic view of Koblensk sitting in the Mosel Valley; it was almost starting to feel like home from home as we had stayed over in Koblensk before on one of the MSA EuroClassic Rallies.

Feeling excessively exhausted, we rolled into the hotel car park at 5.00 pm, emptied the car of our luggage and staggered into the hotel reception, only to discover that we were, in fact, booked into another hotel a couple of miles away – all very deflating at the time. Our hotel was the local Ibis, which didn't bode well for five-star comfort and luxury. Nonetheless, the hotel had been recently refurbished and, indeed, the shower was perhaps the best we'd had in weeks. A refreshing walk back to the Headquarters hotel soon brought us round and we were delighted to hear that Dave and Jo had fared much better, consuming only two litres of oil all day. On reflection they realised that they had been over-enthusiastic yesterday and had been simply pouring in oil until the gearbox was continuously overflowing. Dinner tonight was taken with John and Joan, Dave and Jo, Richard and Nicola, together with Gordon Ketelbey and his wife, Kim, who were over from Sydney. We exchanged cards and arranged to have a beer with them in Sydney later on in the year, when we have arranged to drive the Classic Adelaide Rally. Amusingly, on the notice board last night, there was an instruction from Philip Young and the Rally Organisation, suggesting that all the cars should be washed and fettled ready for their arrival in Paris. This gave rise to a huge amount of discussion (it's amazing what trivial issues generate such serious discussion when travelling within the 'bubble' of a rally like this). Between the "OK, will do" and "Absolutely no chance" factions, it will be interesting to see what happens.

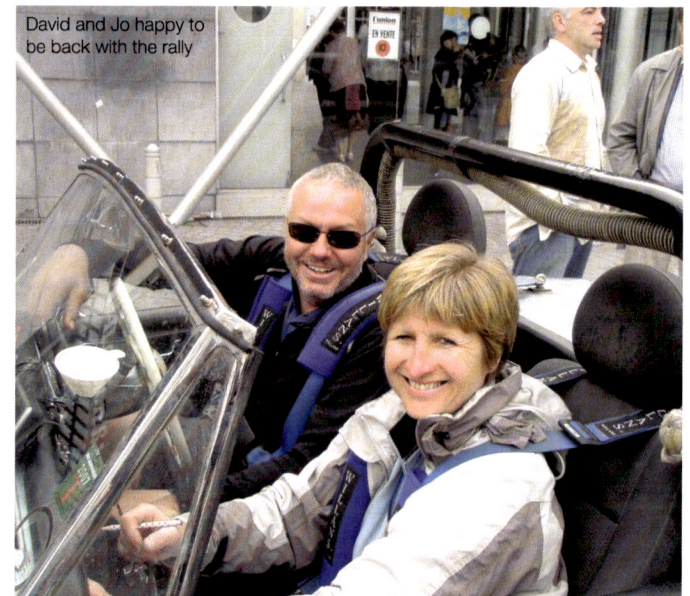

David and Jo happy to be back with the rally

Walking into the rally car park this morning, I bumped into someone whom I knew I had seen before, but just could not place. He was a Russian enthusiast whom we had talked to in Perm and who was following the whole of the latter end of the rally – what an enthusiast. This morning, taking centre stage in the car park, was Pit's Mercedes taxi which some wag had half-cleaned exactly down the centre of the car. Pit was, reputably, unhappy about this as he had been one of the "no chance, get lost" faction and had, indeed, left a notice on his car – "whatever asshole cleaned half my car, please clean the rest of it"! Needless to say, that didn't happen. Our position on this, together with the huge majority of the other crews is that, having driven halfway around the world, we rather felt that the condition of our cars should reflect this – rather than looking as if they had just been driven out of the local car club concours. It was obvious from the appearance of the Chevy that it had endured a tough journey, covered in mud from end to end and winking at everyone with its bashed-in headlamp, now neatly criss-crossed with gaffer tape; she certainly would be staying like this until we were back in Foolow.

Tales still abounded of cars that had had a multitude of problems over the last few weeks. Olaf and Robertus, in their Citroen, were just about to rejoin the rally, having shipped their car back to the Netherlands, replaced the gearbox and were hoping to be back with us that evening. Harry Hickling in his MG SA, had been hobbling along on five cylinders for the last five or six days, David Hall in his Chrysler had a major head gasket problem. Cars that 'disappeared' from the rally for days on end were reappearing, having been worked on for days in backstreet garages – cars were arriving on trucks, by train and, sometimes, catching up by taking shortcuts. All the cars were gathering ready for the final dash into Paris. Amazingly, the Knox, which had dropped a cylinder as far back as the second day of the rally, was still running and, perhaps even more surprisingly, Jan Voboril in his 1916 Lancia Theta was still with us, having, as will be recalled, driven and navigated all the way from Ulaan Baatar on his own!

Our drive this morning was a beautiful trip along the Mosel River Valley towards Luxembourg, past small villages, vineyards, castles and lochs, and it was with a feeling of elation that we pulled into the township of Bernkastel, glanced left to the café where we took some of the local white wine a couple of years ago, and set off on the long climb up the western side of the valley through the vineyards. Suddenly, cresting the rise of the coll, I couldn't seem to engage third gear. There was a Passage Check just over the brow of the hill and we cruised in to find a service crew luckily stationed there. A quick look under the car established that there was something wrong with the selector gear, which, without stripping down the gearbox, was something that they simply couldn't tackle. Yvonne and I had five minutes quick mathematical check to establish whether we could make our next time control within our limits. We were, in fact, 170 miles away but I worked out that, pushing the car along in second-gear, we should just about be able to manage – the thought of losing our gold medal position on the penultimate day was almost unbearable. Setting off rapidly, as every minute would count, we were soon into our stride in

Whew - just made the checkpoint here!

second gear, but it was extremely uncomfortable driving. The engine was racing at maximum revs and the fastest speed we could achieve was only 35 to 38 mph. I was continuously dipping the clutch and attempting to force the car into top gear (we only have 3). Mile after mile passed until, mercifully, after 40 miles of second gear driving – yippee – the gear slipped into top and we were away trying to catch up time as rapidly as possible. Fearful that the problem may recur I left the car in top gear for the whole of the journey, pulling away from traffic lights and tollbooths in 'top' with the accompanying aroma of burning clutch plates. The majority of the rest of our 140 mile drive was relatively easy and we made the checkpoint on time. Chatting to Jon Kennedy, awaiting our appointed time, he reckoned that the gearbox had probably got overheated, and the selector fork seized, but had probably eased now the system had cooled down. As it transpired, the problem never reappeared, but it certainly gave us some heart-stopping moments during that horrendous 40-mile second-gear drive.

The penultimate stop, just before the centre of Reims, was at the caves of a local champagne producer, and suitably relaxed after a sample glass of their produce, we ambled into our parking spot in the square right in the centre of Reims, directly outside our hotel.

Tonight, being the penultimate night of the rally, it will be recalled that the Organisers had promised a massive champagne celebratory dinner for the whole rally in exchange for the work we had to do ourselves in obtaining our entry visas. In great anticipation everybody showered and changed and gathered in the reception lobby of the hotel. To everybody's complete surprise, and to some people's complete annoyance, all of the besuited and befrocked local dignatories who had been invited to welcome the rally, had descended upon our champagne and canapés and consumed the lot! Voices were raised, tempers ran high and the whole atmosphere was charged with emotion. Everyone appreciated that tomorrow night's grand dinner was the absolute finale, to which family and friends had been invited, but tonight was to be the night when the crews celebrated this amazing journey and the camaraderie that had been generated, and here we were with a half-glass of champange and no food whatsoever. The hotel restaurant couldn't cope with 250 people so we decided to move off and search for a restaurant, leaving all the mumbling and shouting behind us. My abiding memory when we vacated the room was of Chris Mower from the Citroen completely losing his temper with Heidi. He had had several burning issues building up over the last few days and this final insult really did tip him over the top. Ten minutes later, ensconced in a pleasant little bistro in the backstreets of Reims, a bottle of wine and an excellent pasta soon smoothed away the frustrations of our 'lost' extravaganza!

It was Saturday 30th June, and our final day of the rally. Until now it really hadn't sunk in that we were so close, what with yesterday's gearbox problems etc. but all we had to do today was a relatively short drive before rolling into Paris. We had a nice and easy late start of 11.10 am, but I was up and out at the car at 7.00 am, checking the oil and water and, once more, topping up the gearbox oil. It was a lovely, sunny morning and as the cars were parked in echelon in one of the main pedestrian precincts in Reims, many of the crews were having coffee in the early morning sun and enjoying the luxury of a late start. Dave and Jo, however, looked a little disappointed as, yet again, oil was streaming from their gearbox and they were genuinely worried about their ability to make this last day. I had a spare gallon of oil, so gave it to them and we all crossed our fingers that they would have no problems on this final run in.

No sooner had we set off on this lovely, sunny morning, than we ran into a wall of damp, mist which was a trifle disappointing – we had always dreamt of crossing the finishing line in brilliant sunshine – hopefully the sun would burst through a little later. We ran on through small country roads, very much as Prince Borghese would have done a hundred years ago, however he wouldn't have come across the increasingly heavy traffic jams that we were to encounter.

Ten miles out of Paris our wishes were granted and the sun rapidly burnt through the cloud to reveal blue skies and brilliant sun. Our final Passage Check was about five miles out of the centre in quite the strangest location on the side of a dual carriageway, where mayhem reigned. There was nowhere to park up on this very busy highway, so rally cars were pulling in, double parking and generally causing great confusion to the local traffic. The 'plan' if, indeed, it was one, was for the cars to travel into the finish in groups of ten. After twenty minutes, we were released and the Chevy was about seventh or eighth down the line in our group of ten. Rally mania took over in our little group and we wove through the traffic in dramatic form,

hooting and cheering to whoever we saw. However, we did notice that the reactions we were getting in France, as indeed we had in Germany, were minimal to say the least. No-one seemed to have the faintest idea of what we had been doing, or what we had achieved. This was in comparison to all the other places we had passed through on our long journey where, over the last five weeks everyone had acknowledged our presence either with huge waves or continuous hooting. Clearly, the more civilised part of the European

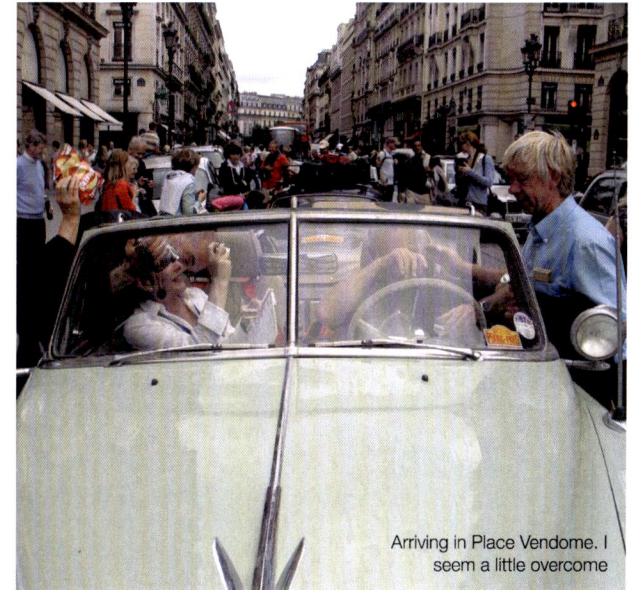
Arriving in Place Vendome. I seem a little overcome

Union were not quite up for displaying their emotions so obviously! Nonetheless, onwards we charged, trying to cling onto the tail of our fast-moving group, flicking in and out from lane to lane. Suddenly, the centre of Paris was upon us, the Seine on our right and Notre Dame and le Louvre to be seen across the river. At last, the traffic stopped for us and we were directed down the final road into la Place de la Concorde. Two right turns and there it was in front of us, the Finishing Line in Place Vendome. There was a huge, welcoming crowd with flags flying, cameras flashing and a glorious reception. We passed a large group of Dave and Jo's friends wearing special 'Welcome to Paris' teeshirts and then, suddenly, leaning into the car were Jim and Carole and Rodger and Jonathan over from Foolow. Carole presented me with a bag of crisps and Yvonne with the inevitable bar of chocolate. What an emotional moment; tears ran down our faces as we hugged each other knowing that we had succeeded in this journey-of-a-lifetime half way around the world. Time seemed to stand still as we were overwhelmed with questions about the rally coming from every quarter. It was difficult to pick out who was asking which question, and find the right superlatives with

Made it! note Carole's present of crisps

which to answer. Slowly, we inched across the Finishing Line and possibly the finest accolade was being presented with our Gold Medals. There seemed to be many

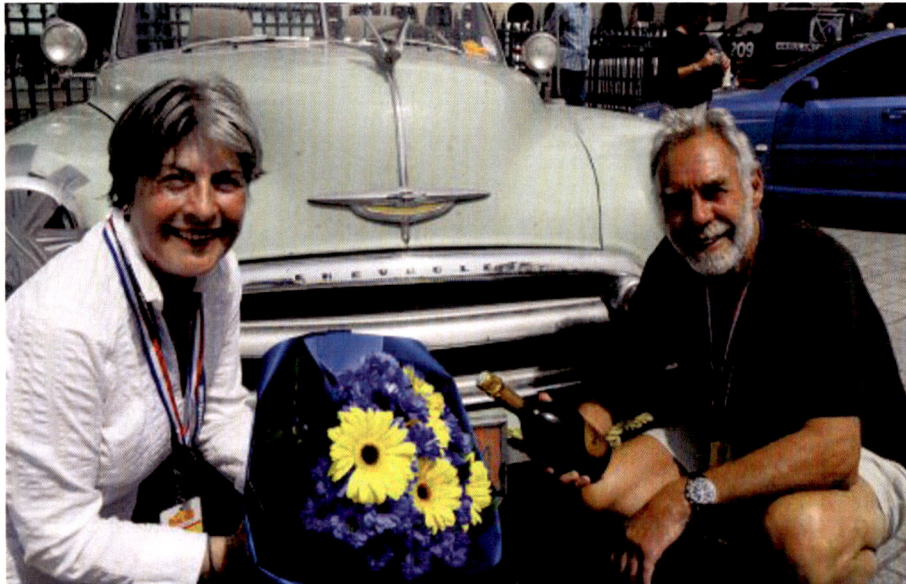

times when we really thought we wouldn't achieve this, but here we were, arm in arm, clutching these most prized awards. (Disappointingly, on close inspection the medals appeared just to be 'gold coloured' – but who cares, it's the achievement that's most important!)

Over the Finishing Line and in to park up in front of the monument in Place Vendome, we were met by Chevrolet Europe, who presented us with a bottle of champange and a large bouquet of flowers and, for the next half-hour, life was a bit of a daze as we were greeted by other friends

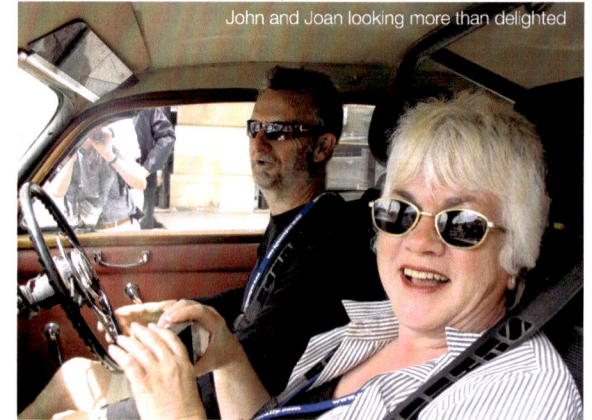
John and Joan looking more than delighted

and rally crews, everyone milling around sharing the absolute relief at having, finally, achieved a life-long ambition. Richard and Anne, from whom I had bought the Chevy, came across to offer their congratulations and, in the distance, we saw Mike and Josie's two sons, Ben and Josh, looking 'cool' as only youngsters do. Behind us John and Joan crossed the line and were instantly enveloped in a group of friends. Dave and Jo's car was almost lost in the sea of white tee-shirts so, luckily, the gearbox had held out.

Blancpain, one of the event's main sponsors, had a shop a little way from the square and everyone was invited back there for champange and nibbles, before slowly but surely retiring to the rather grand Grand Intercontinental Hotel. The first signs of utter

Mike and Josie cross the line

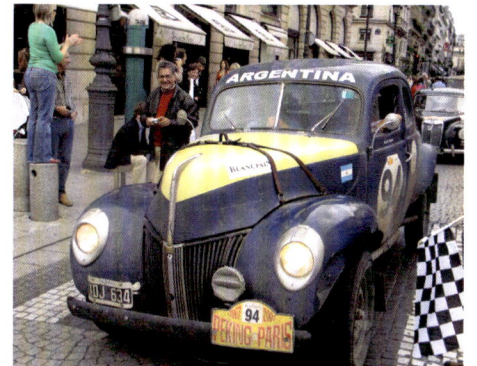

exhaustion swept across us as we sat on the bed arm in arm, just simply coming to terms with, not only the scale of our achievement, but also, the wondrous reception that we'd had a couple of hours earlier.

Eventually, at about 7.30 pm, people started to filter into the bar for the commencement of a fabulous gala dinner. Amazingly, it was almost impossible to recognise the people we had been travelling with over the last five or six weeks, oily overalls, dusty shirts, wrinkled jackets and sweaty tee-shirts, had all been exchanged for ballgowns and black-tie. It was quite amazing to see how well people had cleaned up and it was the cause of much merriment.

Extravaganza in Paris

750 people sat down for a fabulous dinner and prize-giving evening in the extravagant setting of the ballroom at the Grand Hotel. Our guests were Jim and Carole and Rodger and Jonathan, and Denis and Jill with the yellow Rolls-Royce joined our table with two of their friends for a very memorable evening. We were presented with our gold medals, then, together with Richard and Nicola and Jose and Maria, went up to collect our prize as the 'Dry Martinis' had finished as the First Team in the event. More trophies followed with our third in class and sixth overall position. Clearly, we would need a larger sideboard when we returned home.

The finale to the evening was a viewing of the precursor to the rally film, and there were fabulous shots of all the cars in the most extreme conditions, and as we sat there gazing in wonderment at what we had achieved there was hardly a dry eye in the room. Even Philip Young was 'on song'. Philip, as I am sure he would probably acknowledge, is not one of life's great social interacters, but tonight he was on absolute top form with a most impressive speech, praising all of his organisational team, the marshals, the support crews, the sponsors and, of course, the people who made the rally – the competitors.

The only sad note to the evening was that David and Karen Ayre in car no. 1, the Itala, never made the finishing line. There are all sorts of rumours about quite what had happened to them. Stories of them being chased by the police (2007 3-litre Puegot versus 1907 Itala?), their front tyres being shot out in a road block resulting in their eventual arrest. Everybody's heart went out to them having not made the final dinner. Thankfully, common sense at last prevailed and they were released. It is strange how history repeats itself. A hundred year before, Charles Goddard, driving his Dutch Spyker into second place, was arrested by the German police at the request of the French newspaper sponsoring the event, the result of which was that the French de Dions managed to catch up and overtake him.

Slowly, the evening drew to a close and it was very memorable with all the rally crews circulating tables saying fond goodbyes to the people with whom they had spent such memorable times. Addresses and phone numbers were exchanged as we all vowed to meet up somewhere, sometime again in the future. Slowly, and by now wearily, we made our way back to our bedroom as exhaustion swept over us.

We had done it. We'd flaming-well done it!

141

Chapter 15

THE AFTERMATH

The Journey

The next few days were simply a blur, with different emotions overlaying each other at an alarming rate. The first, most noticeable impact, was the immediate loss of the close-knit travelling rally circus. For more than five weeks, our only companions, day and night, were fellow competitors or others generally associated with the rally. Now, in an instant, this had been diluted a hundred times. Families and friends had converged on Paris to meet their nearest and dearest, and straight away the focus was completely different. Instead of languidly sharing a few beers and discussing each day's travails, each crew was now subject to intense interrogation by friends and family. Obviously, during the rally phone calls had been made, texts sent, emails passed backwards and forwards, and weblogs kept up to date, but nonetheless, everyone thirsted for first-hand knowledge of just what it had been like. I suspect now, thinking back, that we all played to the crowds, knowing full well that our moment would be short-lived as we would soon slip back into what would shortly become our more normal way of life.

Yvonne and I took a late breakfast and met up with Jim and Carole and Rodger and Jonathan for a gentle stroll around sunny Paris. Mike and Anne Wilkinson had rented an apartment on the side of the Seine for family and friends, so we called by mid-afternoon for an aperitif and nibbles, but I think the general consensus was that people really wanted to be back on the road again, making for home. Somehow languid tourist days wandering around Paris didn't seem appropriate after the events of the last five weeks.

So, it was the following morning our battered band of four cars that had started out together, John and Joan in the Rover, Dave and Jo in the Sunbeam, Mike and Josie in the Chrysler, and ourselves, struggled out of the centre of Paris, supported only by our old-fashioned maps. Our beloved Garmin sadly turned off. The wretched machine that everyone had found so difficult to master initially, soon had become everybody's firm favourite, and I think everyone was sorry to finally press the 'off' button when we arrived in the Place Vendome.

We journeyed back to Zeebrugge to arrive there ready for the evening boat, only to learn that John and Joan had broken down. Can you believe that. The Rover had, perhaps, been one of the most reliable vehicles on the whole rally, and here they were on the first day after the finish with a broken distributor. We all said at the time, if you're ever going to have a broken distributor, let it be the day after the finish. Nonetheless, a dip into the spares box for John produced the necessary replacement and, before the evening sailing, he had caught up with us.

Hull - nearly home

The chilly Hull coastline arrived at 8.30 am and, once off the boat, we met for a final photo shoot together. Then, in a flash, it was over, Mike and

Josie left for their nearby home in Hull, Dave and Jo were wandering off to High Hoyland, and the Rover and the Chevrolet headed southwest for Foolow and the end of an incredible journey.

We had travelled almost 14,000 kilometres of the world's toughest roads and harshest terrain, and it was exactly as we expected – an amazing adventure, the like of which we shall probably never encounter again. Without question, it was possibly the most arduous endurance rally that has taken place in terms of rugged terrain, passing through some of the most remote areas of the world. Some of the time it was inordinately tough, driving through regions where cars simply hadn't been before. It was hot, it was dusty beyond belief, and every muscle was strained to try to ride the bumps and bashes the car was going through. Nonetheless, we were aware that we were privileged to have the opportunity to visit these extraordinary wildernesses. The images we captured will remain in our minds for ever. At times, in Mongolia, it felt very hard going indeed, but later on during the rally, driving through Siberia, we became aware that, indeed, Mongolia was the highlight of the trip – a thought reflected by many other competitors. I still can't believe that we have passed through the ancient city of Karkourum, the Hanging Monestary and the Buddha caves in Northern China, we had seen ancient ceremonies, traditional dresses and the singing and dancing that heralded our start at the Great Wall of China. We had been welcomed along the whole of our route by the most extraordinary and fascinating collection of people you would ever wish to meet. Cheering children, black-sunglassed Chinese policemen, black-faced Chinese mineworkers, suntanned gnarled Mongolians in traditional dress, oily filthy mechanics, all of whom had continual smiles on their faces. The overall abiding memory is that everybody seemed to be happy to see us, and take part, in their own way, in this enormous endurance rally enterprise. Just as I remember as a youngster standing on the roadside at Barnby Moor welcoming Ann Wisdom on the Monte Carlo Rally, perhaps some of these people will be telling their children that they watched the great 2007 Peking to Paris Rally pass by.

When we commenced the journey, our only objective was to get to Paris come 'Hell or high water', however after the tough crossing of Mongolia, we realised we were doing well in the overall competition and were still on 'gold'. It's amazing how one's objectives can take on a totally different aspect and, indeed, from Mongolia onwards, we were very conscious of trying to maintain our position – all adding to the stress levels. Our little team of four were quite remarkable. The Rover, the Chrysler and the Chevy all took Gold Medals, whilst Dave and Jo in their Sunbeam took a special True Grit award for their amazing efforts in chasing and catching up the rally for nine days.

The Great Petrol Voucher Issue

It will be recalled from earlier, that the organisers persuaded the competitors to very carefully think over the issue of the quantity of petrol that we would expect to use in Mongolia and therefore purchase the appropriate number of petrol vouchers. As no-one wanted to be found to be short of petrol, inevitably everybody ordered far more vouchers than they would really need. The other issue that had been stressed on an almost weekly basis in the pre-rally lead up, was that the quality of petrol we were to expect was to be appalling – hence the need only to purchase petrol through the channels arranged by the organisers.

In truth the whole system turned out to be a complete shambles. Not only were there adequate fuel stations in the small towns we passed through in Mongolia but, more importantly, the octane level available was in the 85/90 region – manifestly better than we had been lead to believe.

The result of the voucher system led to complete chaos. As we had all paid for our fuel in advance, we simply had to go to the appointed garage which, inevitably led to gigantic queues with all the attendant hours and hours of waiting time that this involved, which was the last thing anyone wanted at the end of a tough day's endurance rallying (perhaps the word 'endurance' had wider implications in the eyes of the organisers!). More frustrating was sitting in the gigantic queues looking out across the other petrol stations in the town that were standing empty.

The combination of much better quality fuel than we had been led to believe, more frequent availability than we had expected and the fact that there were no fuel stations available whatsoever on the Mongolian borders, led to a situation where everyone had literally hundreds of litres-worth of pre-paid fuel vouchers for which we later discovered there were no refunds. Certainly, for a day or two (until some other seeming injustice took over) there was a lot of anger vented as it was certainly felt that somebody, somewhere had benefited substantially from the Great Fuel Fandango - we never really knew who, and now I suppose, its better that we didn't!

The People

I suppose in any pastime or hobby, it is inevitable that one meets a large group of people and, certainly, classic car rallying is no exception. The Peking to Paris, however, was particularly exceptional in this respect. Not only were we all together, we were all together for almost six weeks in total, but during that time we all enjoyed or endured an enormous mixture of emotions, from joy to horror, from ecstasy to depression, from wonderment to bewilderment and, I suppose, every other emotion in between, all of which we were sharing with other people on a daily basis. Inevitably, friendships form, some of them merely by the roadside, some of them for the duration of the rally, but many others in various degrees, perhaps for the rest of our lives.

For us it was no exception and, indeed, in the two short years since we left for our adventure we have had untold rendezvous and unexpected liaisons and some downright quirky coincidences.

We had only been back home in Foolow a month or so before a large, brown box was delivered from

'Our' Chevy model

America. Upon opening it, we discovered that Jon Kennedy from the VW Beetle, who it will be recalled owned an identical Chevrolet Bel Air, had posted to us his own model of the car which, by coincidence, was in exactly the colour of our rally Chevrolet. Jon's particular thoughtful touch was to have the model car lettered up with our rally number, 109. I have since added a pair of rally plates to the car and this now stands in pride of place in our kitchen, where we see it every day. A momento we shall never forget. It is our plan, when we next pass through California, to catch up with Jon and thank him personally.

Mick Mykitovich and his wife, Leisia, came over to the UK and travelled through Foolow to see us. We were able to return the visit by meeting up with them later that year on our way to the Classic Adelaide Rally. In Sydney, Andrew joined up with his Mum and Dad and we had a great couple of days with them being shown the sights of Sydney harbour.

Amazingly, the morning we were leaving Sydney we were breakfasting in our hotel, and I was tapped on the shoulder to be greeted by Xavier del Marmol, who was the man, you may recall, who asked me to move over on a driving test as he considered he was a somewhat faster driver than I! Xavier, from Belgium, was passing through Sydney on one day only and we were breakfasting in the same hotel at the same time.

Even more strange, the following day we had flown off to Adelaide for the start of the rally when, having breakfast at a street café in the centre of Adelaide with Dave and Jo, Yvonne spotted a figure walking by, whom she was convinced we had met on the Peking-Paris rally. Following this chap around the corner, we discovered it was Gordon Ketelbey who, with his wife Kim, drove a Cadillac 70 Fleetwood on the rally. Gordon, a native of Sydney, happened to be spending just one day in Adelaide on a court case – stranger than ever. Two breakfasts, two Peking-Paris entrants. We kept our eyes open in vain during breakfast on the third day, but nobody...........

After our participation in the Classic Adelaide rally, we drove across the width of

Australia to Perth, and eventually inched our way back to Melbourne. In Melbourne we were met by Mike and Anne Wilkinson, who entertained the four of us royally for a couple of days. The finale was a gathering of fourteen Peking-Paris entrants, mainly from Australia, but also including David and Adele Cohen from Toronto, who happened to be holidaying in Melbourne at exactly the same time!

A month or two after the finish in Paris, we went on the somewhat more gentle EuroClassic Rally to Porto and Lisbon, which was a great opportunity to meet up with our erstwhile 'Dry Martini' team mates, Jose and Maria. Mike and Jose and Dave and Jo were with us on the Euroclassic rally, and Jose and Maria hosted a small cocktail party in their Porto house before wining and dining a group of us in their favourite restaurant overlooking the Atlantic.

The Celtic Malts Rally last year commenced in Belfast, and we were delighted that Denis and Jill Wilson who had done the Peking-Paris in their magnificent 1927 yellow Rolls Royce 20 Tourer, came to see us off. Geoff and Penny Rawlings were also taking part in the Celtic Malts so, once again, plenty of opportunity to reminisce.

In the last year or so, we have taken part in a rally around Iceland, and have also done the Flying Scotsman – an inaugural rally for pre-War cars – both of these events attracted eight or ten crews from P2P, and I fear that to the rest of our friends we were all very boring as, on a nightly basis, anecdotes and tales of daring do's were exchanged.

On one or two occasions, I have been approached at various car-related functions by people who wanted to exchange stories about Peking-Paris and, I have to confess, that in a couple of instances, I was struggling to actually place these people. Maybe it is the fact that there were 250 people on the event, and it is impossible to remember everyone, maybe due to anno domini but, more likely, the fact that when people are dressed for 'civy street' they look somewhat different from the oily, grizzled, sunburnt figures I had met months beforehand.

Finally, just a few months ago, I was having a beer in our local hostelry, the Barrel Inn on Bretton Edge, noted for its complete remoteness, when there was a tap on my shoulder and Gerry Aitcher re-introduced himself. Now, I knew that Gerry lived somewhere very cosmopolitan in the South, but I was astonished to learn that he has a holiday home in just the next village to us, and here we were, side by side, in this supposedly remote location. Clearly, remote locations are a draw to us both!

John, of course, lives only 250 yards away and we see each other on a very regular basis; every Sunday morning sees the two of us out cycling our 50 or 60 miles in the Peak District hills and, inevitably, at some stage or another, the Peking-Paris subject crops up…….. and, I suppose, simply always will do.

A fascinating situation had started to unfold on the last couple of days of the Rally, when Andrew Mykytovych, the fine young son of Mick, was seen on several occasions in light-hearted conversation with Pamela Reid from the all-lady team of the Sunbeam Rapier. Imagine our astonishment, therefore, a month or two after the rally, to receive an invitation to be guests at their wedding. What a surprise. Nobody had remotely expected this as their relationship had barely been noticed as anything more than friendly discussion between drivers and navigators. It was with great pleasure, therefore, that we joined a half-dozen other P2P rally crews, including Philip Young and Heidi and Jack Pizzie and his TV crew, at their wedding just outside Brighton in March 2008. Many congratulations to them both. Incidentally, Pamela and Andrew have entered the 2010 Peking to Paris Rally.

The Car

Well, I guess that one or two people may be interested to know what happened to The Chevrolet. Inevitably, there are twists and turns to this tale. Initially, when we returned home, the Chevy was washed down, had a cursory cleanout and then was reversed into the garage for an indefinite period. Whilst we had never harboured any specific plans to keep the car and had, indeed, always assumed that eventually she would go, nonetheless a general indifference and apathy, together with building work at home which effectively 'locked' the Chevrolet into the garage, meant that many months passed without any firm decision being made.

Almost twelve months passed by before our building work was completed, and at last the Chevrolet could be accessed once again. We then determined this was the time to make some firm plans. A couple of tentative advertisements in the motoring press brought little or no interest, and eventually we entered the car into the nearby H&H Auction at Buxton in October 2008. Once the decision had been made, I started the feverish work of getting the car ready for presentation at the auction. My plan was to keep the car in its Peking-Paris Rally form but giving the buyer the option to convert it back to a road-going car by offering with it all of the original seating, bumpers, chromework, bracketry etc. etc. I think the options gave the auctioneers somewhat of a nightmare as to how to present the car in their descriptive text. Clearly, its participation in this amazing event would make some good copy, but the dilemma was to what extent this would affect the going price. There were two distinct options; would the car, with its rallying history be seen to have good provenance or, as a direct result of its experiences, would it be seen to be 'shagged out'. Only time would tell.

A month before the auction, I set off with the major clean up of the car. Brighton beach couldn't have contained more sand, no matter how much I swept, vacuumed, dusted, the sand just kept on coming from every conceivable orifice. We did the very best we could, but I suspect the new owners will be finding sand, possibly for the rest of the car's life. Although I say it myself, the car cleaned up remarkably well and looked a picture when I finally finished it two days before the auction. A friend came to call the same afternoon that I finished it and, showing a passing interest, asked if he could look under the bonnet. Twang. The welded bolt that the Mongolian mechanics in Khovd had replaced when our bonnet spring gave way, failed dramatically with the effect that the bonnet crashed down diagonally, gouging yet another groove out of the paintwork on the wing.

This car was definitely going to have the very last word.

The passing friend was so embarrassed, as he felt that the problem was as a direct consequence of his inquisitiveness, that he gave up two hours of his time as we slaved to replace the bolt and reconnect this damaged spring assembly. Quick phone calls followed, cash exchanged hands and our local 'Chips Away' representative was persuaded to make a late night visit to patch up the paintwork. Miraculously, we were ready and the following day I set off on a fine, sunny October morning to drive the car the last ten miles to try and find its new owner.

Initial trepidation about the journey soon waxed away, as I slipped behind the steering wheel and set off on the narrow country lanes to Buxton. Within minutes of leaving home, all familiar sensations came back, the driving position, the lolloping lope of the car, the by-now-familiar cornering sensation, the strange elevated ride. Immediately, I was transported, a moment here in China, a sharp, rough climb and I was passing through the Gobi, a wooded valley brought back recollections of the Altay mountains in Eastern Siberia, the sweeping bends on the way to Smalldale reminded me of some of the time trials in Lithuania. It was all there, and even though the car had tested us to the extreme on many occasions, I could not help but feel a pang of remorse that this would perhaps be the last time we would see her.

By complete coincidence, John was selling his Rover P4 at the same auction and, to our joint delight, both cars sold, ours making exactly the same amount of money that I had paid Richard for the car three years ago - an outcome of which was that I was more than delighted. Strangely, both our cars sold to the same purchaser – an unknown German buyer. John and I could not fathom why someone would want to purchase so variable a pair of cars. We both assumed the purchaser would contact each of us to ask for a little more information or history on the cars, but six months passed by and nothing was heard, and eventually the memories started to slip away.

However, coincidence yet again played a hand. When we were enjoying the final celebratory dinner on the Flying Scotsman in March this year (2009), the indefatigable Andy Inskip, who was a support mechanic on the Flying Scotsman, came across excitably to tell me that the had discovered he was sitting next to a chap from Germany who had, indeed, purchased our Chevrolet. Finally, the two ends of the circle met up and I was introduced to Andreas and, yes, he had bought both of the cars. To this day, I still do not know exactly what his intentions are but we are now in touch by e-mail and, one day, just one day, we may meet our Green Blancmange again.

The Engine

The only other outstanding issue is the saga of the Adrian Bailey engine. As I sit here in Montauroux dictating this, I cannot believe that it is three years ago to within a month since we first found that there was a problem of any sort with the engine, and STILL, STILL, we have no resolution.

I was inevitably stung (in more ways than one) by the engine issue. My overwhelming feeling was one of total frustration and disbelief that I had been let down so badly through such relatively simple issues, by supposedly skilled garagists – if there is such a word, who constantly claimed that they had the morals to hold up their hands if or when any problems arose. What a fool I was to believe such stories. My principals were such that I felt the need to take recourse in the law and am now, more than three years later, wondering whether I am simply wasting my time throwing good money after bad. The whole issue has become mired in purposeless slanging matches carried out by ineffective insurance companies, slow, pedantic lawyers or obdurate 'experts'. Adrian Bailey has appointed an insurance company which, in turn, has appointed a solicitor who has, in turn, appointed an expert witness (who did not give them the advice they required) so they, in turn, appointed yet another expert witness. I, in my turn, have appointed my solicitor who has again appointed an expert and I think my next move is to make my own appointment with the local mental hospital! The facts seem so clear to me – and, indisputable. I have simply not yet met a single person with any mechanical knowledge would could contemplate that enough road dirt could be sucked up from the tarmac roads of the Peak District to completely wreck an American truck-inspired engine within 180 miles. However, the amount of argument, counter-argument and the volume of paper and hot air that has been dispensed on this (certainly as I see it) relatively simple matter, has to be seen to be believed.

However, every time the subject comes to mind, I boil over with anger, which has the effect of reinforcing my determination that there should be a just outcome.

We shall see.

The Thanks

Finally, sincere thanks are due to many people – in no particular order at all……

Keith, who spent so many hours working on the car and enjoyed teaching me some rudimentary mechanics. He was a total inspiration, and a calming influence when we were going through one engine after another. Without Keith I wouldn't have got such a deep knowledge of the car and wouldn't have spent those untold hours lying underneath the car – but never mind, Keith, I'll get you back one day…………

Pete, who rewired the car and quite obviously joined up every wire correctly – we never had a problem………..

Auto Historic, and Bob in particular, for simply digging us out of one of the biggest holes we have ever been in. A complete engine rebuild in two weeks, changing the gearbox almost overnight, together with all the other myriad bits and pieces he sorted………..

Brosterfield Engineering. Nothing seemed to phase Jim, Robert and Peter when they were asked to make all sorts of strange brackets and fittings. They were always on hand with maximum enthusiasm….

Mick at Sheffield Trimming/ Bielowskis. Whilst he made the new carpets etc. most importantly fixed the hood so that the water poured outside the car rather than inside whilst we were travelling through the Stepps of Siberia.

The support teams…..   Andy Inskip always around with a few words of encouragement, just when it was needed…….   Peter and Betty Banham – no rally should be without them!..... Terry Foulkes for a crucial piece of welding in Vilnius.

The Endurance Rally organisation-Philip, Heidi, Kim, Bob and their huge group of helpers without whom the event wouldn't or couldn't have happened.

And, finally….. Yvonne. She has put up with me; the biggest issue of all. Not only did she succumb to the idea, not only did she provide every atom of support whenever needed, not only did she put up with my mood swings, not only did she listen to every argument and counter-argument known to mankind whenever 'issues' arose, not only did she catalogue and list everything in sight, not only did she apparently bake fruit cake for every car on the event (the majority of which I had to eat before, or leave behind), not only did she commit to a first aid course to learn how to cope with everything from headaches to heart attacks, not only did she negotiate her way around the Consulates of possibly the most obdurate countries in the world, not only did she produce sufficient baking to keep several mechanics going day and night for several months on end, not only did she learn and become a perfectionist on the Garmin GP, not only did she navigate her way faultlessly from one side of the world to the other, not only did she sustain both of us for five weeks making fascinating and intriguing lunches from a variety of crispbreads and various spreads, not only was she the fastest tent-erecter and dismantler on the campsite, not only did she prepare and transcribe all the notes we made on the whole journey, not only did she smile and laugh (almost!) all the way round, but she also typed the whole of this book. Yvonne is a star.

Many thanks for following our trip and, in answer to the question that has been asked most frequently, would we do another one?   Watch this space.

Phillip and Yvonne Haslam
May 2009

List of Entrants

No.	Crew	Car and Year	Engine Capacity
Pioneer (Pre 1921 cars)			
1	David Ayre (GB) / Karen Ayre (GB)	1907 – Itala 40	7500
2	Jonathan Turner (GB) / Adam Hartley (GB)	1907 – Itala 40	3000
3	Paul Bessade (F) / Michel Magnin (F) / Marie-Emmanuelle	1911 – Brasier 22/30 Torpedo	3700
4	Daniel Ward (GB) / David Ingleby (GB)	1908 – Talbot 35 HP	5300
5	Michel Laarman (NL) / Antonius Poelsma (NL)	1911 – Knox Type R	7166
6	Scott Anderson (USA) / Gary Robert Fisher (USA)	1909 – Ford Model T	2859
7	Jan Voboril (USA) / Roaldn Moos (USA)	1916 – Lancia Theta	4700
8	Theodore Voukidis (GR / Fabio Longo (I)	1924 – Itala 51B	2813
9	Timothy Clemons (Aus) / Christopher Clemons (Aus)	1917 – Packard Twin Six	6900
10	Ralf Weiss (D) / Kurt Schneiders (D)	1918 – La France Roadster	14500
11	Andrew Fulton (USA) / Warner Bruntjen (USA)	1918 – Essex 6A	2800
12	William Holmes (GB) / Malcolm Corrie (GB)	1919 – La France	14500
13	Neville Jordan (NZ) / Bruce McIlroy (NZ)	1922 – Rolls Royce Silver Ghost	7500
14	Frederick Brown (USA) / Thomas Stevenson (Can)	1923 – Rolls Royce Silver Ghost	7500
15	Albert Eberhard (PT) / Monique Eberhard (PT)	1926 – Rolls Royce Silver Ghost	7428
16	Michael Power (GB) / Anthony Malcolm-Green (GB)	1923 – Vauxhall 30/98	4398
17	Timothy Scott (GB) / John Taylor (GB)	1903 – Mercedes 60HP	9236
Vintageant (Pre 1941) Class 2 - Pre 1931 and Class 3 – Pre 1941			
20	Wilhelmus van Gemert (NL) / Johan de Swart (NL)	1934 – Singer le Mans	933
21	Daniel Brooks (USA) / Matthew Heyself (Can)	1927 – Bugatti Type 44	3000
22	William Erickson (USA) / Steven Dole (USA)	1925 – Buick Pickup Roadster	2550
23	Leighton Pullen (Can) / Judy Pullen (GB)	1938 – Rover 12 Six Light Saloon	1496
24	Dennis Multon (GB) / Pollyanna Multon (GB)	1930 – Alvis 12/50 Beetleback	1635
25	Brian Larkins (GB) / Robin Long (GB)	1932 – Sunbeam 16	2200
26	Andrew Bailey (IRL) / Michael Bailey (IRL)	1929 – Chevrolet Roadster	3500
27	Paul R. Michael (GB) / Glen Grindrod (GB)	1933 – Rolls Royce 20/25	3669
28	Robert Pattison (USA) / Julie Fitzsimmons (Aus)	1928 – Chrysler 65	3200
29	Barrie Frost (Aus) / Lynn de Lacy-Frost	1928 – Chevrolet AB Roadster	2700
30	Pierre-Michel Singer (MC) / Claudine Singer (MC)	1928 – Chrysler 72	3000
31	Jorg Lemberg (D) / Dietmar Binkowska (D)	1927 – Lagonda High Chassis T1	4500
32	Nicholas Bailey (Aus) / Helena Edgill (IRL)	1926 – Bentley 3 litre	3000
33	Harry Hickling (Aus) / Catherine Hickling (Aus)	1938 – MG SA	2288
34	Daniel Rensing (USA) / Michele Shapiro (USA)	1930 – Chevrolet Coupe	3180
35	Horst Friedrichs (D) / Gerhard Lux (D)	1933 – Alvis Speed 20	2655
36	Mark de Ferranti (GB) / Sandra de Ferranti (GB)	1936 – Rolle Royce Coupe	7340
37	Christopher Claridge-Ware (GB) / Anita Claridge-Ware (D)	1933 – Lagonda M45 Tourer	4453
38	Nigel Gambier (GB) / Hugo Upton (GB)	1934 – Lagonda T7	3000
39	Robert Fountain (GB) / Joseph de Giorgi (GB)	1934 – Lagonda M45 Tourer	4553
40	Penelope Rawlings (GB) / Geoffrey Rawlings (GB)	1934 – Talbot 95	2687
41	Christopher Lunn (GB) / Nicola Lunn (GB)	1935 – Lagonda M45 Tourer	4500
42	David Cohen (Can) / Adele Cohen (Can)	1931 – Ford Model A	3300
43	Gerald Acher (GB) / Martin Read (GB)	1931 – Ford Model A Roadster	3225
44	Leonardus Schildkamp (NL) / Lucas Siljpen (NL)	1929 – Lancia Lambda	2570
45	Robert Wilson (IRL) / Susan Wilson (IRL)	1927 – Rolls Royce 20 Tourer	3000
46	Jean-Pierre Muller (CH) / William Medcalf (GB)	1927 – Bentley 4.5 le Mans	4398
47	Rolio Malcolm-Green (GB) / Anthony Crew (GB)	1930 – Delage D6L	3075
48	Harold McNair (NZ) / Anne Thomson (NZ)	1930 – Delage D8S	4050
49	Hans-Dieter Kroenung (D) / Markus Strehle (D)	1924 – Bentley Tourer	2996
50	Robin Grant (GB) / Caroline Wright (GB)	1927 – Bentley Open Tourer	4398
51	Etienne Veen (CH) / Sven Veen (CH)	1927 – Mercedes 630 K Sport	6300
52	Marinus Dingemans (NL) / Helena Schapendonk (NL)	1927 – Mercedes-Benz 630 K	6240
53	Mark Seligman (GB) / Jocelyn Seligman (GB)	1928 – Bentley 4.5 le Mans	4398
54	Robert Abrey (GB) / Jane Abrey (GB)	1928 – Bentley 4.5 le Mans	4398
55	Michael O'Shea (GB) / Sarah O'Shea (IRL)	1948 – Jaguar 3.5 litre Saloon	3500
57	Richard Dangerfield (GB) / Jillian Dangerfield (GB)	1929 – Bentley 4.5	4398
58	Dirk Lindenbergh (NL) / Esther van Vooren (NL)	1929 – Bentley 6.5 Tourer	8000
59	Michael Thompson (GB) / Josephine Thompson (GB)	1929 – Chrysler 75 Roadster	4078
60	Janine Dunkley (GB) / Christopher Dunkley (GB)	1935 – Bentley 3.5 Tourer	3500
61	Gordon Phillips (GB) / Mark Phillips (GB)	1929 – Bentley 4.5 le Mans	4398
62	Kevin Clemens (USA) / Richare Newman (USA)	1929 – Chrysler 75 Roadster	4600
63	Hugh Brogan (GB) / Paul Stead (GB)	1936 – Ford Pilot V8	3622
64	Peter Pivanos (CH) / Bruce Blythe (GB)	1929 – Bentley 6.5 Tourer	6493
65	Ioannis Katsaounis (GR) / Franco Lupi (CH)	1929 – Bentley 6.5 Tourer	6597
66	Anthony Goodwin (GB) / Gillian Goodwin (GB)	1927 – Bentley 6.5 Tourer	6597
67	Roy Williams (GB) / Andrew Davies (GB)	1937 – Riley 16	2443
68	Robert Frankcom (GB) / Julia Frankcom (GB)	1933 – Dodge Roadster	3500
69	Paul Carter (GB) / Vincent Fairclough (GB)	1936 – Bentley Derby 4.25	4250

No.	Crew	Car and Year	Engine Capacity
70	Werner Esch (LU) / Andree Kitzinger (LU)	1936 – la Salle Cadillac Roadster	4098
71	Peter Leighton-Squires (GB) / Neville Burrell (GB)	1939 – Bentley Derby 4.25	4259
72	Marc Rollinger (LU) / Viviane Marie Josee Biel (LU)	1937 – la Salle Cabriolet Sedan	5280
73	Richard Baker (GB) / Peter Boyland (GB)	1937 – Bentley Derby 4.25	4250
74	Jean Steinhauser (LU) / Anne Collard (B)	1940 – la Salle Coupe Cabriolet	5280
75	Olaf Pothoven (NL) / Robertus van den Berg (NL)	1939 – Citroen Traction Avant	2867
76	Charles Stuart-Menteth (GB) / Andrew May (GB)	1940 – Ford)1A	3622
77	David Hall (GB) / Jacqueline Hall (GB)	1929 – Chrysler 77	4275
78	Gerold Leumann (CH) / Hans-Rudolf Portmann (CH)	1926 – Bentley 6.5 litre Tourer	6500
79	Richard Taylor (USA) / Antoinette Taylor (USA)	1940 – Chevrolet Coupe	3501
80	Igot Kolodotschko (GB) / Robert Moore (GB)	1937 – Buick Coupe	2480
81	Engelbertus Kersten (NL) / Berend van den Dool (NL)	1927 – Bentley Speed Six	6500
82	John Refault (GB) / Philip Lunnon (GB)	1938 – Buick Sedan Saloon	2480
83	Gordon Ketelbey (Aus) / Kim Ketelbey (Aus)	1936 – Cadillac 70 Fleetwood	5700
84	Bernard Gateau (USA) / Dina Bennett (USA)	1940 – la Salle Coupe	5277
85	Xavier del Marmol (B) / Catherine Janssens (B)	1937 – Chevrolet Convertible	4000
86	Martti Klikka (SF) / Pirkko Kilkka (SF)	1938 – Packard Coupe 120	4625
87	Paul Merryweather (GB) / Sandra Merryweather (GB)	1938 – Chevrolet Fangio Coupe	3540
88	David Williams (GB) / Sadie Williams (GB)	1938 – Chevrolet Fangio Goupe	3500
89	Alan Grislay (B) / Tracey Curtis-Taylor (GB)	1941 – Chevrolet Fangio Coupe	4250
90	Richard Curtis (GB) / Tengku Idris Shah (MY)	1940 – Chevrolet Fangio Coupe	2998
91	John Hickman (GB) / Philip Hallett (GB)	1934 – Alvis Silver Eagle	3571
92	John Horton (USA) / Robert Brooks (USA)	1940 – Buick Convertible	8000
93	Matthew Bryson (Aus) / Gerald Crown (Aus)	1940 – Buick 4L. Straight Eight	4000
94	Luis F. Bustelio (RA) / Juan P. Vignau (RA)	1940 – Ford Coupe TC	4000
95	Harold Blumenstein (USA) / Alberto Hodari (RA)	1937 – Ford Convertible	3600
96	James W. Taylor (USA) / Frederick Nelan (USA)	1941 – Buick Convertible	3900
98	Francesco Ciriminna (I) / Michele Ingoglia (I)	1948 – Fiat Cabriolet	1100

Classics (Pre 1961)Class 4 – 1941 to 1955, Class 5 – post 1954 to 1961

No.	Crew	Car and Year	Engine Capacity
97	Teresita Aguilar (UY) / Halle Aguilar (UY)	1939 – Chevrolet Coupe TC **	4000
99	John Vincent (GB) / Edwin Hammond (CH	1948 – Austin 16	2199
100	Jose Romao de Sousa (PT) / Maria Romao de Sousa (PT)	1956 – MG Magnette ZA	1798
101	Matthew Keeler (GB) / John Keeler (GB)	1959 – Volkswagen Beetle	1300
102	Garrick Staples (USA) / Jon Kennedy (USA)	1959 – Volkswagen Cabriolet	1500
103	Jens Pilo (DK) / Anne Pilo (DK)	1953 – Bentley R Saloon	4566
104	Nigel Challis (GB) / Michael Pink (GB)	1955 – Landrover Series 1	1997

No.	Crew	Car and Year	Engine Capacity
105	Sally McCarthy (GB) / Carole Harvey (GB)	1954 – Citroen Traction Avant	1911
106	David Roberts (GB) / Joanna Roberts (GB)	1954 – Sunbeam Alpine	2267
107	Alan Crisp (GB) / Christopher Mower (GB)	1950 – Citroen Roadster	1911
108	Michael Wilkinson (Aus) / Anne Wilkinson (Aus)	1951 – Riley RMB	2443
109	Phillip Haslam (GB) / Yvonne Haslam (GB)	1950 – Chevrolet Bel Air	3550
110	Nigel Barton (GB) / Timothy Roupelli (GB)	1950 – Ford Pilot V8	3622
111	Thomas Hayes (IRL) / Andrew Vann (USA)	1951 – Studebaker Starlite Coupe	3785
112	Roberto Choidi (I) / Maria-Rita Degli Esposti (I)	1957 – Alfa Romeo Giulietta TI	1290
113	Simon Chance (GB) / Elizabeth Chance (GB)	1965 – Citroen 2CV6	602
114	John Fallows (GB) / Joan Fallows (GB)	1960 – Rover P4 80	2286
115	Bohodar Mykytowych (Aus) / Andrew Mykytowych (Aus)	1958 – Holden FC	2250
117	Nicholas Marks (GB) / Annabella Marks (GB)	1954 – Lancia Aurelia B205	2400
118	Pamela eid (GB) / Nicola Wainwright (GB)	1960 – Sunbeam Rapier Saloon	1592
119	Hans-Erik Rhodius (B) / Sabine Letzer (B)	1958 – Triumph TR3A	2188
120	David Spurling (GB) / Jonathan Spurling (GB)	1953 – Morgan plus 4	1991
121	Gerald Harrison (GB) / Andrew Douglas (GB)	1959 – Porsche 356A	1600
122	Francis Carey III (USA) / Gary Wales (USA)	1952 – Bentley Drophead	4500
123	Jon Goodwin (GB) / David Goodwin (GB)	1969 – Aston Martin DB6	3995
124	Rolf Korner (D) / Egbert Scheidhauer (D)	1958 – Mercedes Benz 220S	2195
126	Arthur Freeman (USA) / Roger James (USA)	1950 – Ford Coupe TC	4000
127	Roy Stephenson (GB) / Frederick Robinson (GB)	1960 – Aston Martin DB4	4000
128	Richard Ingham (GB) / Judy Ingham (GB)	1967 – Volvo 1800S	1800
129	Richard Worts (GB) / Nicola Shackleton (GB)	1961 – Jaguar Mk II	3794
130	Ulrich Clauss (D) / Hagen Schmid (D)	1964 – Volvo PV544	1780
131	Steven Byrne (GB) / Linda Marston-Weston (GB)	1965 – Aston Martin DB6	3995
132	Hans Peter Lindner (D) / Frank Wiest (D)	1966 – Mercedes 200 Saloon	1988
133	Michael Campbell (GB) / Robin Widdows (GB)	1936 – Bentley Special*	6554
134	Stephen Moore (G / Alan Smith (GB)	1953 – Bentley Special*	5675

Car	Crew	Car	Overall time	Position	Class	Medal
Pioneer Category – Pre 1921 model cars						
16	Frederick Brown / Thomas Stevenson	Rolls Royce Silver Ghost	234:17:49	1		G
15	Neville Jordan / Bruce McIlroy	Rolls Royce Silver Ghost	235:43:52	2		G
9	Theodore Voukidis / Fabio Longo	Itala 51B	238:32:52	3		G
18	Michael Power / Anthony Malcolm-Green	Vauxhall 30/98	246:20:47	4		S
11	Ralf Weiss / Kurt Schneiders	La France Roadster	253:21:37	5		S
3	Paul Bessade / Michel Magnin / Marie-Emmanuelle	Brasier 22/30 Torpedo	273:05:07	6		S
14	William Holmes / Malcolm Corrie	La France	294:48:25	7		S
17	Albert Eberhard / Monique Eberhard	Rolls Royce Silver Ghost	295:03:34	8		B
5	Daniel Ward / David Ingleby	Talbot 35 HP	305:49:47	9		B
1	David Ayre / Karen Ayre	Itala 40	325:50:33	10		
10	Timothy Clemons / Christopher Clemons	Packard twin six	353:37:56	11		B
6	Michel Laarman / Antonius Poelsma	Knox Type R	377:15:22	12		B
12	Andrew Fulton / Warner Bruntjen	Essex 6A	379:41:58	13		B
2	Jonathan Turner / Adam Hartley	Itala 40	411:55:14	14		B
19	Timothy Scott / John Taylor	Mercedes 60HP	443:38:00	15		B
7	Scott Anderson / Gary Robert Fisher	Ford Model T	Ret. Day 7			
8	Jan Voboril / Roland Moos	Lancia Theta	Unclassified			
Vintageant Category – pre 1941 model cars						
88	David Williams / Sadie Williams	Chevrolet Fangio Coupe	225:18:59	1	1	G
85	Xavier del Marmol / Catherine Janssens	Chevrolet Convertible	225:31:36	2	2	G
69	Paul Carter / Vincent Fairclough	Bentley Derby 4.25	225:32:59	3	3	G
87	Paul Merryweather / Sandra Merryweather	Chevrolet Fangio Coupe	225:38:41	4	4	G
35	Horst Friedrichs / Gerhard Lux	Alvis Speed 20	225:41:57	5	5	G
83	Gordon Ketelbey / Kim Ketelbey	Cadillac 70 Fleetwood	226:04:00	6	6	G
78	Gerold Leumann / Hans-Rudolf Portmann	Bentley 6.5 Litre Tourer	226:12:29	7	1	G
59	Michael Thompson / Josephine Thompson	Chrysler 75 Roadster	226:16:19	8	2	G
61	Gordon Phillips / Mark Phillips	Bentley 4.5 Le Mans	226:51:20	9	3	G
54	Robert Abrey / Jane Abrey	Bentley 4.5 Le Mans	227:15:36	10	4	G
50	Robin Grant / Caroline Wright	Bentley Open Tourer	227:24:45	11	5	G
67	Roy Williams / Andrew Davies	Riley 16	227:32:23	12	7	G
68	Robert Frankcom / Julia Frankcom	Dodge Roadster	227:48:32	13	8	G
39	Robert Fountain / Joseph De Giorgi	Lagonda M45 Tourer	227:54:14	14	9	S
24	Dennis Multon / Pollyanna Multon	Alvis 12/50 Beetleback	228:21:00	15	6	G
86	Martti Kiikka / Pirkko Kiikka	Packard Coupe 120	228:21:08	16	10	S
27	Paul R. Michael / Glen Grindrod	Rolls Royce 20/25	228:39:26	17	11	S
79	Richard Taylor / Antoinette Taylor	Chevrolet Coupe	228:48:20	18	12	G
36	Mark de Ferranti / Sandra de Ferranti	Rolls Royce Coupe	228:50:33	19	13	G
77	David Hall / Jacqueline Hall	Chrysler 77	228:57:19	20	7	S
41	Christopher Lunn / Nicola Lunn	Lagonda M45 Tourer	230:15:33	21	14	S
81	Engelbertus Kersten / Berend van den Dool	Bentley Speed Six	230:43:12	22	8	S
20	Wilhelmus Van Gemert / Johan De Swart	Singer Le Mans	240:04:15	23	15	S
55	Michael O'Shea / Sarah O'Shea	Jaguar 3.5 Litre Saloon	241:40:19	24	16	S
94	Luis. F. Bustelo / Juan.P. Vignau	Ford Coupe TC	242:12:09	25	17	S
66	Anthony Goodwin / Gillian Goodwin	Bentley 6.5 Tourer	243:49:53	26	9	S
40	Penelope Rawlings / Geoffrey Rawlings	Talbot 95	245:31:23	27	18	S
91	John Hickman / Philip Hallett	Alvis Silver Eagle	248:38:06	28	19	B
93	Matthew Bryson / Gerald Crown	Buick 4L Straight Eight	249:47:06	29	20	S
26	Andrew Bailey / Michael Bailey	Chevrolet Roadster	254:15:56	30	10	S
37	Christopher Claridge-Ware / Anita Claridge-Ware	Lagonda M45 Tourer	254:40:20	31	21	B
33	Harry Hickling / Catherine Hickling	MG SA	258:24:39	32	22	B
90	Richard Curtis / Tengku Idris Shah	Chevrolet Fangio Coupe	259:03:06	33	23	S
43	Gerald Acher / Martin Read	Ford Model A Roadster	259:19:01	34	11	S
82	John Refault / Philip Lunnon	Buick Sedan Saloon	260:08:19	35	24	S
51	Etienne Veen / Sven Veen	Mercedes 630K Sport	262:22:15	36	12	S
89	Alain Grisay / Tracey Curtis-Taylor	Chevrolet Fangio Coupe	262:59:58	37	25	S
76	Charles Stuart-Menteth / Andrew May	Ford 01A	264:02:45	38	26	B
42	David Cohen / Adele Cohen	Ford Model A	264:06:35	39	13	B
44	Leonardus Schildkamp / Lucas Slijpen	Lancia Lambda	265:01:44	40	14	B
64	Peter Livanos / Bruce Blythe	Bentley 6.5 Tourer	265:30:27	41	15	S
65	Ioannis Katsaounis / Franco Lupi	Bentley 6.5 Tourer	265:41:34	42	16	S
73	Richard Baker / Peter Boyland	Bentley Derby 4.25	266:25:21	43	27	S
52	Marinus Dingemans / Helena Schapendonk	Mercedes-Benz 630 K	267:40:21	44	17	S
74	Jean Steinhauser / Anne Collard	La Salle Coupe Cabriolet	271:22:28	45	28	B
70	Werner Esch / Andree Kitzinger	La Salle Cadillac Roadster	272:31:11	46	29	B
53	Mark Seligman / Jocelyn Seligman	Bentley 4.5 Le Mans	287:23:22	47	18	B
32	Nicholas Bailey / Helena Edgill	Bentley 3 - Litre	295:32:11	48	19	B
34	Daniel Rensing / Michele Shapiro	Chevrolet Coupe	296:49:27	49	20	B
80	Igor Kolodotschko / Robert Moore	Buick Coupe	297:49:14	50	30	B

Car	Crew	Car	Overall time	Position	Class	Medal
38	Nigel Gambier / Hugo Upton	Lagonda T7	300:10:00	51	31	B
48	Harold McNair / Anne Thomson	Delage D8S	303:47:46	52	21	B
47	Rollo Malcolm-Green / Anthony Crew	Delage D6L	307:12:50	53	22	B
46	Jean-Pierre Muller / William Medcalf	Bentley 4.5 Le Mans	307:54:12	54	23	B
75	Olaf Pothoven / Robertus Van Den Berg	Citroen Traction Avant	308:36:20	55	32	B
22	William Erickson / Steven Dole	Buick Pickup Roadster	309:47:40	56	24	B
62	Kevin Clemens / Richard Newman	Chrysler 75 Roadster	313:56:49	57	25	B
45	Robert Wilson / Susan Wilson	Rolls Royce 20 Tourer	317:03:36	58	26	B
92	John Horton / Robert Brooks	Buick Convertible	331:16:11	59	33	B
72	Marc Rollinger / Viviane Marie Josee Biel	La Salle Cabriolet Sedan	336:27:47	60	34	B
84	Bernard Gateau / Dina Bennett	La Salle Coupe	344:13:51	61	35	B
28	Robert Pattison / Julie Fitzsimmons	Chrysler 65	348:16:06	62	27	B
23	Leighton Pullen / Judy Pullen	Rover 12 Six Light Saloon	348:40:36	63	36	B
96	James. W Taylor / Frederick Nelan	Buick Convertible	357:28:02	64	37	B
71	Peter Leighton-Squires / Neville Burrell	Bentley Derby 4.25	367:23:21	65	38	B
98	Francesco Ciriminna / Michele Ingoglia	Fiat Cabriolet	388:14:29	66	39	B
31	Jorg Lemberg / Dietmar Binkowska	Lagonda High Chassis T1	401:25:06	67	28	B
63	Hugh Brogan / Paul Stead	Ford Pilot V8	405:20:46	68	40	
25	Brian Larkins / Robin Long	Sunbeam 16	407:58:00	69	41	B
29	Barrie Frost / Lynn De Lacy Frost	Chevrolet AB Roadster	421:50:37	70	29	B
57	Richard Dangerfield / Jillian Dangerfield	Bentley 4.5	Ret. Day 20			
60	Janine Dunkley / Christopher Dunkley	Bentley 3.5 Tourer	Ret. Day 13			
30	Pierre- Michel Singer / Claudine Singer	Chrysler 72	Ret. Day 8			
21	Daniel Brooks / Matthew Heysel	Bugatti Type 44	Ret. Day 5			
58	Dirk Lindenbergh / Esther Van Vooren	Bentley 6.5 Tourer	Ret. Day 5			
95	Harold Blumenstein / Alberto Hodari	Ford Convertible	Ret. Day 5			

Classic Category – pre 1961 model cars

Car	Crew	Car	Overall time	Position	Class	Medal
132	Hans Peter Lindner / Frank Wiest	Mercedes 200 Saloon	217:05:32	1	1	G
129	Richard Worts / Nicola Shackleton	Jaguar MkII	217:37:20	2	2	G
102	Garrick Staples / Jon Kennedy	Volkswagen Cabriolet	217:37:55	3	3	G
108	Michael Wilkinson / Anne Wilkinson	Riley RMB	218:14:38	4	1	G
111	Thomas Hayes / Thomas Vann	Studebaker Starlite Coupe	219:04:37	5	2	G
109	Phillip Haslam / Yvonne Haslam	Chevrolet Bel Air	220:03:30	6	3	G
114	John Fallows / Joan Fallows	Rover P4 80	220:27:38	7	4	G
113	Simon Chance / Elizabeth Chance	Citroen 2CV6	220:42:00	8	5	G
123	Jon Goodwin / David Goodwin	Aston Martin DB6	229:35:35	9	6	S
115	Bohodar Mykytowych / Andrew Mykytowych	Holden FC	232:17:30	10	7	S

Car	Crew	Car	Overall time	Position	Class	Medal
127	Roy Stephenson / Frederick Robinson	Aston Martin DB4	232:54:03	11	8	S
118	Pamela Reid / Nicola Wainwright	Sunbeam Rapier Saloon	235:40:08	12	9	S
100	Jose Romao de Sousa / Maria Romao De Sousa	MG Magnette ZA	241:13:44	13	10	B
134	Stephen Moore / Alan Smith	Bentley Special	246:24:23		1	S
125	Rolf Korner / Egbert Scheidhauer	Mercedes Benz 220S	248:26:10	14	11	S
131	Steven Byrne / Linda Marston-Weston	Aston Martin DB6	249:08:39	15	12	B
104	Nigel Challis / Michael Pink	Landrover Series 1	257:41:54	16	4	B
128	Richard Ingham / Judy Ingham	Volvo 1800S	259:59:23	17	13	B
117	Nicholas Marks / Annabella Marks	Lancia Aurelia B20S	264:49:49	18	5	B
103	Jens Pilo / Anne Pilo	Bentley R Saloon	264:52:21	19	6	S
105	Sally McCarthy / Carole Harvey	Citroen Traction Avant	274:55:25	20	7	S
112	Roberto Chiodi / Maria-Rita Degli Esposti	Alfa Romeo Giulietta TI	278:57:55	21	14	B
120	David Spurling / Jonathan Spurling	Morgan plus 4	288:15:04	22	8	B
101	Matthew Keeler / John Keeler	Volkswagen Beetle	299:21:55	23	15	B
99	John Vincent / Edwin Hammond	Austin 16	310:41:00	24	9	B
130	Ulrich Clauss / Hagen Schmid	Volvo PV544	315:32:36	25	16	B
97	Teresita Aguilar / Haile Aguilar	Chevrolet Coupe TC	322:47:08	26	10	B
121	Gerald Harrison / Andrew Douglas	Porsche 356A	324:50:12	27	17	B
107	Alan Crisp / Christopher Mower	Citroen Roadster	326:22:00	28	11	B
110	Nigel Barton / Timothy Roupell	Ford Pilot V8	328:54:00	29	12	
126	Arthur Freeman / Roger James	Ford Coupe TC	365:24:00	30	13	B
106	David Roberts / Joanna Roberts	Sunbeam Alpine	376:24:52	31	14	B
122	Francis Carey III / Gary Wales	Bentley Drophead	381:41:56	32	15	B
133	Michael Campbell / Robin Widdows	Bentley Special	Ret. Day 8			
119	Hans-Erik Rhodius / Sabine Letzer	Triumph TR3A	Ret. Day 5			

Spare Box List

Item	Location
ALTERNATOR	Back of BIN 2
ALUMINIUM SHEET	3 open top GREY
AXLE STANDS	Inside L.H. rear wing
BATTERIES	Garmin Box
BEARINGS – MAIN ENGINE	2 OPEN TOP - GREY
BOLTS	4 compartment BLUE HANDLES
BOLTS AND WASHERS – ASSORTED	2 OPEN TOP - GREY
BOWL	Behind spare wheel
BRAKE CYLINDER PISTONS	2 OPEN TOP – GREY
BRAKE CYLINDER SEALS	2 OPEN TOP - GREY
BRAKE CYLINDERS	2 OPEN TOP - GREY
BRAKE FLUID	3 OPEN TOP - GREY
BRAKE HOSES	2 OPEN TOP - GREY
BRAKE SHOES	2 OPEN TOP - GREY
BUCKET	Back of spare wheel
CABLE TIES	6 YELLOW
CARBURETOR KIT	1 PINK
CLUTCH PLATE	2 open top - grey
CLUTCH TOOL	2 open top – grey
CONDENSER	4 compartment BLUE HANDLES
CONROD BEARINGS	2 OPEN TOP - GREY
DISTRIBUTOR CAP	3 OPEN TOP - GREY
EASY START	Spare Tyre
ELECTRICAL CABLES	1 PINK
ELECTRICAL FUSES	4 compartment BLUE HANDLES
EVO-STICK	Tool Bag
EXHAUST BOBBINS	2 open top – grey
EXHAUST EXTENSION	Back L.H. wing
FACET FUEL PUMP	3 OPEN TOP - GREY
FAN BELT	3 OPEN TOP - GREY
FLASK	BIN 2
FLEX HOSE 18 MM DIAMETER	2 OPEN TOP - GREY
FLOOR MATS	BIN 1
FLUORESCENT JACKET	Inside spare wheel
FRONT SHOCK ABSORBER CLEAT	1 PINK
FRONT TRACK ROD ENDS	Wrapped in blue cloth – back of bins by half shafts
FUEL FILTERS	1 PINK
FUNNEL	Back L.H. wing
FUSES - ELEC	4 compartment BLUE HANDLES
GAFFER TAPE	In spare tyre
GALVANISED WIRE	2OPEN TOP - GREY
GASKET PAPER	BIN 1
GASKETS	1 PINK
GASKETS - full set	Floor of Bins
GAZ	Inside bowl behind spare wheel
GREASE	2 open top – grey
GREASE GUN	2 open top – grey
GROMMETS	4 compartment BLUE HANDLES
GUN – GUM EXHAUST REPAIR	5 GREEN
HOSES - TOP AND BOTTOM	3 OPEN TOP - GREY
INLET AND OUTLET VALVES	2 OPEN TOP - GREY
INNER TUBES	3 OPEN TOP - GREY
INSECT WIPES	Inside tyre
INSPECTION LAMP	Back of L.H. wing
INSULTION TAPE	5 GREEN
JUMP LEADS	6 YELLOW
LEATHER	Back of spare wheel
LOCTITE	5 GREEN
MAIN ENGINE BEARINGS	2 OPEN TOP - GREY
MATCHES	With GAZ bottle
NYLON CORD	Toolbag
OIL	In bowl under low level of boot
OIL FILTER	In Spare Tyre
OVERALLS	WITH TOOLS
PETROL FILLER CAP	2 open top – grey
PETROL TANK PATCH	5 GREEN
PICNIC EQUIPMENT	Centre – low level of boot
PLUG LEADS	6 - Yellow
PLUGS 6 no.	1 PINK
POINTS	4 compartment BLUE HANDLES
POLYTHENE BAGS	Back of R.H. corner
POTTI BULBS	Garmin Box
RADWELD	5 GREEN
RAINEX	5 GREEN
ROCKERS	2 open top – grey
S/S TUBING - 3 SHORT LENGTHS	3 OPEN TOP - GREY
SACKING	Back L.H. corner of low level of boot
SEALS - INNER SHAFT	2 open top – grey
SHACKLE PINS	8 VIOLET
SHACKLE SLEEVES	8 VIOLET
SHOCK ABSORBER CLEAT - FRONT	1 PINK
SHOVEL	Back L.H. wing
SPEEDO CABLE	3 OPEN TOP - GREY
SPIGOT BEARING	2 OPEN TOP - GREY
SPONGE	Back of spare wheel
STEERING PIVOT	8 VIOLET
SWARFEGA	Inside tyre
TERRATRIP SENSOR	Garmin Box
TOP AND BOTTOM HOSES	3 OPEN TOP - GREY
TOW TOPE	In Spare Tyre
TUBING S/S - 3 SHORT LENGTHS	3 OPEN TOP - GREY
TYRE INFLATER CANNISTER	6 YELLOW
TYRE PUMP	BOTTOM OF BIN 2
UMBRELLA	Y'S side pocket
UUU BOLT	5 GREEN)
W.D. 40	In spare tyre
WARNING TRIANGLE	Back L.H. wing
WASHERS	4 compartment BLUE HANDLES
WASHERS AND BOLTS – ASSORTED	2 OPEN TOP - GREY
WATER PUMP	3 OPEN TOP - GREY
WHEEL NUTS	4 compartment – blue handles
WHISKEY	BIN 1
WIPER ARM	2 OPEN TOP - GREY
WIPER BLADE	2 OPEN TOP - GREY
WIRE – GALVANISED	2 OPEN TOP - GREY
WORKSHOP MANUAL	Behind driver's seat

MEDICAL KIT

ANTHISAN CREAM			2
ANTISEPTIC WIPES			1
ASPIRIN 300 mg			2
BLANKETS	1	and	2
CHLORPHENAMINE – PIRITON 20 (allergic reaction)			1
CIPROFLOXACIN 500 mg x 20 (severe diarrhoea)			1
CO-AMOXICLAV 625 mg x 15 (other infections)			1
CREPE BANDAGE 1 x 7.5 cm			1
DIORALYTE REHYDRATION			2
DRESSINGS large 28 x 20 cm pad			1
DRESSINGS medium 12 x 10 cm			1
FACE MASK			1
GLOVES			1
IBUPROFEN 200 mg			2
ICE PACK			1
IMODIUM			2
INTRAVENOUS ADMINISTRATION 2			1
INTRAVENOUS CANNULAE 4			1
PARACETAMOL 500 mg			2
PREDNISOLONE - 40 (allergic reaction)			1
SAFETY PINS			1
SAVLON DRY SPRAY			1
SCISSORS			1
SODIUM CHLORIDE BAGS			1
STERI-STRIP would closure strips			1
STICKING PLASTERS			1
SURGICAL TAPE			1
SYRINGES			1
TISSUES			2
TRIANGULAR BANDAGE			1
TWEEZERS			2

Russian Phrase Book

Everyday expressions

Здравстуйте	(Zdravstvitye)	hello, greetings
Досвидания	(dosveedanya)	goodbye
Доброе утро	(dobroye ootro)	good morning
Добрый вечер	(dobriy vyecher)	good evening
Пожалуста	(pozhalsta)	please
Спасибо	(spaseeba)	thank you
Хорошо	(kharasho)	good! Ok
Как по русски?	(kak pa roosski)	what is the Russian for?
Понимаете ли Вы по-англиски?	(ponimayetye li viy po-angleeski?)	Do you understand English?
Я англичани	(Ya angleechanin)	I am an Englishman
Мы англиски	(Muy angleeski)	We are English

Some useful expressions

У вас есть (вода)?	(oo vas yest (voda))	do you have any (water)?
(Бензин)	(benzeen)	(petrol)
Мне нужно помощь	(mnye noozhna pamoshch)	I need help
Где?	(gdye)	where?
Где стоит (мост)?	(gdye stoyeet (mosst)	where is (the bridge)?
Где стоит больница?	(gdye stoyeet balneetsa)	where is the hospital?
Сколко стоит?	(skolka stoyeet)	how much?
Сколко я Вам должен?	(skolko ya vam dolzhen)	how much do I owe you?
Когда?	(kogda)	when?
Пажалиста, напишите это	(pazhalsata, napisheetye eta)	please write that down

Numbers

Нуль	(nool)	none, zero
Один	(adeen)	one
Два	(dva)	two
Три	(tree)	three
Четыре	(cheteerye)	four
Пят	(pyat)	five
Шесть	(shyest)	six
Семь	(syem)	seven
Восемь	(vosyem)	eight
Девять	(dyevit)	nine
Десять	(dyesit)	ten
Одиннадцать	(adeennadsat)	eleven (12-19 add 'nadsat' to 2-9)

Машина	(mashina)	car
Автомобиль	(avtomobeel)	car (automobile)
Вода	(voda)	water
Бензин	(byenzeen)	petrol
Керосин	(keroseen)	kerosene, diesel
Масло	(masla)	oil
Гидралическое масло	(gidraleecheskoye masla)	hydraulic oil
Смазка	(smazka)	grease
Колёсная мазь	(kalyosnaya maz)	axle or bearing grease
Колесо	(kolyeso)	wheel
Запасное колесо	(zapacnoye kolyeso)	spare wheel
Переднее колесо	(pyerednoye kolyeso)	front wheel
Задное колесо	(zadnyoye kolyeso)	back wheel
Тормоз	(tormoz)	brake
Тормозной башмак	(tormoznoy bashmak)	brake shoe
Шина	(sheena)	tyre
Запальная свеча	(zapalnaya svyecha)	spark plug
Карбюратор	(karbyoorator)	carburettor
Фильтр	(filtre)	filter
Мне нужно фильтровать бензина	(mnye noozhna filtrovat benzeena)	I need to filter the petrol
Радиатор	(radiator)	radiator
Переднее ось	(pyerednoye oss)	front axle
Задное ось	(zadnoye oss)	rear axle

Some you may not need!

Вам нужно поехать в санаторий (vam noozhna payekhat v sanatoriyi)	you need to go to a sanatorium
Верблюди здесь очень высокомерный (Verbloodi zdyes ochen viysokomerniy)	here the camels are very supercilious
Медведь глотал мои запонки (Myedved glotal mayi zaponki)	a bear has swallowed my cuff-links
Где живут дикие помойниций? (gdye zheevoot deekye pamoynitsee)	Where do the wild washerwomen live?
Где слуаетесь вечеринка? (gdye sloochayetes vyechereenka)	Where is the soirée?
Вы меня досаждаете, Я возвращаю Домой с первым самолетом ! (Vuy minya dosazhdayetye, ya vozvrashayoo damoy sperveem camolyetom)	You P**s me off and I am b*******g off home on the next plane

АПТЕКА   drugstore

1950 CHEVROLET 'BEL AIR' SKETCHES

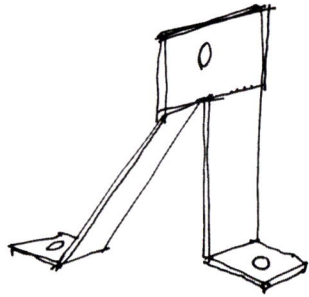

SKETCH VIEW

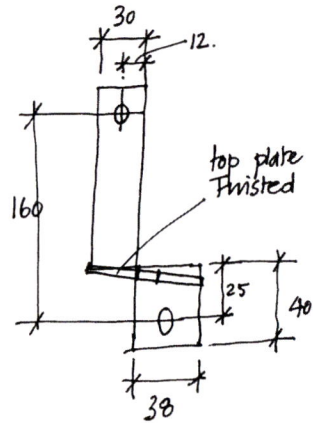

top plate
twisted

30
12.
160
25
40
38

PLAN VIEW

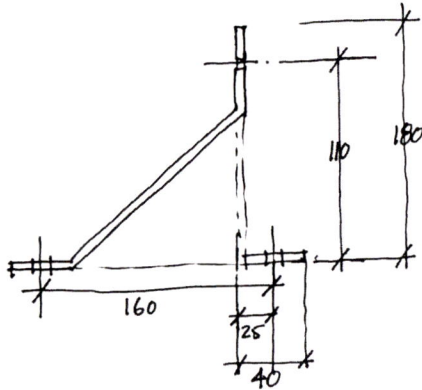

110
180
160
25
40

SIDE VIEW

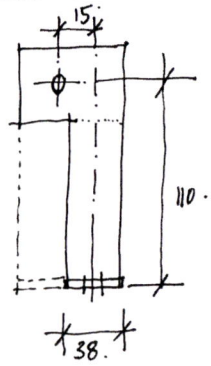

15
110.
38.

FRONT VIEW

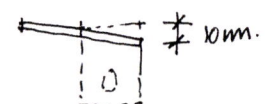

10mm.

TOP PLATE TWIST.

SEAT BELT BRACKET

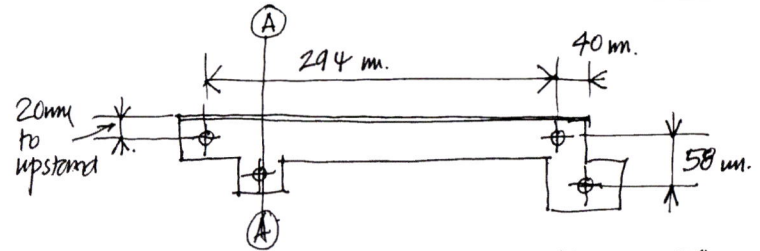

A

294 mm.
40 mm.

20mm
to
upstand

58 mm.

A

PLAN OF SIDE RAILS 1" thns. 1" handed.

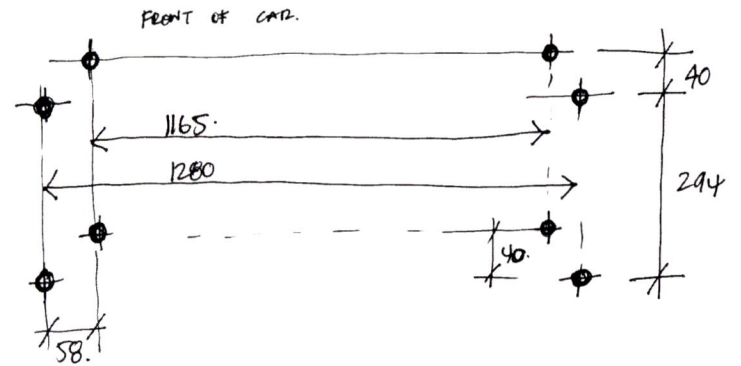

FRONT OF CAR.

40
1165.
1280
294
40
58.

PLAN OF CAR FLOOR — EXISTING HOLES.

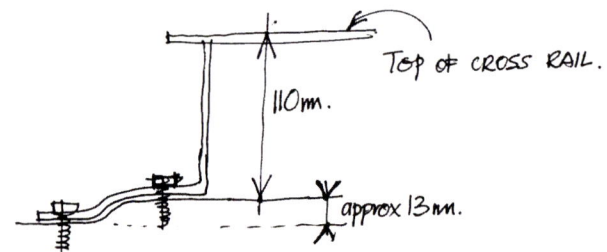

TOP OF CROSS RAIL.

110mm.

approx 13mm.

CROSS SECTION. A-A

SEATING FRAME

200   200   550

pencils

light

book slots.

flask / bottle holders.

180.

120.

TERRATRIP.

GPS.

340.

200

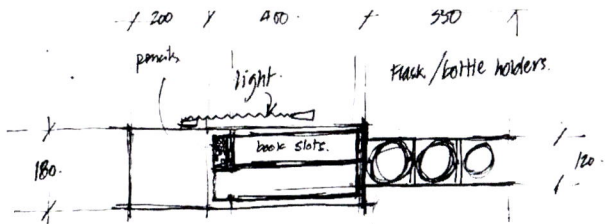

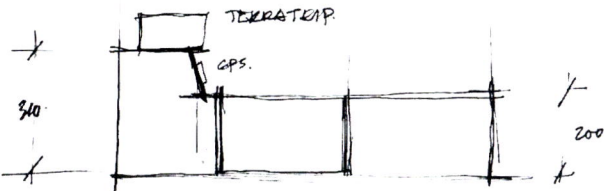

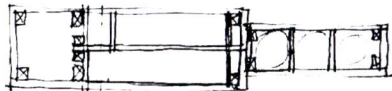

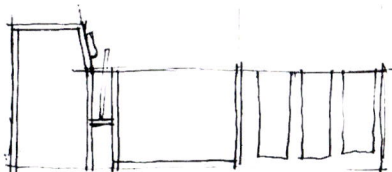

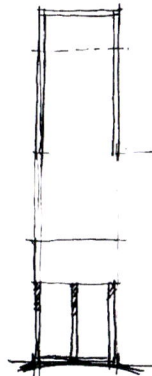

book slot long enough for chipboard.
Terratrip.
GPS.
cigarette holder connection.
stop watch
rally light.
Jack plug for pods

4lb. RADIATOR PRESSURE CAP

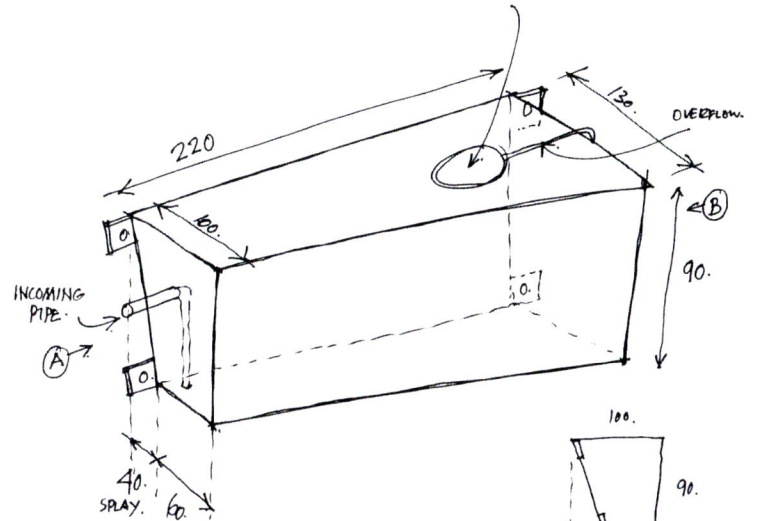

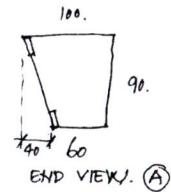

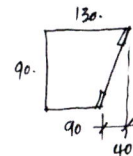

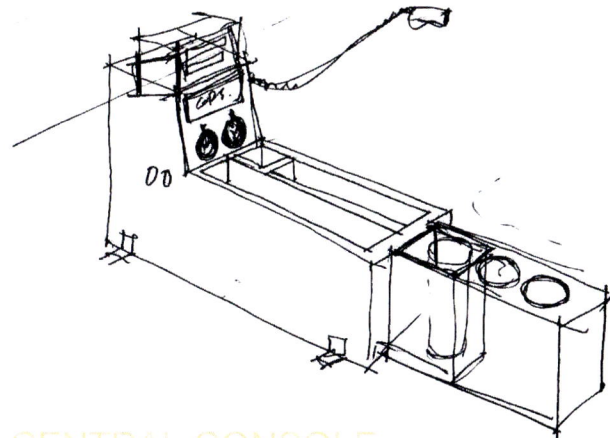

220

100.

130.

OVERFLOW.

90.

INCOMING PIPE.

40.
SPLAY.   60.

100.

90.

40   60

END VIEW. (A)

130.

90.

90   40

GPS.

OO

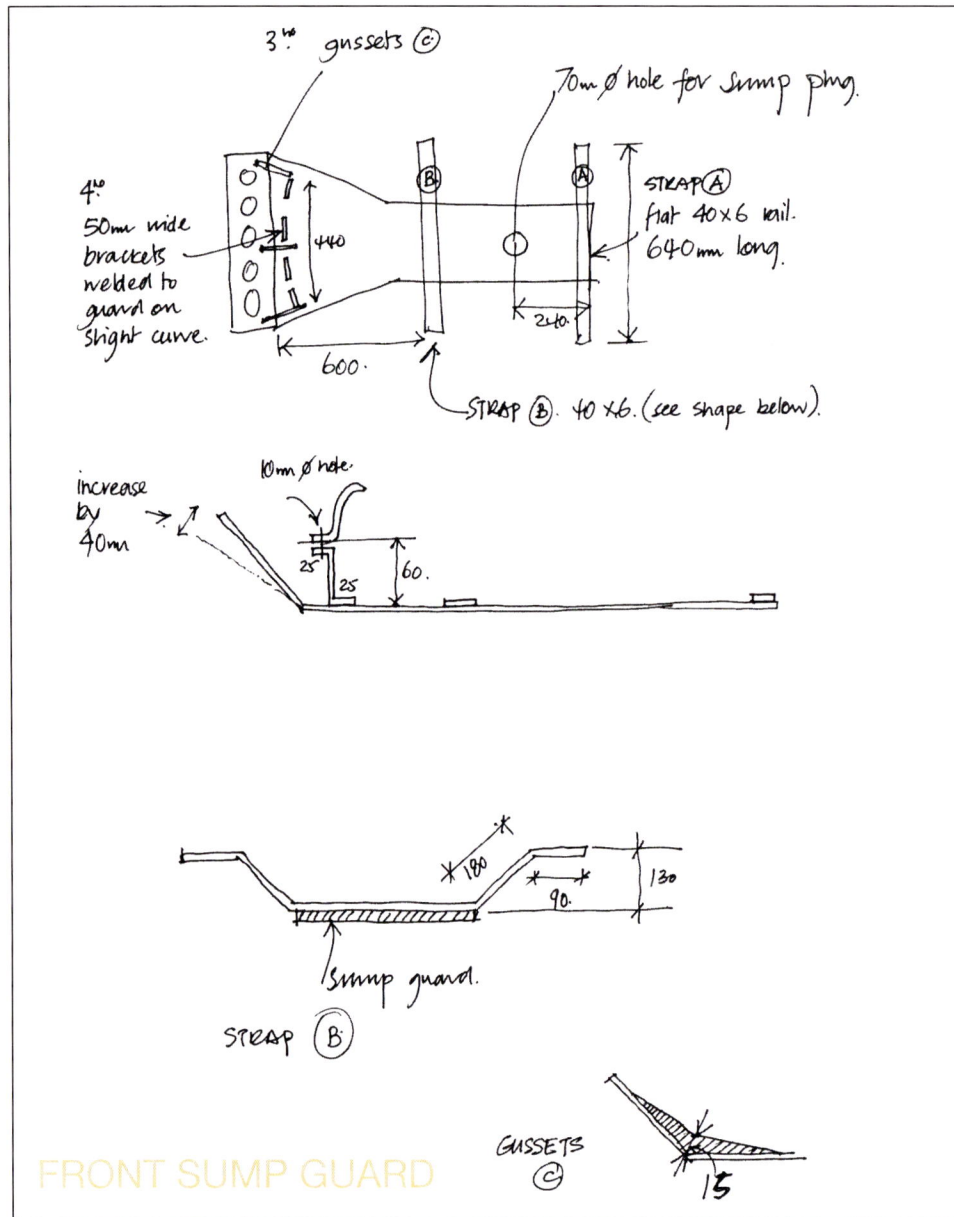

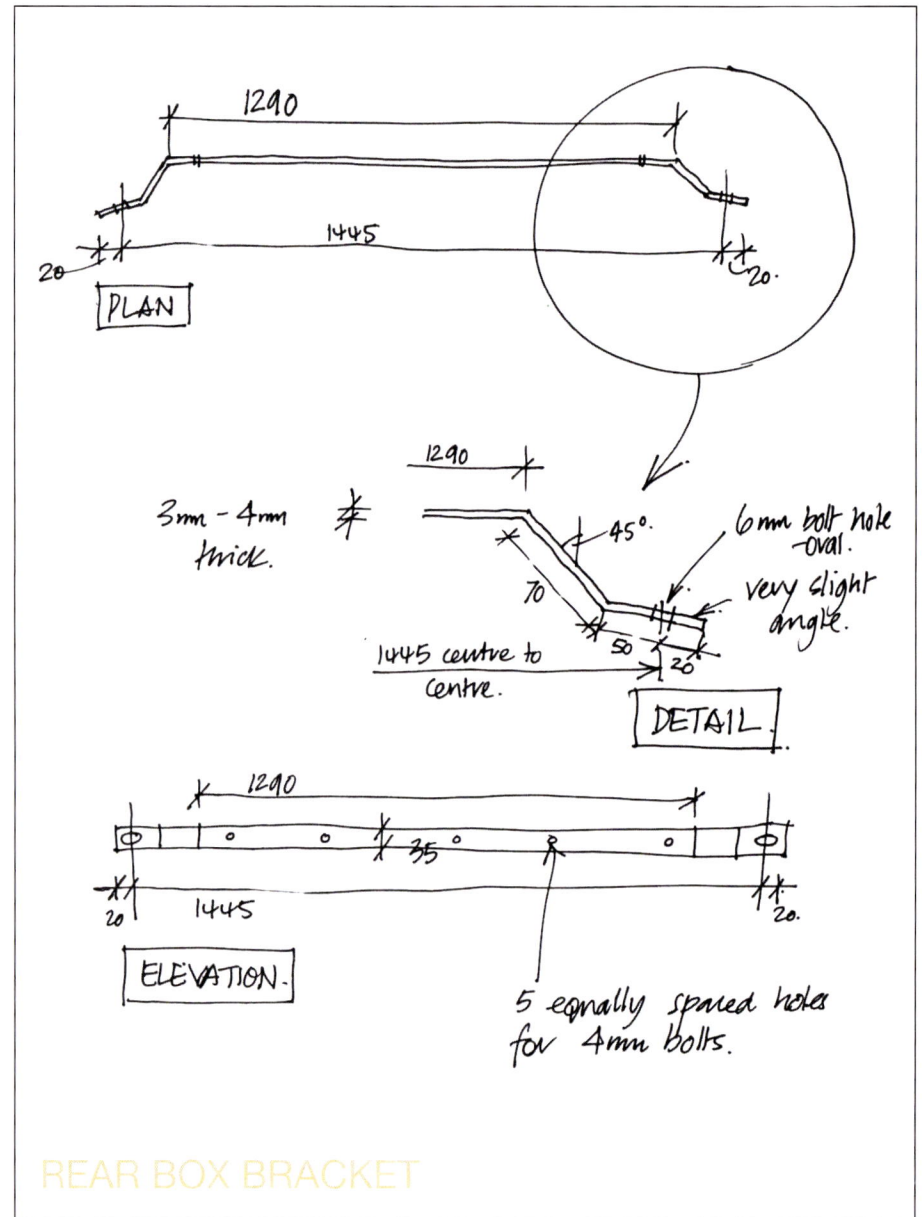

FRONT SUMP GUARD

3^{10} gussets ©

$70m \emptyset$ hole for sump plug.

4^{10} 50mm wide brackets welded to guard on slight curve.

STRAP Ⓐ flat 40×6 rail. $640mm$ long.

STRAP Ⓑ. 40×6. (see shape below).

440

600.

240.

increase by 40mm

10mm $\emptyset$ hole.

25   25   60.

180   90.   130

sump guard.

STRAP Ⓑ

GUSSETS ©   15

REAR BOX BRACKET

1290

1445

20   20.

PLAN

3mm - 4mm thick.

1290   45°

70   50   20

1445 centre to centre.

6mm bolt hole oval.

very slight angle.

DETAIL

1290

1445   35°

20   20.

ELEVATION.

5 equally spaced holes for 4mm bolts.

PHILLIP HASLAM

Born as a young child in Sheffield, led a sheltered life running a small architectural practice for thirty years, before retiring in 2006 to concentrate on preparation for the Peking to Paris Rally. A latecomer to rallying, has taken part in a variety of events – Scottish Malts, Euroclassic, Mille Miglia, Classic Adelaide, Red Rock Rally, Mille Millas, Tour of Iceland – but nothing quite so adventurous as the Peking to Paris.

Relaxation before this came in the somewhat frenetic activities of cycling, swimming, running and all things athletic. (Has no pretensions of becoming a writer).

YVONNE HASLAM

Born as an even younger child in Sheffield. Led a busy business career involved in the running of a large portfolio of properties on behalf of a major furniture retailer. Was swept off her feet by a well-known cyclist cum architect.

Envisaging a quiet life in the Derbyshire countryside, baking and gardening, she agreed to marrying the aforementioned and was somewhat taken aback to discover that she had been swept into the crazy world of classic car rallying. Her life has never been the same since.

159